A PANORAMA
OF GERMAN LITERATURE
From 1871 to 1931

A PANORAMA

OF

GERMAN LITERATURE

From 1871 to 1931

BY

FÉLIX BERTAUX

TRANSLATED WITH BIBLIOGRAPHIES BY

JOHN J. TROUNSTINE

WHITTLESEY HOUSE

M c G R A W - H I L L   B O O K   C O M P A N Y,   I N C.

New York

PUBLISHED BY WHITTLESEY HOUSE
A division of the McGraw-Hill Book Company, Inc.

Printed in the United States of America by The Maple Press Co., York, Pa.

Contents

PART I

From Naturalism to Symbolism, and the Individualist Reaction (1882–1890)

PART II

The Development and Differentiation of Literary Trends (1890–1914)

CONTENTS

PART III

The Quest for Fresh Orientations

PART I

From Naturalism to Symbolism, and the
Individualist Reaction

(1882–1890)

Antecedents

IN THE course of the half-century—from 1871 to 1918—
during which the Hohenzollern Empire endured,
Germany underwent a transformation which seemed
little short of miraculous even to the Germans themselves. The idealism that had once been extolled by
Madame de Staël seemed banished forever from a
country suddenly modernized and bursting with realistic
energy. But in spite of appearances there was no true
cleavage between the Germany of Goethe and the Germany of Bismarck. When time has given proper perspective, we shall see that they were attached one to the
other by a bond which we are now inclined to forget.
Idealism and realism, coexistent in Goethe's day, were
likewise coexistent in the Germany of the Empire. The
psychical forces at work alternated from one extreme
to the other, but were always rooted in a humanity
not fundamentally altered by differences of time and
place. Any effort to explain modern Germany in terms
of a transition from idealism to realism is therefore likely
to fail; the explanation lies rather in a study of the interaction of idealism and realism under the stress of historical events.

In a country wont to lament its lack of traditions this
persistence of a latent tradition may seem a curious
phenomenon. Equally curious was the "revolution"
which German writers began only a dozen years after
the foundation of the Empire—a revolution of the spirit,
which continued throughout the whole reign of William
II. This revolution had not a little to do with the moral

downfall of the Hohenzollern régime, whose material downfall has served to incite the "revolutionists" to even greater activity. It opened up horizons of thought which embraced all Europe and all humanity, and which, though but dimly viewed in a distant ideal future by the opposition groups of pre-War days, seem clearly defined and real to the rising generation of today. Revolution, indeed, is an inexact term with which to describe the movement; it was rather a phase in the evolution of a Germany seeking her true relation to the modern world.

This evolution was all-embracing. Literary phenomena were closely linked with political, economic, and social phenomena. Modern German literature attracts us as much because of its richness in documents bearing upon this metamorphosis of mind and soul as because of its literary content.

The changes which occurred cannot be properly interpreted unless we keep one essential fact in mind: Germany, like Italy, did not achieve nationhood until four centuries after the appointed time. It was therefore with an intensity heightened by long frustration that the Germans aspired toward the unity whose spiritual and temporal fruits neighboring civilizations had long enjoyed. This explains the explosive character of German spiritual development once the formation of the Reich had given it free rein. Some have seen in this explosiveness a sign of youth, the vigor of an adolescent people ready to leap in a transport of passion upon older, feebler races. But as a matter of fact its explanation must be sought in the past—a past which, in spite of many differences, has much in common with the past of Italy.

The long years of somnolence through which the old German states passed brought about a gradual building up of tension, from unrealized dreams and unsatisfied

desires, which made possible the extraordinary burst
of energy that modern Germany has displayed. The
Thirty Years War by no means annihilated Germany's
heritage from the Middle Ages and the Renaissance.
On the contrary, enough of this heritage was preserved
to contribute to the rebirth of a whole ideology in the
eighteenth century and to a tremendous material expansion in the nineteenth. It is a common error to suppose
that German civilization started afresh in 1870. The
events of 1870 were merely one of that civilization's
consequences; they served only to stimulate an already
existing desire to broaden and continue its development.
Far-seeing Germans had long realized what the relative
values of the several phases of this development were to
be.

Until the formation of the Empire, German civilization had been municipal in character; that is to say, it
had borne its finest fruit in the free towns and in the
cities of the Hanseatic League. Its expansion had been
limited by political circumstances. In the seventeenth
century its supporters were the rich bourgeois. It took
shelter in patrician dwellings which were like isolated
islets, and it remained out of touch both with the common people, who were cut off from it entirely, and with
the princely courts, where all eyes were turned toward
Versailles.

The awakening came in the second half of the eighteenth century—the effervescent period of *Sturm und
Drang*. The youth of that day, whose enthusiasm was
shared by the young Goethe, cast about for a source of
inspiration suitable to a divided and impotent Germany
and capable of endowing her at least with spiritual
unity. Their return to nature—a nature *à la Rousseau*
but at the same time distinctively German—was a
reaction against the hold of French culture on the coun-

try. Their difficulty lay in determining the essential character of the German spirit which was to be restored to its rightful place. *Was ist deutsch?* The question has been asked ever since. Wagner and Nietzsche took it up again in the nineteenth century, and during the Empire German writers devoted a good part of their efforts to seeking an answer. The chief subject of German literature until 1914 was Germany itself; the chief character was the German, appearing and reappearing under every imaginable guise. So true is this statement that as a whole the literature of the period gives the impression of being one vast *Entwicklungsroman* detailing the physical and spiritual development of a collective hero, the German people. The conflicts to be resolved all represent conflicts between the opposing tendencies which were then struggling for mastery of the German national consciousness and influencing its evolution.

It is difficult for a Frenchman to conceive of such conflicts. In France, harmony between the individual ethos and the national ethos has so long been clearly established that French society has been spared the uneasiness arising from uncertainty in this regard. Rather, the danger has been the likelihood of too firm a certainty, of a crystallization which hampers evolution. The literature born of that French society, in spite of changes and in spite of the rise of varying schools of thought, has in essence remained unmistakably French. Cosmopolitanism and patriotism, monarchism and republicanism, State and individual, have become integrated in the Gallic mind; and the Frenchman has traditions which tend to silence those parts of himself that cannot thus be integrated. But this acquisition of a sort of abstract personality or universality means the sacrifice of certain irrational elements which are themselves universal in character. The danger of arriving at too exact a conception of the relation between the individual and society is that we may reach a false conception of humanity as it really exists; for there always remains a part of the problem of that relation which cannot be solved by purely rational means.

The danger which German society ran was exactly the reverse. It lay in an uncertainty as to this relation which arose at once from historical circumstances and from the German's congenital predilection for chiaroscuro. This is not to deny that the German has a passionate interest in Mediterranean clarity, or to deny that the intellect has assumed an increasingly important rôle in German thinking. Yet the German feels a repugnance for dry rationality, an unwillingness to renounce the attractions of the obscurer depths of the soul.

When the *Stürmer und Dränger* of the eighteenth century set out to define the German genius, they called the primitive past to their aid. Indeed, like their romanticist successors, they were satisfied that the Middle Ages were the true and only source of inspiration for the German people, and spent nearly half a century digging up medieval epics, medieval legends and medieval songs. Ancient myths were resuscitated with a strange combination of artistry and naïveté. Poets totally unable to achieve Goethe's sovereign detachment industriously began to recreate a world suited to the Germany of their day—a Germany greedy for fictions and illusions because in them she believed she was discovering her true self at last. Thus arose a wave of historicism, born of a desire for definition on the part of a generation of Germans who could conceive of defining themselves only in terms of the past; nationalism was the reaction against an excessive cosmopolitanism which had gone before.

The inspiration which these men discovered in the past was almost musical in effect—a Proteus of sound and fury, intoxicated with his own metamorphoses. Uncertain of spirit, they were eager for help from any source, finding none in themselves; the result was that they let themselves be carried away by a sort of pantheistic religiosity. This in turn gave birth to a heady, effusive literature which called upon the individual to identify himself with nature in order to partake of its power. While it was far from bringing elasticity of spirit to men of romantic temper, at least it gave them the impression of a soothing contact with the infinite. The great risk they ran was that they would confuse the infinite with the merely exaggerated, sink in the quicksands of a dull reality, and, by erecting their poor objects of reverence into symbols, slip into sterile illusion. Goethe, when he felt himself sliding, had strength enough to hold back. He sensed in time the need for self-restraint. His classicism represented an effort to reconcile the Promethean genius, which exalts the human being to godhood, with the genius of Pantheism, which stoops to kiss the hem of Nature's robe. Desire and renunciation, freedom and submissiveness, were harmonized in him in a rhythm which could become a humanism representing new reality for the Europe of his day.

But the mass of the German people could not follow Goethe in his humanism. They had first to be made conscious merely of their German-ness. The nineteenth-century Germans had to go through the process of achieving a sense of political unity before they were prepared to listen to Goethe's advice that if they ever were to become true Germans, they must go above and beyond what is German and German only. "Poets and thinkers," in an effort to find in the past a basis for this new national spirit, brought forth a whole apparatus of historical research which represented a strange alliance of science and poetic imagination. Their strength was in their aspiration toward the heroic life; their weakness lay in their delight in imaginary figures, which led them to hail a Siegfried in every Philistine and to see in a Thuringian hillock the mountain from which would emerge a Barbarossa endowed with all the attributes of Wotan. As their ardor grew, fed by their desire to create a new empire of the German Nation in the image of the Holy Roman Empire, their brains began to whirl with visions reminiscent of Wagnerian opera. Gustav Freytag, following the Prussian armies across eastern France in 1870, went so far as to imply that in their ranks he had rediscovered the ancient German heroes whom he had glorified in his novels, and that in the thundering passage of the Uhlans he heard the hoofbeats of the horse of Attila!

The more imaginative writers, under the influence of this kind of auto-suggestion, reached the point where they began to take their hallucinations for reality, and considered as mere hallucination the reality clamoring around them. In spite of its power, they considered this reality inadequate; they felt that it must be enlarged, that its outline must be extended until they could breathe into it the elements of fantasy of which their dreams were made. Their excitement became almost convulsive; their tendency to confuse the real and the chimerical turned to megalomania. The German national consciousness, though stimulated by this sort of popular literature, risked perversion at its hands. So passionate a preoccupation with a single motif threatened to prejudice all the others. Those writers were prophets who could prophesy only under the suggestive influence of the past. The future, according to them, was to develop backwards. Attempting the first clear definition of essential Germanity, they were led to identify it with the dead, to picture the future Germany as a sort of cardboard Valhalla.

As this concept of German national consciousness progressed, the liberal concept whose impact had first been felt by the young Goethe, then by "Young Germany," was all but swallowed up. The disappointing results of the Revolution of 1848 caused its temporary disappearance, and though the German people could hear echoes of it from those who were in exile at the time, even these exiles, suffering, like Heine, from a repressed patriotism, came to believe that it was more urgent to achieve a Germany politically unified than a Germany free in spirit.

The inspiration which Goethe had drawn from other lands and other times did find asylum with a few writers like Hebbel and Georg Büchner; but it was a hundred years before Büchner's revolutionary genius finally succeeded in stirring his compatriots' hearts. Between the isolated, or the exiled, and those who were making literature the tool of nationalism, there was scarcely anyone except those writers who had remained provincial or academic. They refused to place their art at the service of a political cause, nor did they make any effort to achieve the *tour de force* of which Goethe had shown himself capable: to set up a *Welt- und Lebensanschauung*, an all-embracing view of man and the universe in a novel, a poem, or a play, without sacrificing their independence of imagination. They had accepted Goethe's cult of the beautiful and practiced it with religious devotion; but when it came to the question of nobility, they were unable or unwilling to follow him. The spontaneous lyric quality which had been rediscovered by Herder, Goethe, Brentano, and Eichendorff had turned insipid by the time it had passed through Mörike and Geibel to Heyse. A swarm of rhymsters was feeding the steel-helmeted German giant on sentimental slop, and Heyse's novels served merely to stimulate the

ANTECEDENTS

imaginations of those who still drew their inspiration from Italy.

German idealism, which was by no means a mere figment of Madame de Staël's imagination, but which, fed by the confused aspirations of the German people, had burned with a clear, white flame between Königsberg, Berlin, Weimar, and Heidelberg, seemed nevertheless on the eve of 1870 to have fallen into decay. Wilhelm Scherer showed that he felt this to be true when he terminated his history of German literature with the death of Goethe. Yet this apparent decadence of idealism was in reality only a temporary eclipse. The amazing constellation of the geniuses of Weimar had set, without one star of the first magnitude to replace it. This is a common enough phenomenon in the history of human society. Equally common is the refusal of a people proud of the idealism of its leaders to follow those leaders to the high plane to which that idealism has carried them. For the moment, the Germans were turning the inspiration they had derived from the great men of Goethe's day to purely utilitarian ends, to the achievement of political unity of the Reich—a material blessing whose possession seemed prerequisite to the full enjoyment of the spiritual blessings preached to them for so long. The laying of the foundations of a spiritual Fatherland, of a philosophy and a literature essentially German, had been possible even without a politically unified Germany. But if this German culture was to achieve power and influence, then a German nation, a German political entity, was essential.

The problem of the German writers after 1870 and the establishment of the Empire was to decide whether the emphasis should be placed on the word "German" or the word "culture"—in other words, whether German culture, freed from historicism and become modern at last, was to imply merely an aggregation of individuals driven together from purely material interests, or a development of the individual to the point where he has solved his material problems through the group and has at the same time preserved intact his dignity as an independent human personality.

CHAPTER I

The Surrender of the Idealistic Conventions to Realism

BUT FOR their vehemence there was nothing surprising in Nietzsche's statements that the victory of Germany in 1870 was not the victory of a superior over an inferior civilization, that power was likely to dull the intellect of a nation, and that there was grave danger of the destruction of the German spirit in the service of the German Empire. Such diverse figures as Jakob Burkhardt, Wilhelm Scherer, V. Fischer, and even Richard Wagner had already given voice to their uneasiness at the expansionist policies of the Reich, and to their fear that the spiritual life of the nation would thereby be compromised. The feverish speculation of the *Gründerjahre* had ended in a panic. The giddy years of the establishment of the Empire were followed by a period of malaise, and as early as 1880 several German writers were already expressing pessimistic views.

The first to recover from their intoxication discovered that the big stick of *Realpolitik* was not going to suffice in providing the German people with the new civilization and the nobility of life which they had been led to expect. There was a substantial distance between aspiration and realization. This distance had been spanned on the material plane, but not on the spiritual.

In 1885, fifteen years after the establishment of the Empire and at a time when literature should have been in the full flush of modernization, German literature suffered a distinct slump. Poets were still writing gilded lyrics about moonlight and ivy-covered walls. Gustav Freytag's realistic novels were little more than works of propaganda. If it was true that the schoolmaster had been the creator of modern Germany, then modern writers were certainly offering the public a Germany created in the schoolmaster's image. Spielhagen's novels, though they were painted with good critical sense on a wide canvas, did not rise above the level of theses. Germany had no social novel which could be considered an artistic creation. German writers were still led astray by historicism. Their favorite characters were Norns and the legendary Germanic heroes. Even the younger writers like Bleibtreu and Hauptmann yielded in their early days to this temptation. Clichés took the place of observation; an imitative imagination took the place of psychology. Haunted by the past and the grandiloquent expression which they gave to it, German writers were prevented from seeking their inspiration in the grandeur of the present.

The German drama, which had always been important among a people who attend the theatre with almost religious devotion, was equally reluctant to take up modern ways. Wagnerian opera represented a revival of genius so far as the music itself was concerned, but the Wagnerian conception of a synthesis of the arts, as it was to be found in primitive Greece, was directly opposed to the spirit of the age; the development of new modes of artistic expression resulted rather in an increasing diversity of artistic genres. Wagner and others served as examples of what could be accomplished by combining the sensibility of the poet with that of the musician or painter, but they made no contribution to the effort to return to a truly German art, integrated in all its forms. Wagnerian opera was confused and laboriously naïve. In it devotion to art became a religion; but its gods were those of a *papier mâché* Germanism, and its heroes, divorced from the music, seemed artificial. Unfortunately those who were influenced by Wagner borrowed only this artificiality, which seemed to satisfy their public. As late as 1890, Wildenbruch, a cousin of the Hohenzollerns, achieved enormous success by filling the stage with his forbears, engaged in predicting the victory of Sedan five centuries before it occurred. It was precisely such sentimentalists who won the crowds. Sentimentality and patriotism went hand in hand. Where art in all its forms might have sprung from the truly fresh and naïve lyricism of the *Lied*, it was corrupted by the Bovaryism of bearded giants. And it was not exempt from sensuality. Wagner's music, like Mackart's painting, stirred the turbid depths of the senses, and the "simple-minded psychology" denounced by Nietzsche made it impossible to distinguish what was divine and what was human, all too human, in desires concerning the nature of which writers as well as their public delighted to delude themselves.

Illusionism is the only word for this deviation from idealism in which mawkish conventions mask appetites almost hysterical. When Nietzsche broke with Wagner he was satisfying a desire for intellectual cleanliness. But it required an *élite* to share his repugnance for insincerity toward oneself, his courage in seeking freedom of the spirit, and it was not until 1890 that he was to find an audience. Indeed it was not until several years after the World War that cold rationality was really to come into its rightful place.

Had it not been for the fact that the changes through which European literature was passing were not yet understood in the Germany of 1880, the impulse to set up a revised standard of values might have come from abroad. But the Russians had not yet been translated into German; Ibsen, living in Munich, was ignored by his hosts, and the few of his plays which were presented in Germany were badly received; Whitman's work was known only to a few of the younger writers like Schlaf. With the exception of Shakespeare, whose plays were a part of German repertory, there was little interest in English literature. Indeed, and this seems strange, it was not until 1926 that English literature had any appreciable influence upon the Germans at all. No attention was paid to the brothers Hart when they earlier preached the example of Fielding and the English novelists of the great tradition. The German novel continued to be conceived as an *Enzyklopädie des Lebens*.

But German life had changed. It had become so rich and so complicated that it was difficult to find room for it in a novel, however encyclopedic, or to express its evolution through the career of an individual hero. The tradition begun by *Wilhelm Meister* demanded too much of the writer; it would have required an amazing genius to conform to it in the face of the increasing difficulty of combining breadth with profundity. Theodor Storm* was no more than a dreamy storyteller, a poet with a delightful knack of fusing landscapes with spiritual attitudes. Only Gottfried Keller† in Zurich might seem a worthy heir to the tradition of Goethe. His novel *Der grüne Heinrich* is the story of a massive personality, powerless to integrate itself. In it there are strength and robustness enough for a really great work, but Keller lacked the gift of complete self-expression. His own character, and his career as an unsuccessful painter turned town clerk,

* THEODOR STORM (1817–1888). Note especially *Immensee; Aquis submersus; Renate; Der Schimmelreiter.*

† GOTTFRIED KELLER (1819–1890). Note especially *Der grüne Heinrich; Die Leute von Seldwyla; Martin Salander; Züricher Novellen; Sieben Legenden; Gedichte.*

made it impossible for him to achieve the full flowering of genius which had been Goethe's. His work was too cluttered with detail to be great, too hesitant to gain even the full effect of the detail. It was nevertheless influential and helpful, precisely because of its confusion and its hesitancy, which reflected a sturdy vitality seeking expression. Keller was a realist who escaped platitudes, and he made more than one bold expedition into the untrod mysteries of the real. It is little wonder that André Gide was delighted by the chapter in which Keller penetrates into the byways of the adolescent mind. Anticipating Freud, Wedekind, Jean Schlumberger, Roger Martin du Gard, and even Gide himself, Keller bit deep into the opacity of formalistic psychology. His writings palpitate with life—the life of the common people in a democracy, observed with sly good sense. The individual, for Keller, is important chiefly because of his relation to the whole, and Keller seeks out this relation with a touching dignity. Keller succeeds in making clear the rich combination of achievement and frustration in the existence of the humble, with their dreams, their escapes, their preoccupations.

Perhaps Gottfried Keller's work—his somewhat prosy lyricism and his often poetic prose—is that of a minor artist. But he was an artist nevertheless, if only because of an eye that could see and a heart whose sympathy went out to all living things without denying the right of the intelligence to pry into the fabric of life. His intelligence is always conscious of its limitations; his warm heart seeks to press beyond them. As a result his writing often contains outbursts of feeling that are like the flowers of spring in a mountain country, lovely, delayed blossoms. Keller was one of those who, given nothing to begin with, have to gain everything at the price of hard experience. Such men can sometimes reinvent life, giving it new meaning. Like Goethe, although without Goethe's success, Keller set out to rise above realism and romanticism by reducing them to the status of elements of a broad human wisdom in which reason and sensibility are both employed to the full, and serve each to urge the other on. Gottfried Keller might have been the father of the moderns. But in spite of the favor with which he was received, the fact that he came from Switzerland made it impossible for him to gain the interest of expansionist Germany.

Keller's compatriot, Conrad Ferdinand Meyer,* had even less influence. He was distinguished by his ability to express a tormented sensibility and a quivering sensuality with restrained purity of line. But what he had to offer was a taste for the perfect, the finished, whereas the young German moderns were hurling themselves bodily upon the infinity of matter and cared little what imperfections might be found in their work.

These moderns ultimately turned rather toward Zola for their inspiration. Zola made several very different contributions to the modernization of German literature, and his is the credit in part for inspiring German writers to turn again to a broad poetic and critical view of the whole of life at a time when they were alternating between microscopic treatments of fact and vast empty structures of thought.

In 1883, however, the Frenchman's work was available in Germany only in translations which greatly coarsened its effect; it was considered a sort of scatological curiosity. Indeed a member of the Reichstag denounced Zola's writings as dangerous to public morality. The public itself much preferred the frothier importations from Paris, and nearly a quarter of the royalties paid by

---

* C. F. MEYER (1825–1898). Note especially *Huttens letzte Tage; Jürg Jenatsch; Gedichte; Der Heilige; Die Richterin; Die Versuchung des Pescara.*

German theatres at the time went to authors of music-hall skits. A new type of German philistine had arisen, at once patriotic and self-indulgent, who savored the virtues of his own people more fully if, upon emerging from a music hall in which a French skit was being played, he could rub his hands together and say: "Thank God we Germans are not like that!" Meanwhile German critics were praising French writers of a still different type—Dumas, Augier, Sardou; but the public considered them too cruelly realistic and refused to have anything to do with them. German audiences were Gallomaniac, on the principle that after great victories one can permit oneself small defeats; but their Gallomania was limited to the lighter types of writing, and did credit neither to Germany nor to France. It took the cleansing influence of naturalism to reëstablish literary relations between the two countries on a plane worthy of both.

From Paris a German writer, Michael Georg Conrad,* exhorted his compatriots to realize that the military defeat of France had been followed by a great cultural renaissance. In 1884 he founded the Munich review, *Die Gesellschaft*, which was to acquaint the Germans with the new school of French painters and with the new French literary movement as well. The contacts which some of the German painters† had already established with the French, from Millet to Courbet and Manet, were extended into the literary field. Through Conrad's efforts some of the younger German writers became devotees of Zola, and found in him what their elders had too often neglected to cultivate—the link between German civilization and the civilization not only of France but of Europe as a whole.

* M. G. CONRAD (1846–1928), *Parisiana*, 1880; *Französische Charakterköpfe*, 1881; *Lutetia*, 1883; *Lutetias Töchter*, 1883; *Was die Isar rauscht*, 1887.
† Among others Leibl and Liebermann.

The naturalist movement gains its significance from the fact that the chief aim of these writers was to be "modern." "*Die Moderne*" was their battle cry. Their object was not to tear down the Bismarckian structure, but to pierce openings in its feudal walls and thus to make passage for the new cultural currents which were sweeping across Europe. The benefit which German literature and German spiritual life was to derive from their efforts was in direct proportion to their individual talents, which were not always great. The period left few names worth remembering, and even these few diminish when judged by standards stricter than those applied by the public and the over-indulgent critics of their own times. Today German literature between 1880 and 1890 takes on the aspect of an indistinct cloud of dust, but it is a dust cloud bursting with vitality. From this literature much can be learned concerning the evolution of German taste, to which it yielded after fruitlessly attempting to shape it. Naturalism and symbolism, considered as literary schools, are interesting today chiefly because they reflected the state of mind of the contemporary public; the few strong personalities of the period interest us chiefly because they were in active opposition to that state of mind. In the two taken together we have two aspects of the inner life of Germany which complement rather than contradict each other.

CHAPTER II

The Naturalist Revolution in Berlin and Munich —the Younger Literary Generation in Search of a "Modern" German Culture

1. *Naturalism Considered as a Broadening of the German Spirit*

THE IMAGE of diastole and systole which Goethe applied to the activity of the spirit serves equally well to characterize the spiritual rhythm of the young German writers who between 1880 and 1890 were bringing about the literary revolution. During the first part of the movement, which may be considered as lasting until 1887, naturalism represented for them a broadening of the German spirit. Later, when they were in the reaction which accompanied disappointment, it came to mean a subordination of the human spirit to universal determinism.

Their early feeling of elation arose both from the spirit of the time in which they lived and from the spirit of the race whose swelling vitality they shared. Julius and Heinrich Hart, Arno Holz, Hermann Conradi, Paul Ernst were all born on the border line between the bourgeoisie and the common people, that is to say, in the petty official and petty tradesman classes—the very milieux which were most astonishingly affected by the modernization of Germany.* Conradi baptized them

* Cf. KARL SCHEFFLER, *Der junge Tobias*, 1927.

with the name which best describes them today—"candidates for a future." These young writers made scarcely any distinction between their individual future and the future of the nation. Yet they had the independence to conceive of that future as shaped by spiritual as well as material forces. They were "real-idealists," as the brothers Hart called themselves, and they aspired to a life of strong emotion as well as to a life of power.

Nearly all of them brought a sense of nature, a quasi-mystical adoration of Pan, from the plains of Westphalia, the forests of the Harz Mountains, the country scenes where they had passed their childhood. This nature worship was strengthened by their contacts with romanticism, and as a result of political events was metamorphosed into a worship of Germany as such. Indeed, their pan-Germanism was often an unconscious pantheism. As ten-year-olds they had stood before bulletin boards which announced victories over the French, and had watched the hostility between Prussia and the other German states melt away as the German nation came to life like a body stretching its limbs in joyous self-awakening and self-realization. It was inconceivable to them that these victories and this joy should not be things of the spirit also. "*Es war Frühling,*" wrote Nietzsche, "*und alles Holz stand in jungem Saft.*"

Berlin exercised a strong attraction upon these young writers. Between 1880 and 1890 they flocked in increasing numbers to the capital, where they could feel the mounting wave which Julius Hart had recognized as that which was to carry them on its crest. There were, of course, some Germans hostile to rationalism or enamored of complexity, who still refused to grant Berlin's claim to the title of capital. But the tempo of life in the former residences of the great had slowed down noticeably; a new and important concept was born: the distinction between capital and province. It was not only the common people who rushed from the provinces to the "*Millionenstadt*," submerging a native racial strain which had already begun to lose its distinctive character. Intellectuals, too, came from every point of the compass, attracted by the cosmopolitan atmosphere of the capital. That Berlin exercised no real catalytic action is true enough. It had not become a capital in the sense that Vienna and Paris are capitals, for it lacked a tradition to bring unity out of the diversity of individual groups. It could offer inspiration only within limits. But does France really draw her inspiration from Paris itself? Does the capital which Goethe so greatly admired do much more than offer an opportunity for an exchange of views between the "best minds" of the nation? In such a rôle, Berlin was not a bad successor to Weimar. A caustic rationalism which spares nothing is perhaps as necessary for the creation of a nation as is a Mephistopheles for divine creation.

Berlin's lack of ancient buildings, its modern intensity of life, and the feverish instability resulting from its cosmopolitanism may sometimes have hindered the German people in their effort to achieve national form, but at the same time these things prevented crystallization, prevented what was merely temporary from being taken as final. The majority of the members of the Academy which was founded in Berlin at this time—from the brothers Mann to Döblin—were representatives of the most advanced literary and political thought of the country. The setting up of the Academy seemed in itself to consecrate once for all Berlin's dynamic power to attract writers and artists from all over the country, in spite of their desire for solitude. They all wanted at least to approach for a moment this dynamo which served as a central distributing agency for the high-tension current of the time. The Berlin market set standards of values for the publishers and art galleries of Leipzig and Frankfort and Munich. Although Berlin was perhaps not a place of residence, it was certainly the chief crossroads of a Germany which looked toward Russia and the Orient as well as toward the West, and traffic both national and international continued to increase. One might seek elsewhere for the heart-beat of Germany, but the brain was undoubtedly Berlin.

However this may be, Berlin was undeniably the capital of the naturalists and played a decisive rôle in this initial movement of contemporary German literature. The great city, with its outstretched tentacles, offered beginners a colossal example of *things* as distinct from *ideas*. Writers, caught in the grip of their senses, broke at last with bookish tradition and arm chair idealism. Meditation was largely displaced by observation, and observation in turn gave way to passionate excitement. The turmoil of city streets, the ferment of ideas in cosmopolitan coteries, was a potion all the more intoxicating since these young men took it on an empty stomach. The wine of Bohemianism went to their heads. New messiahs appeared periodically: Conradi raved to eager listeners behind closed doors; Arno Holz played the prophet beside belching factory chimneys; Karl Bleibtreu in the *Würzburger Brau* proclaimed his empire over barmaids and ʃan outmoded literature. It required all the humor and common sense of the brothers Hart to calm overwrought passions and to reconcile over-emotional artists who had yielded to anarchic impulses in an atmosphere of effervescence that recalled the days of *Sturm und Drang*.

In these "revolutionary" passions there were two distinct motifs: the national and the social. The military victory over France had stimulated the German will to power, but had kept it on the material plane upon which it had been established. This victory brought with it forgetfulness of the imponderables which had prepared it and made it possible; idealism was repudiated as involving too much suffering. Success deludes those who achieve it into misconceiving its nature, and it was partly because of their personal failures that the writers who were declassé at the time were ultimately destined to discover what was lacking in the Reich. The Berliner, Bleibtreu,* went so far as publicly to denounce Spartan Prussia for being insensible to intellectual values. The country which had permitted Kleist to commit suicide and had not yet provided a pension for Liliencron, was reproached with neglect of the arts and letters. The system of *Realpolitik* was termed a negation of true culture. Germany was beginning to luxuriate in a material well-being which still chiefly affected the parvenu class that was eclipsing the old wealthy bourgeoisie.

The splendor of giant cities could not hide the underlying poverty, nor could it answer the demands of a growing working class which, as contemporary election figures impressively indicate, was turning increasingly to socialism—a socialism which did not yet constitute a political threat. For while Berlin was still thrilling over the Hodel assassination, over monster mass meetings and the "*Sozialistengesetz*," Bismarck, exactly as if he were training his mastiffs at Varzin, was taming the *Sozialdemokratie* by bringing forth first the muzzle of restraint and then the biscuit of State Socialism. The result was that the socialism of the writers, from Henckell to Bruno Wille (1860–1928), was sapped of vitality, twisted into banal protests and dreams of universities and theatres for the common people.

* KARL BLEIBTREU (1859–1928).

The literary stimulus came from Zola,* and *Germinal* was its beginning. In his work writers who still had everything to learn found a clear formula. Zola's careful observation was less of an attraction to them than the combination of lyricism and romanticism bursting forth from within realism, with imagination coloring and magnifying sparse facts. They recognized in Zola an art closely related to their own tradition. The undammed flood, the power to evoke elementary nature and the mass of humanity, recalled scenes from Goethe's early work. In this "revolutionary outburst," whose discovery filled Bleibtreu and his friends with exultation, was a source of inspiration which, though softened, was to make itself felt in Hauptmann's *Die Weber*. From Zola these Germans learned not only to give breadth and scope to a literature which in Germany as well as in France had degenerated into miniature, and lacked even the merit of psychological finesse; they learned also to put humanity into their work with an unstinting hand. The brothers Hart praised Zola for his courage, and considered him more moral than the academicians. There sprang up a current of sincerity in writing which ran to join Nietzsche's amoralism at the other end of the horizon. Democrats and aristocrats were engaged in a common struggle against a lying optimism and a simple-minded state of bliss. Their pessimism opened the way for the regeneration which Heinrich von Stein demanded.

Until 1885 this group of writers produced nothing save doctrines and manifestos, programs which were lyrics and lyrics which were programs. One after another, following the Hart brothers' *Kritische Waffengänge*, came Bleibtreu's *Revolution der Literatur*, Arno Holz's *Das Buch der Zeit*, and the anthology *Moderne Dichter-*

* Whom Michael Georg Conrad of Munich had not long before loudly introduced to Germany.

charaktere. Although Holz brought in a "modern" note in his glorification of city suburbs and of springtime on city streets, it was still little more than a debauch of sentimentality and fancy. Nothing had yet been gained for art—no technique invented, no creative criticism. Patriotism was keeping house with socialism, realism with idealism. Reason remained optional; feeling was obligatory. Since everyone wanted everything, no one could make up his mind to a choice. Art was confounded with desire. It was a sort of applied art—to be applied with all one's emotional forces to every objective reality. The poets represented in *Moderne Dichtercharaktere* are not finished personalities, but beginners who have mistaken their hope for power. They were so overjoyed to "feel themselves Germans" that like Henckell (1864–1929) they thought: "We are the Universe; we are the lords, the masters. We are the measure of all things. We carry forward the struggle, ours is the triumph. Within us burns the pure flame of truth."

Even Hermann Conradi, the most intelligent of the group, preached a literature of paroxysm and inspiration. "The spirit which animates our writing can stand by itself unassisted, for it is the spirit of the country, the spirit of a nation awakened from sleep. It springs from the depths of the Germanic soul." Nevertheless, since Conradi was a violent individualist, he placed his hope not in the expansion of the collective soul, but in individual talent, for which he demanded a development which should be "complete, unlimited, unconditional." And while his megalomania misled him into a belief in the possibility of "remaking the Universe by casting into the crucible the individual ego with all its uncertainties, all its motivating forces, whether worthy or unworthy," he still saw that "the innovators, the rebels, are thus in opposition to the forces which now dominate society."

Already the pleasing sensation of "belonging to a collectivity, of being one with it, of living only for the community," was beginning to conflict with the will to "enter upon an era of great souls and deep feeling."

2. *Naturalism Considered as a Subordination to Universal Determinism*

The great fault of the enthusiasts who had conceived their revolution as an expansion of the German spirit was a complete lack of restraint. Where were restraining influences to come from? These men would have nothing to do with the restraints represented by bourgeois morality, the police, the military, or the schools. Of the last, with their tendency to standardize the human product in order to render it "utilizable," they had particularly hateful memories.* The school system succeeded perhaps in imposing uniformity upon the masses, but artistic temperaments it merely excited to revolt.

As a matter of fact, the only prenaturalist who had the truly artistic disposition was Hermann Conradi,† and he alone refused to yield to the system. His volcanic temperament reminds one of Vallès, of Lautréamont, of Rimbaud. He was a revolutionist who never experienced a political revolution, and an artist, who died before the artistic revolution could take place. He was also one of the few young writers of the day who was familiar with the work of Dostoievski and who had read and under-

---

* Literature is full of protests against the coercive educational system of that day. Cf. FONTANE, CONRADI; ARNO HOLZ, *Der erste Schultag;* THOMAS MANN, *Die Buddenbrooks;* HEINRICH MANN, *Der Untertan;* WEDEKIND, *Frühlingserwachen;* HERMANN HESSE, *Peter Camenzind* and *Unterm Rad;* EMIL STRAUSS, *Freund Hein;* OTTO FLAKE, *Freitagskind;* LEONHARD FRANK, *Die Ursache;* REIMANN, *Till.*

† HERMANN CONRADI (1862–1890); *Lieder eines Sünders,* 1887; *Phrasen,* 1887; *Wilhelm II, und die junge Generation,* 1889; *Adam Mensch,* 1889.

stood Nietzsche; but he died of poverty at thirty, before he had had time to orient himself. Nietzsche made clear to him that Prussia represented an artistic style, and Conradi learned to appreciate the stiffening of the Prussian aristocrat against "the pantheism that was driving Germany into a stupor"; but he could not stomach the Prussian military spirit. He was a psychologist and sociologist born before his time, and he realized that in Germany nationalism and socialism were merely two aspects of authority. In 1889 he denounced their junction as Germany's greatest ill, though Spengler was later to see in it the one hope of salvation.

With an astonishing prophetic sense Conradi predicted that his generation would be led to slaughter by William II, and that liberty would be buried to the strains of Wagnerian music. The essays and the two novels, in which he analyzed the faulty standards of his time so brutally as to be condemned by the courts, will remain as a key to the psychology of the years 1885 to 1890, and his *Lieder eines Sünders* fall little short of being a great lyric work. He was to Nietzsche what Lenz had been to Goethe.

A luckier man was to find what Conradi was seeking. His successive states of mind and spirit were like a revolution periodically renewed and never reaching its goal. In fact his work is chiefly interesting because he was continuously questioning all things afresh. His thinking differed from the rationalism of those revolutionaries for whom revolution meant substituting for the existing order a power sprung full-armed from the human brain. He was not a doctrinaire who desired to destroy or dominate definite elements; his was an explosive temperament exasperated by any limitations at all. When the world failed to conform to his desire, he saw only two alternatives: destroy the world or destroy the desire. His philosophy was a philosophy of extremes which denied the right either to take a middle course or to set up a formal oscillatory movement from one extreme to the other. He conceived of himself neither as an artist nor as a repository of wisdom, but as a gambler, and he was willing to risk everything he had. He represented an explosion of individualism, and his individualism was an anarchical rising up of the intelligence, the sensibilities, and the instincts. Like his associates, he demanded complete hyperesthesia. The result was a literature of bludgeon-like power.

There are similar elements of violence in the writings of Rimbaud and the French *surréalistes*. But in these French equivalents there was less breadth and more art; sensibility was more closely analyzed by the intellect; and even at the height of the literary revolution there was a tendency toward organization in the classic pattern, just as classicism had patterned itself on the monarchy. The revolutionary tradition in the rest of Europe had passed through modifications during the course of centuries; in Germany it had scarcely changed at all. There is something of the legendary Faust in the *Sturm und Drang* period. We may call it titanism, demonism, or simply "*Sehnsucht*"—eternal appetite; it remains essentially what it was in the *Götterdämmerung* myth, the desire for total destruction so that creation may begin anew. "*Stirb und werde*"—die and be born afresh—die so that a new life may begin. Strong personalities like Goethe's Faust call upon inner restraints to bring contradictory forces into harmony. They seek in the chaos of the present a more complex order for the future. But others usually progress from revolution to complete submission and end, like Karl Moor turning himself over to the police, by giving themselves over to restraints outside themselves.

This was what Conradi's fellows did. They were not so much active revolutionists as men who submitted passively to revolution, and they ended by adapting themselves to their surroundings. Disappointed in their hopes of inspiring the masses with their own conception of reality, they let themselves be inspired by the masses. At first they believed that they could create a new and greater Germany merely by getting emotionally excited about it. Failing in this, they began to ask themselves whether that greater Germany could not best be brought into being by exactly the opposite means—complete subordination. The dynamism of an explosive was followed by the dynamism of a liquid which takes the shape of its container.

The new group, which these writers founded in 1887, was named from a word of command used in the cavalry: "*Durch!*" They were still concerned with piercing an opening in the feudal walls of Bismarckian Germany, but by a different means. The capital city and modern German society in general had assumed in their eyes the aspect of the Slav goddess Pschipolniza, who put embarrassing questions to the Spreewald harvesters come to break in upon her mysteries. They could not answer her enigmas without first going away to think. Thus an exodus to the suburbs began. Niederschönhausen, to which fled Holz and Schlaf; Erkner, where Gerhart Hauptmann entertained; Friedrichshagen, where the presence of the Hart brothers brought *la vie de Bohème* to the open fields—all these became colonies for alternate discussion and meditation. Against a background of lakes and pine trees, the new theories were built up in quiet and repose.

Literary groups increased in number and added new recruits of bourgeois origin. A sense of balance come down from conservative milieux permitted them to make a more economical use of their sensibilities, a more profitable use of their talent. They saw enough evidences of success around them so that their pessimism, which was social in origin, was dispelled before the national optimism. This national optimism in its turn served to revive personal hopes in new forms. The young writers of the day passed from a naturalism which implied doing violence to nature to a naturalism conceived as a blossoming within the Reich itself. In an acceptance of existing facts it seemed to them that each temperament could come into its own. They were still idealists, but idealists for whom the ideal was conformity with the real. This process of adaptation was greatly assisted by the good humor of the Rhinelander Wilhelm Bölsche, the dialectic of the Prussian Arno Holz, the gentleness of Johannes Schlaf, the forbearance of Gerhart Hauptmann, and the boyish insouciance of Otto Erich Hartleben.

The air was filled with a spirit of conciliation. Thinking was less cramped. Bölsche had lived in Paris, Hauptmann in Italy and Switzerland. At last something existed for them beyond a Berlin bubbling like a sorcerer's cauldron. In addition to a broader experience of the world they had acquired a taste for study. Bölsche worked at natural history, Johannes Schlaf at philology. Hauptmann was attracted by turns to agriculture, to sculpture, to the natural sciences, to political science, and to psycho-physiology. After he had sat under Haeckel in Jena he came to Berlin to listen to the voices of the masters, to learn from his friends, from his books, and from life. Ibsen's plays finally reached Berlin, and between 1887 and 1890 were tremendously successful. At the same time, Antoine visited the German capital with his *Théâtre Libre*. Germans who had known only the Zola of *Germinal* discovered the Zola of *Thérèse Raquin*. The figure of the Goncourts showed above the horizon. The naturalist movement, which had at first been chiefly concerned with verse and criticism, now turned toward the theatre, and having attacked national, social, and moral questions began to occupy itself with problems of esthetics and literary technique.

Ideology and methods changed. Arno Holz, recognizing the inanity of doctrines improvised in the rush of city streets, learned to use libraries. The young writers felt the need to lean upon the science and knowledge of their century, which was largely German in inspiration. These things had already, since Renan's time, strongly influenced French literature, and now they began to have their effect upon the Germans also.

German writers still needed an esthetic formula before they could proceed to artistic creation. Holz realized that Zola could not be fully understood without studying his doctrine of the experimental novel, and went on from there to study Claude Bernard and Proudhon. Taine's contribution was to teach the Germans how to use the milieu as hero, for the milieu is the only hero which realist esthetics permits. Darwinism and Marx's materialistic conception of history were at the source of the new literary stream, but it was swelled and turned in its course by French contributions. An esthetic dogma was taking shape, and modern German culture was being given a higher, artistic form—in short, a style.

The spirit in which this task was undertaken was the spirit of absolute determinism which, if science was right, ruled the universe. Whatever the doubts with which the older masters had qualified their faith in science, they were discarded by the disciples. These latter were radical —the word in German has kept its old sense of "fundamental"—and, insisting that an idea be carried through to its logical conclusion, which meant to them examined to its very foundations, they set out to destroy all the reservations which their predecessors had maintained. The earlier writers had tried to retain their mastery over experience, whose value they realized to be relative. The revolutionaries who claimed to stem from them and to reach beyond their limitations were in reality submissive, which explains their zeal to make objective reality complete master of the human personality. The doctrine that man is subordinate to the external universe, which they accepted as philosophers and applied like scientists in a laboratory, became on the plane of art the type of "petty fatalism" which Nietzsche was denouncing; but Nietzsche had as yet no listeners.

Wilhelm Bölsche,* who was later to achieve a success nearly as great as Fabre's with novels based on natural history, set up in 1887 a system of esthetics growing out of the natural sciences. The influence of his little brochure must not be exaggerated, but it is characteristic of the tendency of the times and represents at least one aspect of the naturalist faith toward which the members of the *Durch* were turning. An absolute determinism rules the universe. The restricting force at work in it is at once realistic and idealistic. To recognize it and to yield to it is to go with, instead of against, divine nature, which takes care of us better than we can take care of ourselves. The evolution which is taking place in nature would become senseless if it had no consummation. For Bölsche the modern civilization of Germany was a boundary. The higher form of being is that which results from an application of the Darwinian law, nature's masterpiece of selection. The literature which should represent this definitive form of civilization should borrow its methods from the scientist, and should find its inspiration in a

* WILHELM BÖLSCHE (1861–   ). For bibliography, see p. 287.

ervent, instinctive submission to the laws which control all the organisms of nature. Beauty in a work of art should be the beauty of the snowflake, whose marvelous crystalline forms are the result of the operation of nature's laws. This doctrine, carried to its logical conclusion, results of course in an absurdity: a zoölogical conception of life and art.

Arno Holz* was a Prussian; he lacked the amorous reverence which the pantheists felt for the organic, undifferentiated mass of nature. He sought on another plane the absolute truth which his group demanded. A thinker who reasoned like a geometrician, he invented the formula of "rational realism." During a sojourn in Paris he discovered Zola's theoretical writings, and after having bowed before them in fainting submission he arose again to set out upon his own path. Zola's formula— a slice of nature seen through a human temperament— seemed to Holz to involve one capital sin: it left the door wide open to temperament. This, he felt, accounted for the "romantic tra-la-la" with which the French naturalist's work was tainted. Once this fact was recognized, nothing remained but to carry the experimental theory to its ultimate conclusion, to solve the equation by eliminating the unknown—which meant eliminating temperament.

Holz now understood what Ibsen had said and what he himself had felt: that the time for poetry was gone. He attributed his previous failures to poetry and lyricism, which he now attempted to suppress in himself as arising from a valuable but dangerous subjectivity. The personality of the writer was the unknown which brought failure. He ridiculed Proudhon's "delightfully imbecile" state-

* ARNO HOLZ (1863-1929), *Buch der Zeit*, 1885; *Die Kunst, ihr Wesen und ihre Gesetze*, 1890-92; *Neue Gleise* (in collab. with J. Schlaf) 1891; *Phantasus*, 1899; *Revolution der Lyrik*, 1899; *Das ausgewählte Werk*, 1918.

ment that "the greatest artist is he who is the greatest idealist." Taine he excused for having believed that art, "taking nature as its object, makes manifest now a deep aspect of its intimate being, now a higher moment in its development," but only because of Taine's "great merit" in insisting that the work of art is always the product of the milieu with which the artist works. Zola, poor man, had gone only part way. Holz came to his aid with an open letter written in French which proclaimed that "the Master could rest easy." His disciples would "put his principles to the test which he himself had demanded," and would "bring naturalism to its full intensity."

Thus in the formula "Art = Nature − X," it was no longer necessary to substitute for "X" the unknown, temperament. "X," discovered by Holz, was the means of expression at the artist's disposal and his cleverness in making use of them. Marx had applied his formula of transformism to the social activities of man; all that was necessary now was to apply that formula to esthetic activity. The organized individual depends upon his milieu, the workman on his tools, the writer on the language which is his means of expression. Thus the literary revolution became a revolution in the means of literary expression.

Holz's deductions bore impressive witness to the need for the absolute which was felt at the time. The masters who had inspired the work of the Berlin naturalists had retained their sense of the relative. To them, science left room for doubt; the world as they saw it remained a hierarchy; in it the highest place was given not to the external object but to the human personality, not to fact but to thought. Their disciples, however, reversed this scale of values, and by carrying to extremes their desire sometimes for the absolute, sometimes for the relative eliminated everything except the gregarious elements in life and in the art which sought to express that life.

Nevertheless, the literature about to arise in Germany, whether it resulted from following established principles or from reaction against them, was in a real sense a new and modern literature. The proclamation of the need for a new literary technique was of capital importance. The experiments of Holz and Schlaf came as a revelation to writers who had previously paid but little attention to form. The two men worked well together, Schlaf's feminine receptivity giving body to the dry concepts of Holz's intellect. They spent a winter in experimentation; the resultant stories and essays really set German literature upon a new path.

Their originality lay in the tools they used. The language which they brought to the service of naturalism closely approached the "copied from nature" type of speech which had been demanded in the preface to the Goncourts' *Henriette Maréchal*, but drew its power from a different source. It was the language spoken by the common people, written down just as the people spoke it: interjections, hesitations indicated by dots, unfinished phrases ending in mumbles or in drunken sobs, in an effort to express whatever was expressible of a thought which did not wholly emerge from the mind. It was speech given depth by its very awkwardness, and moving because of the intensity of the feelings expressed— now resignation to inexplicable fate, now an explosion which for a flash of time seems to lift up the whole weight of the world; awkward and sometimes pathetic grammatical errors in which confusion is a reflection of psychological incoherence; barbarisms of the suburbs or the provinces. The color and savor of the Berlin dialect in Holz's work or the Silesian dialect in Hauptmann's— all these were a far cry from the literary language in which the Goncourts wrote, or for that matter from the language, at once literary and admirably of the people, which Goethe made Gretchen speak.

The truth to which the naturalists adhered was too natural to be a perfect art form, but it made a pleasant contrast with the falsities of academic language. Conventional platitudes were being discarded. The danger lay in the likelihood of falling into photographic, phonographic accuracy of representation and in the dullness of soul in characters conceived as mere extensions of the social machine, just as the workman was considered a mere extension of the industrial machine. "*Man wird doch die reine Maschine,*" cries one of the female characters in Holz's and Schlaf's play *Die Familie Selicke*. Heroism in their eyes lay in accepting the rôle of victim. Others were to appear later, to bring the human personality back to its proper position; meanwhile Holz and Schlaf had at least given the younger German literary generation a working formula. Gerhart Hauptmann, ever gracious, did well-merited homage to the two authors of *Papa Hamlet* and *Die Familie Selicke* by dedicating his first play, *Vor Sonnenaufgang*, to them. Later, become more prudent, he implied his desire to escape from the limitations of their formula by withdrawing the dedication.

During the season 1889–1890, German naturalism came down from the upper regions of theory to face the Berlin theatre public. The *Freie Bühne* was founded by a committee which included Maximilian Harden (who later resigned when Hauptmann came in); Otto Brahm, the future director of the *Deutsches Theater;* and Paul Schlenther, who was later to go to Vienna as director of the *Burgtheater*. The movement, which was shortly thereafter to spread to the officially consecrated theatres, began in this *Théâtre Libre* which had been founded in imitation of Antoine's. *The Power of Darkness*, *Thérèse Raquin*, *Henriette Maréchal*, Ibsen's *Ghosts* and his *Lady of the Sea*, *Die Familie Selicke*, and *Vor Sonnenaufgang* were all played there. The opening of Hauptmann's *Vor Sonnenaufgang* was the "*bataille d'Hernani*" of German naturalism. At first the bourgeois public cried out against its crudity, but ended by capitulating. And the critics followed after.

Old Fontane* hailed the appearance of a "New Continent," and though he was seventy took up again his career as a novelist and sturdily set to work to follow the lead of the younger writers. These later Fontane novels represent the actual achievement, by a graceful, practiced writer, of the aspirations which led the younger writers only as far as experimentation. Fontane was a descendant of Protestant French refugees who had settled in the Mark of Brandenburg, whose austere charm he caught admirably in his writing—a type of Frenchman who had much in common with a certain type of Prussian intellectual. His coldness to imaginative and sentimental confusion, his tolerant and human rationalism, his good-humored scepticism, accompanied by a clear sense of the seriousness of life, all led him to feel himself more closely allied to the Potsdam of Frederick II than to the new German literary generation. Over these younger writers he had the advantage of greater perspective both in time and in wisdom. He was over-modest when he called himself a "conversationalist." He was far more than that; he was a psychologist, and an extremely subtle one. His novels of Berlin life contain no mere rudimentary characters—parvenus, housewives dreamy or domestic, officers, professors, aristocrats,

* THEODOR FONTANE (1819–1898); note especially *Wanderungen durch die Mark Brandenburg*, 1862–1881; *Irrungen, Wirrungen*, 1888; *Stine*, 1890; *Frau Jenny Treibel*, 1892; *Effi Briest*, 1895; *Die Poggenpuhls*, 1896; *Der Stechlin*, 1899.

bourgeois, and so on. His was a keen analytical sense which seized upon nuances of character, and an art which was easily capable of depicting their manifestations. His style indeed was conversational, with all the nonchalance and even the negligence of conversation, but it gave the very impression of reality which Holz and Schlaf were seeking. But his was a selective reality; he resisted the temptation to push his characterizations to the point of caricature. Humor served him as a sufficient tool—not the humor of the ironist proud in his intellectual superiority, but a kindly humor halfway between the humor of Anatole France and the humor of the English, which Fontane appreciated to the full. The dominant note was not bitterness or roguery, but a broad sympathy for all living things, whether on the rise or on the decline, together with an amused and amusing astonishment at social or worldly forms crystallized in mechanical stiffness, which resulted in laughter at the expense of the noble who was no more than a noble, the bourgeois who was no more than a bourgeois, and the military man who was that and nothing more.

Through Fontane's characters one catches a glimpse of the author himself—not, indeed, a genius, but certainly a splendid example of a highly human artist whose mind was open to the new ideas of his time, who was happy to be able to discern the rising sap of socialism and the virtues of industrialism beneath blemishes which he made no attempt to hide, who was attracted by new techniques and new systems of ethics, and who was a liberal in the noblest sense of the word—that is to say, man who drew his inspiration both from an evolutionary process which was moving in the direction of democracy and from a tradition which was essentially aristocratic.

Few of the works of the younger men attained the quality of Fontane's writings. Hauptmann's *Vor Sonnen-*

aufgang represented a sensible application of Zola's formulas, but its characters were still smothered by Darwinist and Marxist superstitions, and not until 1892 did Hauptmann, with *Die Weber*, approach Zola's epic breadth of treatment and at last show himself capable of producing a work in which he freed himself from dogma and gave his personal nostalgia free rein. It was this partial flight into a dream world of his own, which added to naturalism a sort of Germanic classicism, that accounts for his ability to continue to represent the naturalists to the present day.

The value of the manifestos of 1890 lay in the fact that they served as an inspiration for the future. The whole field of reality stood ready to be reconquered. Naturalist literature accepted everything which had previously passed as ugly, vulgar, or lacking in significance, and took up again the tradition of Albrecht Dürer and the young Goethe, who had found beauty in the smallest manifestations of the sensible world. The scrutiny to which the *Stürmer und Dränger* of the eighteenth century, inspired by Shakespeare and their own love of common things, had subjected the life of the humble was now broadened to include a greatly enlarged society, and it seemed only proper that literature should reflect this enlargement. On the moral side, the field of observation was likewise broadened. "Social pity" themes still loosed floods of sentimentality, but there was room for more than the "good sentiments which go to make bad literature." The lower instincts and the problem of sensuality took their places as proper subject matter for art as well as for psychology.

The spirit in which literary artists now began to approach their material was far broader than that of Bölsche and Holz. Hauptmann, for example, was not concerned with forcing literature into harmony with some recognized and immutable truth; he sought to discover in the sea of appearances elements of a truth that was ever changing. The analysis of the external, concrete world was carried to the limit, and though an accompanying synthesis was not achieved, at least the way was prepared for creative work. The application of the analytical spirit to the inner life indicated a new courage of which the "idealists" had been incapable. The wave of amoralism which arose with Wedekind, in a form less aristocratic than Nietzsche's, indicated a new desire to get down to the fundamentals of morality. But the chief contribution to the artistic spirit was the enthusiasm with which the younger writers girded up their loins to take possession of the whole of reality. The senses were given complete liberty, both as a means of acquiring knowledge and as a means of gratification. Especially important was a sort of re-education of the eye in a country where for some time an artificial idealistic formality has prevented poets and artists from looking at anything save the clouds. Writers, inspired by painters, ran the risk of attempting to do the latter's work without the proper means of expression, but at least they greatly benefited by the acquisition of new ways of seeing and feeling, and in consequence the universe which they conjured up took on new color and savor. Eyes which could see and ears which could hear restored to it its picturesque and musical qualities. All that was lacking now was the requisite vigor to extricate these reconquered riches from their formlessness, and shortly after 1890 this too was to be available. But before turning to a study of these newer literary figures it will be worth while to compare the aims of naturalism with the total of its accomplishments.

Once the naturalist formula was invented there was no lack of writers to make use of it. In so far as the drama was concerned, as early as 1889 Sudermann,* in *Die Ehre*, used it as seasoning for his own style. He had a good sense of theatre, but made no pretense to greatness. A clever story-teller, he achieved even in France the easy success which often comes to hybrid artists. But his rôle was limited to furnishing the department store buyer the merchandise of realism. Otto Erich Hartleben's plays and stories, on the other hand, were free from false esthetic appeals, but on the whole Hartleben was only a capable follower of Maupassant who never equalled his master. The playwright Max Halbe had poetic genius, but contributed nothing which had not already been better done by Ibsen or Hauptmann. So far as the effect of the evolution of naturalism on the drama is concerned, Hauptmann and Wedekind are the only two names worth remembering.

In the field of the novel there was tremendous productivity. Almost anyone can write a realistic novel, and it would be useless to try to study in detail the works of a great number of honest literary craftsmen each of whom added a brush-stroke to the great picture of contemporary society which was being painted. The metropolis, the provinces, the proletariat in the factories and on the farms, the department store and the small shop, the barracks, the army, the officer and the non-commissioned officer, the professor and the student, men who were men and women who were feminists, fathers of families and adolescent boys and girls—each was proper material for a novel and each found its novelist.

These novels were like monographs. The "encyclopedic novel" was broken up into little pieces. Life in its infinite but concrete diversity was looked at not as centering about the author or as colored by his personality, but rather as seen in its relation to the concrete objects to

* Hermann Sudermann, 1857–1928.

which his personality is subservient. As it appeared in these novels life was made up of hundreds of thousands of interesting laboratory notes, so that the whole became a study in micrography. The effect was of swarming rather than of development, produced by creatures who believed themselves to be creators. Earlier generations had sought an orientation of the national life in terms of what was past and far away; these writers sought it in the present and in their immediate surroundings. The stage was completely occupied by the collectivity. The great majority of realistic novels of the period might have carried as an epigraph the words: "*So sind wir.*" They gave a magnified importance to common realities by repeating in a thousand voices: "This is what we are!" without once aspiring to anything beyond this.

There were also many women novelists of considerable talent. But since their work differed scarcely at all from the work of the men, and does not make one feel that its absence would have been noticed, and since, in short, these women writers created nothing irreplaceable, they can well be omitted from a study whose chief purpose is to point out the general evolution of the literature of the day.

CHAPTER III

Symbolism as a Normal Development of Naturalism

NATURALISM had scarcely reached a position of influence when Hermann Bahr, in 1889, announced that it was to be superseded. Bahr was an Austrian novelist and essayist of eclectic temper, and had already acquired the reputation of foreseeing the coming fashion before anyone else. He had just returned from Paris, where he had made an extremely intelligent study of the contemporary French literary movement. The future seemed to Bahr to lie in something beyond naturalism. Following his lead, the Germans discovered Baudelaire, Verlaine, Mallarmé, Huysmans, Maeterlinck. Shortly after its equivalent had taken place in France, there began in Germany a reaction against the crass realism of the moment in favor of either a "*réalisme qui sent bon*" of the Goncourt variety, or of symbolism. This was not a mere mechanical imitation of the French; it was less a French influence than an interaction of French and German influences. Once more something that was originally German returned to Germany through the intermediary of France.

French symbolism owed much that was good and much that was bad to the German romantics who flourished from the end of the eighteenth century until the time of Richard Wagner. The French had shown their originality by achieving through preciseness what others had sought to achieve through vagueness and confusion; by inventing conventions which rendered new ideas communicable; by giving artistic values to things which had been floating in mid-air. The danger for the French had been that they would check the development of these new ideas; their merit was that they had channeled them and placed them in circulation. In Verlaine the Germans rediscovered the musical quality which had always charmed them. Mallarmé appealed to their taste for profundity; he offered them an invitation to plastic expression, and at the same time initiated them into the worship of form. They ended by agreeing with him that form can contain spirit without necessarily doing itself violence. Even Maeterlinck had some influence; his contribution was to re-acquaint the Germans with their own Novalis, who was the source of Maeterlinck's inspiration.

The neo-romanticism of the years following 1890 was not so much a reaction from naturalism as a normal development of it. Nowhere in Europe had naturalism lived up to the standards which it had set itself. Romanticism, steadily driven out, invariably popped in again by a different door. Zola and Ibsen attracted interest as much by their elementary symbolism as by their equally elementary realism. In the work of these writers the Germans sensed something which they themselves felt strongly. They had only to yield to their desire to express it, to their nostalgia for something beyond what the visible world could offer, in order to find themselves moving rapidly toward symbolism. The ego, which in their great desire to achieve objectivity they had tried to suppress, was by no means dead. It had merely been smothered under the mass of objective realities superimposed upon it. Unable to affirm its sovereignty through these objective realities, it now sought to identify itself in them as in so many symbols. The writer who had lost his identity, as a person, found it again by means of the symbol, which acted as a sort of diffuse, impersonal ego. When the ego thus reappeared in the mass of objective reality it had sufficient concreteness to satisfy such writers, say, as Hofmannsthal. Others, however, were not content with this shift from physiological impressionism to psychological impressionism. They considered such an abandonment to sensation merely a sign of decadence; no matter how delicate or how artistic the writer's sensibilities, it resulted in a literature of esthetes, for whom art is Narcissism and Narcissism false.

Largely through Nietzsche's influence there ultimately came about an aristocratic affirmation of the ego—no longer one of the thousand parasitical egos which in Bergson's view develop within the fundamental ego, but an ego powerful enough to confront all of life boldly, having mastered both life and itself. As naturalism thus spread into different channels, counter-currents sprang up. Liliencron and Dehmel, thanks to Nietzsche, were not to be satisfied, the one with pure impressionism, the other with pure socialism. Nietzsche inspired their lyricism with a Dionysiac element; helped Stefan George to work out an elaboration of the human personality along aristocratic lines; assisted the Mann brothers in their effort to bring into being once again the novel of spontaneity. It is with this aspect to Nietzsche's work that any study of the newer writers, who were creators rather than mere reflectors, must begin.

CHAPTER IV

Nietzsche and the Resurrection of the German Spirit—the Promethean Spirit versus Pantheism

NIETZSCHE is ordinarily considered a difficult and dangerous writer. Yet so far as difficulty is concerned, his work is not difficult in form—he rightly prided himself on having done as much for the language of Goethe as Goethe had done for the language of Martin Luther, and he wrote a German as beautiful and as clear as any ever written—but in substance his ideas, at first glance changing and inconsistent, actually correspond to the unity of life, whose mingled order and complexity he was attempting to grasp. As for being dangerous, Nietzsche is dangerous only to those who read him in haphazard fashion, selecting what flatters their own passionate desires and thus doing violence to a tissue of living thought so delicate that it can only be appreciated if it is approached dispassionately. He would have considered himself a bad teacher had he been unable to teach his disciples to get along without him. His work is such that it must be studied as a whole, approached with the care and disinterestedness of the scientist, and, if necessary, read antagonistically.*

Strictly speaking, Nietzsche might be considered merely as a profoundly inspired poet, and his reputation would be secure on this ground alone, if only because the flame with which he was consumed kept alight in a

---

* FRIEDRICH NIETZSCHE (1844–1890), *Gesammelte Werke*, 1900.

few people an exceptional fervor for the noble and the beautiful. But there was also a Nietzsche who was a thinker. He was a born oppositionist, and his ideas represented an absolute reaction against the ideas of his time. Determinism was then carrying the day. Impressionism, whether physiological or psychological, whether naturalism or in process of evolution toward symbolism, was only the artistic aspect of the yielding of the soul to invasion by the things of the objective universe. Basically it was pantheism in modern dress. Nietzsche set up in opposition to it the Promethean spirit, the right to struggle against fate. His ideas seem complex, but they are all included within one central idea: that man can lift himself above nature, and can lift man himself above man—a process which implies the bringing about not of a master-slave relation, but a development within the individual.

The problems which Nietzsche set himself are our problems today. The Superman is merely a poet, very pure, very gentle, and very solitary, who seeks the answer to the ever-present question: How can a man lift himself up to the plane where he really deserves the name of man? This process of raising oneself to a new stature implies no mere acceptance of a fixed relation between a given self and a given world, whether a relation of subordination or of domination; it implies the desire that through each other both self and world should elevate themselves. It is the duty of each man to repeat the sum of human education within himself. Nietzsche, taking up again the task of educating the human personality to which Goethe had consecrated his life, followed Goethe's methods. Like his predecessor, he sought his examples in the heroes, the artists, the saints of the past; his aim was to unify their disparate virtues and to make this unified virtue his own. He sought in the traditions of the past whatever manifested man's desire to uplift himself. He felt that such manifestations were to be found in every great era and in every civilization, among Germans as well as among the French moralists and the Greeks. He dreamed of a synthesis which should unify classical reason with romantic religiosity through a fusion of all conflicting forms and beliefs. During the period of his enthusiasm for the musical drama and for the Dionysism of pre-Socratic Greece, he believed in the omnipotence of instinct, that demon within man which sweeps him suddenly upward to magnificent heights. During his rationalist period, he believed the source of uplifting power to lie not in that type of reason which reduces the world to petty causes and effects and the soul to petty virtues, but in a lucid intelligence which frees the spirit by dominating the confused impulses of instinct. During the *Zarathustra* period he sought to rise above both reason and instinct through an inspiration springing from the elementary man, but at the same time imposing upon him such restraints that his power is increased tenfold and turned toward self-elevation.

Naturally those who seek inspiration from Nietzsche find differing kinds of inspiration in the successive phases of the evolution of his thought. Each discovers the Nietzsche he seeks, but none can afford to forget that, for the great amoralist, inspiration was always equivalent to the will to reach a higher moral elevation. In the field of ideas there are several Nietzsches, but in so far as his general aim is concerned there is only one: a Nietzsche seeking the maximum purity at the same time that he seeks the maximum profundity and the maximum freedom. Those who seek Nietzsche's inspiration must not believe that it will be easily obtained. Freedom as Nietzsche understands it is a conquest of the self, and a conquest achieved only with great difficulty. *Zarathustra* is not a revelation; it is a doctrine of gradual and heroic sublimation.

Nietzsche was at once the last source to which nineteenth-century Europe turned for inspiration and the first prophet of the Europe of the future. The reason was that he was at first concerned merely with absorbing what was diffuse in his surroundings, and only later gave it back, like a lens concentrating rays from many sources and sending them out again as one hot beam. The influence which Richard Wagner had upon him was merely one incident in the period of absorption which preceded the period of radiation.

Nietzsche has been accused of infinite scorn. This is true, but his scorn was greatest for those objects of his hatred which he felt within himself, and his will to power was directed toward converting the conflicting forces within him into spiritual strength. The Superman, whose title he borrowed from Goethe, is neither the character in sub-Nietzschean novels who crushes the weak,* nor is he the oversimplified concept of humanity in evolution, full of gross confidence in transformism. Nietzsche's Superman is a symbol—the conception of a growth, a development toward a higher elevation taking place within an individual ego more subtle than that of Julien Sorel, forcing itself against its own resistance, and moved by the aristocratic desire to lift itself above its desire, to find itself on a higher plane. In contradistinction to the "*Teilmensch*," the man who remains fragmentary within his own limitations of space and time, the Superman is the "*Gesamtmensch*," the whole man that Goethe sought

---

* "The Voyager and his shadows" would be a subject worth treating. Since Paul Adam, errors in the interpretation of Nietzschean thought have been so widespread that M. Julien Benda, although this does not weaken his theory, has failed to discover in Nietzsche his best ally against "the treason of the intellectuals."

to be and who achieves universality less through knowledge than through the will and the power to encompass all
of life entire—an ideal of culture, of humanism, which was
to be taken up, after Goethe and Nietzsche, by the best
representatives of the new German spirituality, from
George to Scheler.

The power which motivated Nietzsche was not dissimilar to the particular form of *élan vital* which was
actuating the Germany of his day. While France was
drawing in upon herself, gathering her forces, Germany
was going through a process of free spiritual expansion.
Nietzsche benefited by this "rising of the sap," and
suffered also from the morbid uncertainties of the early
years of the Empire. Beneath an exterior which seemed
perfectly healthy, developed what he called "*Fäulnis
vor der Reife*," a decomposition before maturity. The
germs of decadence which were abroad in Europe became
virulent when they attacked a civilization which had
been wrenched out of its old equilibrium and turned into
an organism that was expanding like a forced plant and
whose powers of resistance were therefore low. As these
germs worked, ambition turned to megalomania.

Nietzsche felt the impact of contemporary European
ideas—the religion of science, Darwinism, the material
interpretation of history, socialism, industrialism, imper-
ialism; and in most cases he fought them. One could write
their history by referring to his works alone. Though
he wrote against them, even as he fought them he absorbed some of their strength. They represented energy
which was important merely because of its violence, and
Nietzsche, while he denied the ends to which it was
turned, nevertheless accepted it. His, however, was a
conditional acceptance. He wished that energy to be not
passive, yielding to conventions imposed by a history and
a science based upon a false scale of values, but creative,

bringing into being a set of values which are to be found neither in things nor in facts, *Amor fati*—but the destiny which he loved, as Goethe had, was not a determinist destiny existing outside the self; it was incarnate in the individual. *"Ich bin ein Verhängnis"*—I am a destiny. To make such a statement presupposes that one know oneself entire, and wish to be superior to oneself.

Thus Nietzsche's conception of human evolution was influenced by the scientific ideas of his day, but it escaped the zoölogic aspects of the other philosophies based upon the principle of natural selection. Nietzsche sought more than merely to reach visible heights on a wave of happy accidents. He sought a hierarchy, and he was not content, like Gobineau's followers, with the conception of the suzerainty of a blond pirate. His struggle was not for existence but for the achievement of a higher life; his hierarchy was to be spiritual. In that hierarchy order was to be brought about on a basis of reason, but not a cold, dialectic reason. There is also the logic of passion, a reason far more inclusive than that of merely rational people, a reason which is always in process of evolution, always assimilating the irrational. Its rôle is to examine all things without exception and to cause to emerge from each a concept of value.

All this presupposes the exploration of space and time, research—to be followed by creative selection—into the limitless riches revealed. Passionately Nietzsche gave himself up to the task. Even his most violent hatreds were merely the sign of a tender watchfulness that made great demands upon its object. The fact that he exiled himself from Germany and felt at home only in Nice; the fact that he criticized Germany and found his proper spiritual climate in the regions frequented by Montaigne and Stendhal, does not mean that he was anti-German. He had set out in quest of a new humanism, and his problem was so vast that it stood far above any idea of nationality.

Nietzsche's way of showing his love for Germany was to pray that she might have opponents. The opponents he chose for himself were a self-satisfied Germany and a self-satisfied Europe, whose very self-satisfaction was a sign of mediocrity. His was the dissatisfaction of a man tormented with an ideal of perfection. He saw the necessity of powerful adversaries, the necessity of an opposing power to force one to self-development. In the Europe of his dream, the enemy would no longer be the neighboring state—the adversary who opposes you, so to speak, on a horizontal plane—but the things which are in oneself, of oneself, above which one must rise. French civilization would no longer be set against German civilization, classicism against romanticism, the spirit of reason against the spirit of music. Synthesis would be possible, and this synthesis, instead of being an artistic formula like Wagner's, in which a variety of heterogeneous motifs were merely juxtaposed, would imply a complete fusion of all the esthetic and ethical systems of Europe with a view to raising the whole Continent to a nobler way of life.

Such an objective implies first of all an extraordinary effort of the intelligence. Our epoch lives, just as Nietzsche (who anticipated us) lived, under the twin signs of relativity and simultaneity. The older categories of thought have lost whatever semblance of the absolute they had. Rationalism, intellectualism, romanticism, mysticism, Christianity, deism, atheism—none of these any longer satisfies the mind. Differing views of the arts, the sciences, technology, politics, morality, religion, all show the same blind will to recover a lost unity. Yet the intelligence of the artist or the cold intellect of the scientist is not competent to establish a true bond between such diverse conceptions. If our view of the world is successfully to be refashioned in harmony with life, we need for the task the "intelligence-passion" which Nietzsche represented. This force, opposed to dilettantism, that inventor of Utopias, is the sole force capable of restoring to the human personality, its identity and sovereignty, for it is the only force which calls upon the whole of our being. Nietzsche's aristocratic individualism is not the affirmation of an existing ego, but the development of an ego through a constant process of self-domination. Superman, hero, saint, artist are only so many symbols denoting the diverse forms into which chance throws this ego.

Theoretically one ego has as great a chance for development as another. But in practice—and this is one of the points upon which Nietzsche breaks with democracy—each man goes only so far as his individual virtue can carry him. From the Nietzschean point of view the ideal of freedom not only triumphed in the nineteenth century but, perhaps because of this very triumph, turned decadent in the same period. Whether bourgeoisie or proletariat, those who embraced that ideal took too crude a view of it. They were fascinated by a civilization which was synonymous with physical well-being, and they sought freedom merely the better to indulge themselves.

The result was that they either turned away in disgust from their very self-indulgence, finding that the liberty they had wooed like a harlot was too easily conquered to be worth the conquering, or, believing themselves cheated in the favors for which they had crudely pleaded, as a means of revenge proclaimed the sovereignty of necessity. Nietzsche shared neither their conception of freedom nor their conception of necessity. He gave a new meaning to both concepts, believing that one did not necessarily exclude the other but that on the contrary a subtle relationship could exist between them.

Nietzsche's teachings do not lead to the establishment of particular cults. They tend rather to keep the spirit free of obligations, ready to meet changing situations, but still retaining the religious ardor which makes life a succession of profound experiences. His great value was that he set an example of the man who could "*unlernen*," forget his formulas, unlearn what he knew, and match the enrichment of that changing whole, the universe, with an enrichment of that whole *par excellence*, the human personality. Coming into a society which was concerned with passively reflecting the objective world about it, he served as the stimulus that encouraged man to throw off the burden of the world of things, which threatened to smother him. In Germany itself he made many converts to Goethe's view that to build a civilization, an art, or a morality of true nobility, the first necessity is the education of the ego, the achievement of an inner style.* Quite apart from his direct influence upon Stefan George, Liliencron, Dehmel, and the Mann brothers, he set up fresh currents which served to break the stagnation into which German artistic and literary creation had fallen as the final result of naturalistic and neo-romantic impressionism. Outside Germany he is still a strong influence upon those who declare that they

* It is not mere chance that Thomas Mann (*Brief an Hermann Keyserling*) recalls the letter in which Wilhelm Meister says to Werner: "Ich weiss nicht, wie es in fremden Ländern ist, aber in Deutschland ist nur dem Edelmann eine gewisse allgemeine, wenn ich sagen darf, personelle Ausbildung möglich. Ein Bürger kann sich Verdienst erwerben und allenfalls seinen Geist ausbilden; seine Persönlichkeit geht aber verloren, er mag sich stellen, wie er will. Er darf nicht fragen: Was bist du? Sondern nur: Was hast du? . . . er soll einzelne Fähigkeiten ausbilden, um brauchbar zu werden, und es wird schon vorausgesetzt, dass in seinem Wesen keine Harmonie sei, noch sein dürfe, weil er, um sich auf eine Weise brauchbar zu machen, alles übrige vernachlässigen muss."

"love in themselves only that which they are capable of becoming."

It is unfortunate that there is space for only passing reference to a name which should stand side by side with Nietzsche's—that of Carl Spitteler*—not because of any influence which the German philosopher-poet and the Swiss poet-philosopher had upon each other, but because they belonged to the same spiritual family, each recognizing the other's greatness but each achieving greatness from his own individual virtue. Nietzsche was a volcano spewing up to the universe the universe which it had swallowed. Spitteler, the author of *Prometheus und Epimetheus* and of *Olympischer Frühlung*, represented a universality still in chaotic state—an Alpine chaos full of admirable contrasts of light and shadow. In it Prometheus is young again, and has the humor which Nietzsche lacked. Spitteler's farces of the gods interrupting the drama of salvation in Shakespearean fashion, his depiction of the crudeness allied with subtle tenderness of primitive humanity, represent life at its beginning stages—an inspiring freshness often lacking in more sophisticated thinkers. Spitteler fully deserves to stand side by side with Nietzsche.

* CARL SPITTELER (1845–1923). In addition to his poetic works note *Literarische Gleichnisse*, 1892; *Lachende Wahrheiten*, 1898.

PART II

The Development and Differentiation of
Literary Trends

(1890–1914)

CHAPTER I

The Theatre

1. *Gerhart Hauptmann*—The Drama of Desire*

THE MEMBERS of the Berlin and Munich naturalist groups, in spite of their search for a rigorously accurate definition of what was essentially German—a definition of the collective being of the race in terms of particular time and particular place—had great difficulty in suppressing their own secret, individual desire to embrace nature in its indeterminate totality, to discover, in the tissue of poetry which underlies objective reality, the symbols of an ego truer and more inclusive than the national or the social ego. The reason that Gerhart Hauptmann's writings remain the finest product of German naturalism is that, while they represent a milieu whose substance flowers in them, they seek at the same time to reach far above and beyond that milieu and to become in their entirety an unending drama of nostalgia.

On Hauptmann's theatre the final curtain falls in vain; the end of the play leaves the problem unsolved; one realizes that the drama must go on afterward—a drama which is at once of the author and of his epoch, the endlessly posed problem of human destiny. Hauptmann is neither an analyst nor a moralist. He is a poet, in the original sense of the word. To call him a lyric poet, a

---

* GERHART HAUPTMANN (1862–   ). For bibliography, see p. 299.

dramatic poet, an epic poet, would be to attempt to confine him to categories which cannot contain him. He is in some degree all of these things; but if one must seek limitations to his talent, one must seek elsewhere than in the range of his artistic activity. His receptivity is tremendous; he receives stimuli from every direction. His intuition is equally great; there is scarcely a color, a form, or a movement in living reality which escapes him. He welcomed his milieu and his times with open arms.

Places, spiritual attitudes, ideas, sensibilities all had their effect on him. He was a *Stimmungsmensch;* he vibrated to the least breath; and like a delicate instrument he responded to a whole gamut of scattered notes which not only roused echoes but set up subtle harmonies within him. His song does not rise like Zarathustra's—a swelling anthem that dominates the plain. He stayed close to the murmur of the masses, a musician accompanying a choir for which he had not written the music himself. The sounds which came to him from beyond appeared only as fragments of broken melody. He was waiting for something greater, for the swelling of another melody that would not merely complete itself to the satisfaction of the ear but that would also express himself and his century. No such melody has arisen, as an expression of either Hauptmann or his time. But we still await its coming.

Those who knew him in his youth called him "the silent Hauptmann." His portraits all show him as a listener. In them life is in suspension, like the figure in Böcklin's painting who looks backward over one shoulder in an attempt to surprise the silent secrets of the forest into which Pan has entered at midday to dream. In Hauptmann's tense features there is an almost imperceptible quiver. There is something troubled in the eyes and in the brow, behind which is a mind that has not yet achieved comprehension of the cosmos. Behind that veiled expression is a persistent question. Hauptmann found only temporary satisfaction in Haeckel's teachings concerning the enigmas of the universe. He seized upon contemporary science, but, unlike Holz and Bölsche, failed to find an inspiring and soothing dogma in it. On the contrary, for Hauptmann science only deepened the mystery. The many objects of his faith represented to him not so much positions to be defended as inspirations to push farther ahead. What he drew from life and experience served only to feed his love of living. He set out to consume himself, and he never felt that he had lived enough.

By 1892, when the success of his *Die Weber* marked the triumph of the younger group of writers, Hauptmann had already, within himself, outdistanced the younger writers' movement. Some of these men were "candidates for a future," risen out of the common people, attempting to profit by the growing power that was in Germany and to turn it to ideal ends, but either breaking themselves against the resistance of the milieu for which they wrote or adapting themselves to its tastes in order to harness its power to their own ends. Others were bourgeois, flirting with both socialism and nationalism, and finding in the doctrines of Marx and Darwin something to satisfy the requirements of their national feelings, their conception of humanity, their taste for science, and their need for a modern code of esthetics. Hauptmann, on the contrary, was neither of the bourgeoisie nor of the common people. He served as a link between them, which is different from seeking a compromise between them. And though he was sympathetic with these younger writers' views, he was not satisfied.

He was fortunate enough, throughout a youth spent in Silesia, to remain in close contact with a population of

farmers and workmen, which differed markedly from
the industrial proletariat that the Berlin naturalists
knew—a population which retained a sturdy, salty
personality of its own. He knew the odor of cut clover, of
plowed earth. His writing has sap in it; it bursts with
colorful earthy notes like poppies in a dun field of
ideology. It has a freshness which sets it apart from the
rustic idylls of George Sand, and a powerful sensuality
which is, however, far from the erotomania of Zola's
imitators. Finally, it leaves room for the play of an
imagination that seeks to transfigure objective reality.

The question was how this transfiguration was to be
accomplished. Hauptmann hesitated before a variety of
methods. When he was twenty he wanted to be a sculptor.
In the sculptors' ateliers of Rome and Breslau he had an
opportunity to rid himself of any inclination to wallow
voluptuously in formlessness; his poetry has the usual
vague background of romanticism, but the foreground
stands out in full relief, peopled with figures given plastic
reality. When he came to Berlin he wanted at first to be
an actor; and when he was finally carried away by literature, he was able to put his stage experience to practical
use in his plays.

Unlike most of his young friends in Berlin, Hauptmann
had not deliberately chosen literature as a means of
subjugating the external world without the unpleasant
necessity of first subjugating oneself. He began by first
exploring that external world, whose existence seemed
to him as important as his own, and he saw in literature
only one of many possible methods of giving expression
to life. When he finally turned to writing, he discovered
that he was possessed of an unusual facility. But though
literature permitted him to use his creative talents
economically, it did not prevent him from seeking to
understand and develop his own personality. Gradually

ıe settled down to a rhythm of life in which periods of ;athering strength alternated with bursts of creative ːnergy, and periods of a search for equilibrium alter- ıated with adventurous expeditions into the unknown. During his Berlin period, he used the lake region between Erkner and Friedrichshagen as a refuge from the hurly- ﹣urly of the capital. Soon he turned to Schreiberhau, in ıis native Silesia, for a haven from which he could look ﹣ut in peace upon the agitation all around him. Trips to America, to Italy, and later to Greece broadened his ﹣utlook. In his work naturalism for the first time reached beyond the boundaries of the Berlin suburbs.

From the very beginning, from *Promethidenlos* to *Griechischer Frühling* and *Der Bogen des Odysseus*, Hauptmann showed himself to be a realist who had found realities other than those of the Hohenzollern Empire. Sometimes he yielded to the attractions of material grandeur, to the colossal, as in his Friedrich, in *Atlantis*, who never felt so much respect for the spirit of his time as when he stood before a modern ocean liner whose power, at once real and fantastic, seemed to him to bear clear witness to the fact that the modern age is not without poetry and that the inventions of modern engineers are indeed more romantically audacious than any poet's dream. But Hauptmann knew when to draw back. Like other writers he praised those things which can be given objective reality, but he realized that when they have actually been given such reality they are very likely to turn vulgar.

He did not conceive the new civilization at whose foundation he was working, together with his race, as consisting entirely of factories and dispensaries, of applications of science and the arts, of the fusion of hygiene and esthetics, designed, in an atmosphere of suburban homes and exposition grounds, to bring

physical well-being to the masses. He re-introduced into
the conception of that civilization the conception of the
human soul which the theoreticians all about him had
sought either to exclude or to warp to their own ends
and in this conception he brought back not the sentimentality ruined by a century of abuse which had provoked Nietzsche to terrible laughter, but a true feeling
for humanity that sought to deepen its life, and for
something in that humanity which cried for deliverance.
The doctrinaire naturalists were trying to define essential
Germanism in terms of the Germany of the present.
Hauptmann sensed what was European in the German
and made no distinction between contemporary civilization and the civilization of the Renaissance, of the Middle
Ages, or of Greece. To understand, it seemed to him
necessary to seize upon everything, to attack problems
by other means than the intellect alone, and above to
be careful never to believe in the solution of those problems by the mere invention of a system or a technique.

Hauptmann escaped formulas, in an age when science
was dogmatic and the formula supreme in literature as
well as in other fields. Not that he did not take advantage
of formulas—he was remarkably clever at it. But while
he tried them all, he remained prisoner to none. Formulas
were to him like the multiple resources of language that a
writer uses to give expression to his teeming inspiration.
He underwent many influences, but he never let himself
be submerged by them. He profited by the movement
which Zola began in France: *Germinal* served as the
shock which produced *Die Weber*. But Hauptmann's
characters—bourgeois or common people, miners, weavers, truckmen, stationmasters, preachers, intellectuals,
painters—are German to the marrow.

The chief benefit Hauptmann received from the French
and from Ibsen was a training in technique; but his

period of experimentation did not end by his accepting the stencils of the naturalists and the neo-romanticists. He turned to Shakespeare and to Molière; but instead of writing imitations of *Macbeth* and *L'Avare*, he wrote *Schluck und Jau*, the *Winterballade*, and *Kollege Crampton*. From Kleist he learned how to bring a plot to crisis and dénouement, but when he wrote *Der Biberpelz* in imitation of Kleist's *Der zerbrochene Krug* he succeeded in creating a satire of the police courts of the 1890's that was wholly original. His contact with Arno Holz is an excellent example of his method of borrowing. Hauptmann was then working on his first play. He had so much to say after three thrilling years in Berlin that there was grave danger that he would turn his drama into the kind of monologue which often ruins the theatrical value of German plays. Holz read him *Papa Hamlet*, and immediately Hauptmann saw the value of fragmentary dialogue, saw the great usefulness of a speech reflecting the little unexpected gestures of ordinary conversation and spoken with the inflexions and deformations of habit or passion. The use of dialect permitted him not only to express the subtleties of the feelings of the people, but also those subtleties of thought which Montaigne said required Gascon for their full expression. But Hauptmann left photographic realism to others; he set out to observe life and to watch its development. Not that he believed this development to follow the rules of logic. He could not bring himself to do to a multiple, richly irregular whole, that violence through which the classicists had achieved unity and simplicity. Herein lie his strength and his limitations.

The process through which, during ten years of youth, he absorbed everything about him was rather a process of passive absorption than the methodical investigation of a Wilhelm Meister. Hauptmann was impregnating his ego; to fertilize it was more important to him than actual creation. He was an autodidact in search of teachers. At Jena he had studied under Haeckel; in Berlin he worked at sociology; in Zurich at psycho-physiology. Max Müller's studies in the history of religion strengthened in him a sentimental mysticism that was fed by everything he touched. But it was precisely because of this religiosity, which emerges continually, from *Der Apostel* (1890) to *Der Narr in Christo Emanuel Quint* (1910) and *Der Ketzer von Soana* (1918), and which tinctures all his work, that he was able to escape the crystallized ideology of his time. The way in which he made successive use of the naturalist and then the neo-romantic formulas is evidence of his eclecticism rather than of any faith in the modern esthetic. His conception of realism was just as much to depict the revolt of the fifteenth-century peasant in *Florian Geyer* as that of the modern proletariat in *Die Weber*. And so surely did he seize upon what was permanent in the accidental, and what was universal human truth in the most concrete details and the most abnormal images, that today we can reach a better understanding of the Soviet revolution through a reading of Hauptmann's *Florian Geyer*.

Hauptmann's intuitional powers are a combination of the *Einfühlung* of the estheticians, the *Anschauung* of the philosophers, and the *Hohe Intuition* of Faust. Through *Einfühlung* the subject's sensibility penetrates the object and reaches an understanding of it from within by sensing every fold of meaning. The *Anschauung* is, in its first stages, a form of knowledge obtained from the aspect of the object by the use of not only the sense of sight but of all the other senses as well. The objective world, with its outlines, its colors, its tactile values, its savor, and its sound is reconstituted in a sort of semi-consciousness. The reality thus introduced within us is fragmentary, but it nevertheless retains, like Proust's *Madeleine*, the power to evoke all reality. If then to these two the third form of intuition is added, the *Hohe Intuition*, the brief moment of illumination in which the parts are shown in their relation to the whole, we shall have a view of the world which not only includes all sensible reality but approaches Deity.

Hauptmann has avoided those forms of inspiration which involve the ecstatic state. His revelations of the divine do not come to him, as they come to Lord Chandos in Hofmannsthal's masterpiece, from unreal beings and objects, but from human beings in which one feels a continual rebirth of the spirit. Hauptmann thinks in terms of flesh-and-blood characters. His most striking creations are not intellectual types, but simple people. His rustics, whether men or women, represent a primitive humanity which no literature before his time had depicted with such sincerity. In France, in spite of their willingness to try anything, the realists could not rid themselves of a certain citified dryness; the realist psychologist modelled himself on the *salons*, in which lively analysis led to immediately expressible conclusions.

The French, even when, under Freud's influence, they plumb the depths of the unknown, cannot refrain from fashioning their characters after their own intellectual desires. Even their most illogical characters smack of the author's logic; their simplicity, from which complexity is not excluded, may be greater than nature's, but they lack the gripping, elementary power that nature exerts upon us. Balzac's peasants are not so much peasants as manifestations of the Balzacian intelligence. Zola's peasants spring not from the soil but from a human brain; they embody an idea, and what picturesque intensity they possess arises from the author's romanticism. Not until André Chamson do we feel that peasant life is again bound up with natural forces in a sort of late-flowering paganism—a paganism only slightly modified by Christianity and by rationalism, and that remains naïve on the edge of our sophisticated civilization, which it does not understand and which in turn does not understand it. Only painters like Bastien-Lepage were able to avoid the dry intellectual approach and to sense in this pagan world enough of poetry to make it unnecessary to introduce poetic elements from without, such as the embellishments of a Fromentin or even of a Millet.

In Germany Hauptmann alone succeeded in freeing this domain from literary claptrap, and by methods other than Hardy used in England. Nor did he limit himself to photographic impressions of village life such as Ladislas Reymont was producing in Poland. Hauptmann approached rustic nature both as a rustic and as a painter. He did not come, like Loth in *Vor Sonnenaufgang*, to observe, to take notes, to verify pre-established theories. His spirit was free, he could forget that he was a cultivated man; his cultivation served only to permit him to express what in pagan, peasant fashion he felt. He benefited by the tremendous education of the senses which German impressionism provided, and went on to enter into communion with beings who were still entirely sensory, but from whom he was distinguished by his ability to express their sensations on the plane of art.

Hauptmann's was an art not concerned with note-taking or with over-stuffing its substance. He neither slipped into the *pointilliste* error nor was he taken in by the romanticist techniques of multiplication and intensification. From *Die Weber* to *Rose Bernd*, the intensity of his work arises from the sobriety of the detail. His characters speak seldom, which is one reason for their strength. They are like the writer whom Thomas Mann amused himself by depicting in *Der Zauberberg*—Peeperkorn, who could never complete his sentences, but whose stammerings were not without grandeur. They resemble Hauptmann himself, who gives the impression that what he might say, what he lets you guess, is more important than what he actually says. His Rose Bernd cannot translate into words the emotions which sweep through her, but she suggests what the animal sluggishness of her tongue prevents her from expressing.

Especially in Germany, this art of suggestion can some-times become as powerful as the art of perfect expression. When Hanna, wife of the truckman Henschel, restrains her lover from fleeing at her husband's approach, she can think of only one thing to say: "*Der Teufel ist los*"— "The Devil's let loose"! The expletive, probably purely instinctive, gives no indication of what is going to happen. What actually does happen escapes classic deliberations, takes place on the threshold of conscious-ness, in the region of pure impulse. Up to the moment when the tragedy floating in the air suddenly crystal-lizes, nothing out of the ordinary occurs—only the unfaithful wife, the husband drinking with the man who has betrayed him—a good-natured giant of a husband who wishes no harm to anyone but who is driven mad by the feeling that a destructive fate has been steadily pressing down upon him, upon his horses, his first wife, his first child—and so the chain proceeds. How can he understand? Where and toward whom can he turn? He goes to the grave of his dead wife and begs her for a sign. None is forthcoming. The seen and the unseen, the sensible and the supra-sensible, surround us, wrap the individual in black immensity. He struggles in the toils of life. He is undifferentiated from, undissociated from the perceptible and from the occult substances of nature, and he acts as they do. He is no more himself than an impotent power, creating and destroying with one and the same uncompleted and uncompletable, unexplained and inexplicable gesture.

Thus Hauptmann's view of life, in some ways so modern and so new, nevertheless represents a return to German pantheism. The bases of Goethe's art were both this pantheism and a conception of the concrete to which he clung tenaciously. But Goethe's images were clear-cut, symbols expressive of the multiple aspects of a thought in which intellect was sovereign; whereas Hauptmann's images, or rather, his characters, remain, like Rodin's figures, attached by their extremities to the block from which they are hewn. A gesture, a feature, a contrast of light and shadow give them a relief rare in a literature tending toward the picturesque and the musical rather than the plastic, but bodies and souls nevertheless retain their connection with the whole of nature, with the poetry of the limitless. Hélène Kraus is not cut free of the rich soil from which she springs like a luxuriant flooer, nor Rose Bernd from Priapus, hidden beneath the grassy slope on which she lies, nor the priest from the powerful forces of nature loosed by the spring upon the mountain of Soana.

In this last work Hauptmann treated the case of a new Abbé Mouret by the usual methods of description and analysis, but in his preceding works he limited himself to description and interpretation. He sets up two forces and leaves them working against each other: on the one hand, nature in its indivisible totality; on the other, the human spirit, indivisible but seeking to escape from its indivisibility, at once happy and unhappy in the realization of its oneness, struggling to differentiate itself but unable to forego adhesion. The drama lies therefore in the conflict between two aspirations—the desire to become one with Pan, and the desire to achieve individual personality. They are desires which, in spite of their religious aspects, can find no religion to reconcile them.

On a higher level than these simple people is the representative character which Hauptmann first tried to draw in *Einsame Menschen*—the great lonely individual to whom he gave successively the names of Vockerath, the preacher; Heinrich, the bellfounder; Florian Geyer, the revolutionary leader; Michael Kramer, the painter; and Gabriel Schilling, the dreamer who stood with outstretched hands waiting for the sea to take him to its depths. Ideas are never entirely communicable, desires never completely realizable. There is no communion possible either with nature or with man except through death. In any case, death is the only true reward of the seekers of man, who are also seekers of God; death terminates their struggles and lends those struggles their final perfection.

With these beliefs as a basis, Hauptmann drifted toward the drama as his natural means of expression. It is true that in his novels and stories—*Bahnwärter Thiel*, *Der Apostel*, *Der Narr in Christo Emanuel Quint*, *Atlantis*, *Der Ketzer von Soana*, *Die Insel der Grossen Mutter*—and in his epics—*Anna* and *Till Eulenspiegel*— he sought to achieve a view of the universe in which dramatic treatment was replaced by the broader, more reposeful treatment of the epic. It is true that in his later work he has sought relief from dramatic tension such as Anatole France permitted himself in his later novels. Indeed, from *Kollege Crampton* on, his humor allowed him to avoid heavy pessimism, and *Der Biberpelz* is one of the half-dozen really excellent German comedies. But all these things—laughter, lyricism, calm wisdom—were merely attitudes which contributed to and were integrated with his main attitude—the tragic—and which did not essentially modify it. To express that tragic conception of the world, however, he required a dramatic formula less rigid than that of the classicists, less limited than that of the naturalists. He drew his inspiration from all sources. There is a breath of Christianity in his work, side by side with pantheism. He rejected neither the early Christians nor the Protestant reformers, as is evidenced by the fact that he wrote both *Der Apostel* and *Der Narr in Christo*.

There was in him also something of the messianism of the German Empire, though it was not a megalomania. In Hauptmann the human stands far above the national, just as in his *Festspiel* (1913) he created the figure of an Athenian Germany majestically insensible to "*rabies nationalis.*" The human is in turn dominated by the divine, by the infinite love and the infinite melancholy inspired by the spectacle of a creation not yet completed, a dream pushing ever onward toward the goal of an unrealized, unknown perfection. André Gide called *Die Weber* "a powerful drama which I admire and which at the same time exasperates me." Was his exasperation not the same exasperation that is caused by looking upon life itself, which is forever cheating us of the answers to our questions? To avoid trying to answer life's questions for her, to be eager to know ourselves, to collaborate in nature's work of art—that, in Gide's own definition, is the task of the true artist.

Problems themselves therefore attracted Hauptmann more than their solutions. He was struck by man's ignorance not only of the divine but of the human. His play *Friedensfest*, in which, through no fault of their own and in spite of their best efforts to reach an understanding, the members of a family find themselves first strangers to one another and finally enemies, is only one act in the great drama which Hauptmann feels to be weighing upon humanity, its principal character being fate. But Hauptmann's fate lacks the mechanical character of the fate of the Marxist and Darwinist writers. Sociology and physiology have their part in explaining its manifestations, but there is room left for poetry—a poetry allied to myth.

The poet is a watcher at the bedside of a humanity continually in birth-pangs. He assists in the delivery, but he does not believe that even through him that delivery is ever complete. Even in exceptional individuals, humanity, like the masses who go to make it up, lacks the words to express itself completely, lacks the knowledge to rule itself. Hauptmann turned to the common people as subjects for his writings, and brought them constantly upon his stage, less because this was the fashion at the time than because he felt a real affinity for them. And the common people who provide him with character after character are always the common people of *Florian Geyer*—impulsive, anarchical, at once denying authority and appealing to it, wedded to justice and bringing about injustice, desiring good and doing evil. Its leaders, like Luther, first sing its glories and then condemn it as one condemns a mad dog. Others, the generous of soul like Geyer, die for lack of ability to control it. But when they give up their control they do not give up hope. "Music! . . . more music!" the dying Geyer cries. His friend Besenmeyer, the rector, argues that "Reason is not the accursed slut which Luther considers her, but the fundamental source of truth." Geyer's philosophic testament might well be Hauptmann's: "I have lived in the consoling conviction which persuaded Count Eberhart of Würtemberg to found the University of Tübingen. I have helped dig the well of life, so that everywhere, mysteriously, a humanity gone mad may drink of the waters of wisdom which extinguish the fires of unreason."

"Mysteriously"—with Hauptmann we seem always to be witnessing the celebration of a mystery which has nothing to do with the established churches. His work breathes a mute, inexigent prayer. The soul is swept upward toward a conception of the inexpressible that is not only diffused throughout the world of objective reality but that swells in the hearts of a humanity which must be allowed to stammer passionately on. When he gives common names to the naïve objects of his love, he is not showing disrespect for the silence due to deep realities, but is avoiding the danger of thinking in terms of quintessences and thus losing contact with humanity.

Hauptmann has taken from German tradition that which is perhaps best in it—a secret intellectual humility before the universe, a naïve and yet philosophic ability to adore, to be awed in the face of a world whose very obscurity may nourish the soul. Distinctions between realism and romanticism fall away. Reality becomes poetry unrecognized; poetry is reality revealed. The world owes Hauptmann a debt of gratitude for never having ceased to seek that revelation.

Hauptmann's melancholy must not be confused with pessimism. It is simply a more subtle optimism, a more profound hope than that of the theorists of the *Neuland*, the organizers of a modern scientific civilization. Nor is it purely intellectual. It arises as much from the heart as from the intelligence, and both are caught in the network of the universe. The heart neither wishes nor is able to free itself from this network. It yields to the *Sehnsucht*, the call of desire which makes the voices of Hauptmann's characters tremble and which, though it has no formal cult, is as certain as religious faith. Its strength is that of life itself, projected beyond the immediate present. The poet is in sympathy with the totality of life. He does not seek to disengage his own ego from it; he lets himself share its confused power. Hauptmann's originality lies neither in a Nietzschean struggle with the elements of life, in an effort to bring order into them, nor in an Olympian detachment. It lies rather in a tenderness which is compounded of *Mitleid*, compassion, pity for the suffering, and *Mitgenuss*, gladness, participation in all that is gladness.

This tenderness sometimes expresses itself in terms of the social pity then in fashion, but it is essentially very different. Hauptmann's characters, even when crushed or in wretched revolt, do not have the physical and moral poverty of the proletarian masses depicted by the naturalists. They burst the confines of the naturalist formula. Hauptmann's masses are not mere waves of nameless people. Like Goethe, he shows us characters detached from the mass, characters each with its own individual gestures, each with its own unforgettable voice. Upon Hauptmann's characters the milieu from which they spring does not act like a sponge, absorbing everything into formlessness. The grandeur of the whole, as in Rembrandt's religious etchings, arises from the sum of individual characters, each unique in its humility. Hauptmann's men and women of the people are not unfortunates conscious only of their misfortune, degraded by their work, by misery, by vice and heredity. They retain the robustness of the rustic; like Goethe's Marguerite, they burst out in spontaneous laughter between spasms of somber passion. Their sensibility is not a controlled sensibility, but neither is it merely animal. Hauptmann was not attracted by the facile effects to be obtained from bestiality. He has his own way of being at once democrat and aristocrat. He feels and makes clear the inner nobility of his characters; and these characters are not entirely, irremediably dependent upon

the circumstances in which they are placed. His view of
the life of humble people is not invariably tragic, for
their existence is tragic only by moments, accidentally.
Their good humor helps them to overcome their daily
misfortunes; their good sense leads them to accept tran-
quilly whatever comes; and it was from this attitude,
rather than from the pedantic theories of the determinists, that Hauptmann drew his inspiration.

The suffering which he accepts as a *leit-motif* arises
from beyond the confines of the immediate physical
milieu. It is not merely the suffering of the oppressed
masses. His characters protest against circumstance not
as members of a lower social order, but as uncertain
souls whose uncertainty has nothing to do with particular
place or time. Theirs is Hauptmann's own protest, the
protest of all who are born with an inexplicable wound,
a sickness which is never to be cured, which can scarcely
be diagnosed, and which is perhaps only the sickness
of life itself for the aware, the knowledge of the eternal
misery of man which Goethe called so great that no
human soul could comprehend it.

Individual lives seem to Hauptmann to be moving
down blind alleys. An invisible hand guides the drama
to its dénouement. Will plays no part in Hauptmann's
dramas, and even passion has a hesitant aspect. His
heroes incarnate both *das Leidende* and *das Leiden-
schaftliche*. They are swayed by great passions, but at
the same time they are endowed with great patience
to await their passions' end. The drama in which Hauptmann places them is not a drama of action but a drama
of situation, and the author seldom finds an escape
for the central figure save in suicide. That central
figure, however, clothed in a different aspect and with
a different name, comes to life again and again in subse-
quent dramas. *Einsame Menschen, Die versunkene Glocke,*

and *Gabriel Schillings Flucht* are all dramas of solitude among those one loves—the same character confronted afresh with the same situation. Hélène Kraus, Rose Bernd, and Griselda are the same women, controlled by the same law of desire. The poet transposes his inner tragedy from the medium of naturalism to that of symbolism, from the real to the legendary, in successive phases and with characters resuscitated from play to play.

The tragedy lies always in the feeling that man, whether he struggle with beast or angel, is certain always to be worsted. As lover he bungles his love, as revolutionist his revolution, as reformer his reform, as artist his work—just as the Creator bungled the Creation. But the struggle is never given up. Michael Kramer, into whose creation Hauptmann put his greatest seriousness, will never finish the painting of Christ to which he has dedicated his life. He lacks the artist's power to project his own ego on an heroic scale, to fashion a world in his own image. But nevertheless he feels that by his effort to "drive out ruthlessly the petty bourgeois soul," he has contributed something toward setting humanity free. Confronted by his unfinished creation, just as when he was confronted by the body of the son whose suicide destroyed another of his hopes, he is still sustained by a mystic faith which makes him raise Beethoven's death mask in his hands and murmur: "Death is the sweetest form of life, the masterpiece of eternal love!"

2. *Frank Wedekind*—*The Anti-Bourgeois Drama*

To call Frank Wedekind anti-bourgeois is perhaps an over-simplification, but it is a true enough description

* FRANK WEDEKIND (1864–1918) note especially *Frühlingserwachen*, 1891; *Erdgeist*, 1895; *Der Kammersänger*, 1899; *Mine-Haha*, 1901; *Der Marquis von Keith*, 1901; *Die Büchse der Pandora*, 1902; *So ist das Leben*, 1902; *Die vier Jahreszeiten*, 1905; *Feuerwerk*, 1905.

of the impression left by his work. Judged by either his
life or his writings, he was a born antagonist. No matter
what he came in contact with, his first move was invariably to try his strength against it, to set himself
up as an opponent who gives no mercy and expects
none. Advertising director of the firm of Maggi in
Zurich; author of novels and plays whose substance was
wrenched from the living flesh; an actor who dramatized
himself openly before literary gatherings and played out
the drama with a fierce verisimilitude before society,
the public, and himself, he struck a lion-tamer's attitude,
believed that he alone of all men was capable of depicting
truly the superb and terrible beast that is man. In the
relative freedom of that beast he found his own freedom,
which was relative also.

He had absolutely no sentiment. He had only an
instinct—it is difficult to tell whether it was hate or
love, but which he conceived as primitive brutality—
that turned him against anything which smacked of
compromise. When Wedekind attacked Hauptmann he
was attacking all who showed indecision, all the hesi-
tators who were afraid of alcohol, afraid of a kiss,
afraid of evil. He gave a literal interpretation to passages
from Nietzsche which were themselves not without a
literary tinge, and on that basis attacked all literature.
To show that books were false, he called to witness
people who had never read a book, people "whose sole
rule of action is the simplest animal instinct." To attack
goodness, he pointed out the power to overcome evil
which lies in evil itself. The basis of his plays and of his
life is the duality of that instinct of evil, the antagonism
that it contains within itself. The tragedy of life, in
Wedekind's view, is that often the moralist, and some
times he who is amoral, looks upon a good deed as a
bad one and believes to be good one which turns out
to be bad.

Before he turned his attack upon his own amoralism, Wedekind set out to attack the contemporary educational system, which swallowed up lives still wholly instinct and forced them to conform to the requirements of an organized society. In *Frühlingserwachen* (1891) he depicted adolescent youth, tormented with vague sensual desires, being strangled by parents and teachers who were determined to impose upon it "iron discipline, moral principles, moral restraints," even if houses of correction had to be employed for the purpose. He saw all bourgeois society organized with the single purpose of applying the very discipline against which he was revolting. "My whole talent rests upon the disagreeable fact that I cannot breathe a bourgeois atmosphere," he makes his character Keith, the adventurer, say. Wedekind said that he felt himself most at home in Munich, because of the "frenzy of mute saturnalia in the air."

Lulu, the heroine of his *Erdgeist* (1897) and of *Büchse der Pandora* (1903), the superb "creature without a soul" who carried both men and women, lovers and the Lesbian, Geschwitz, along with her in her bacchic frenzy, was intended to represent the power of the senses, whose legitimacy Wedekind was striving to establish, like Rabbi Ezra telling his son that carnal pleasure is not only an invention of the devil, but is also sanctioned by God. Wedekind centered the problems of morality about the problem of sex. Of the many forms of sensuality which lend themselves to artistic presentation his choice was overwhelmingly for the sexual instinct, and he frequently confused virility with salaciousness. Lulu finally becomes sex incarnate, so powerful that nothing can withstand her save the knife of Jack the Ripper. Wedekind's cruelty of observation and statement reminds one of Strindberg. After depicting a situation

that freezes the blood, in language that makes the hear
stand still, he bursts forth like Heine with a laugh whicl
seems to say: "But this is life, as life is lived!" Hi
character Keith, attempting to turn his final downfal
into a mere graceful pirouette, says lightly: "Tragic
Come, come. Just a little slip!"

The true Wedekind must be sought in the play, *De
Marquis von Keith*. The hero is a false marquis wh
finally comes to grief. He is a lover who conceives hi
love as a sexual orgy and drives his wife to suicide, onl
to be in turn abandoned by a mistress who refuses t
share his downfall. He is a crook who sets out to buil
a bawdy house with stolen bourgeois money, only to b
unmasked and left to see the bourgeois themselves buil
the bawdy house and profit by the crook's idea. In shor
morality pays big dividends.

The irony of this attitude conceals a secret incor
sistency. Wedekind was attacking himself just as muc
as he was attacking the world, for although he considere
himself an outlaw he called upon existing laws to justif
a kind of law which he conceived as true. The traged
of this anti-bourgeois life lay in the fact that he secretl
desired the same things as the bourgeoisie which h
pretended to scorn, and was attempting first to remak
the bourgeois in his own image. His instinctive respe
for authority shows clearly through the preface t
Büchse der Pandora, in which he thanks the judges wh
condemned the book for having forced him to disciplir
himself. His desire for repose is clearly implied in h
reverence for the Church, that haven of wound
souls.

The spirit of revolt in Wedekind's characters, the
is not truly Nietzschean; it lies somewhere on the out
limits of Nietzschean amorality. It is the spirit of
weakling who, in order to avoid slipping down one pre

pice, throws himself over the opposite one. In taking a tragic view of the petty conventions of the bourgeoisie, Wedekind only falls into the pettiness of Bohemia, and his supposed liberation is merely that of the slave who has changed his master. For the tyranny of bourgeois conventions he merely substituted the tyranny of the senses. His revolt against the vulgarity of bourgeois restraints failed to free him from essential vulgarity. He stated a faith, indeed, but in the sincerity of his statement there was something of pretense. He was likewise an artist, but precisely because of this element of pretense. He catches his audience in an extraordinarily powerful physical grip, but only by appealing to the physical thin parts. In passing final judgment upon him we are inclined to ask ourselves whether what we have really seen is not Prometheus selling matches on the sidewalk.

CHAPTER II

Lyricism

1. *Liliencron* and Dehmel—Impressionism and Dionysism*

To ATTEMPT to make Detlev von Liliencron seem greater than he was would be to do him a disservice. He is at his best only when he is represented in his actual magnitude. Then he is a true poet, whose great gift was naturalness. Unlike the naturalist school, he did not need to seek nature in his surroundings; nature was already within him. He had no need to investigate nature objectively; he felt nature and had the gift of unrestricted expression. In 1884, when he published his *Adjutantenritte*, he was forty. Germany had never before had a poet who dared so openly to be himself, and who showed so much grace in the process. Here were no metaphysical or idealogical overtones, no pantheistic ecstasy, no intoxication with the musical, no effort to comprehend the cosmos or to express the soul of humanity. Here was a man revealed—a man who

---

* DETLEV VON LILIENCRON (1844–1909), *Gesammelte Werke*, Schuster & Löffler Verlag (12 vol.). *Adjutantenritte*, 1884; *Gedichte*, 1889; *Der Haidegänger und andere Gedichte*, 1890; *Neue Gedichte*, 1891.

Early poems reprinted in complete edition: *Kämpfe und Spiele, Kämpfe und Ziele, Nebel und Sonne*, 1900; *Bunte Beute*, 1903; *Poggfred*, 1896–1908; *Balladenchronik*, 1906; *Ausgewählte Gedichte*, 1896; Prose: *Kriegsnovellen*, 1888–1895; other short stories collected in 1900 in *Aus Marsch und Geest; Könige und Bauern; Roggen und Weizen;* Novels: *Breide Hummelsbüttel*, 1886; *Der Mäcen*, 1890; *Mit dem linken Ellbogen*, 1899; *Leben und Lüge*, 1908.

yielded to the appeal of the senses, but who did so brilliantly, in the manner of the born artist. He represented the beginning of a type of German poetry which is best described by saying that La Fontaine might have written it had he been not a courtier of the days of Louis XIV but a young lieutenant in the armies of 1866 or 1870, or that Musset might have written it had he remained a page and forever taken life as lightly as he took women, whether countesses or shepherdesses. Yet withal Liliencron was a modern, taking his inspiration from the aspect of his times rather than from books. Like Turgenev, he was a huntsman; like Maupassant, a lover of the shores of the sea. Yet though he loved to dream in the open air, he did not give himself over wholly to dreaming; his gun was always loaded, his mind always prepared for action. He seemed always to be saying to himself: "On the one hand is the world, at once adorable and detestable—adorable for the pleasures that I find in it, detestable for the meannesses; on the other hand there is myself, Detlev, moving through that world with a plume in my hat and a bold smile on my lips, full of the bravado of the well-born gentleman who greets each meanness of fate with the Frenchman's cry: '*Je m'en fiche!*'"

Liliencron might have been merely the loyal, spirited officer, naïvely swearing by his Emperor and his flag, treating his adversary chivalrously because he respected in that adversary the sense of honor which he himself felt so strongly. He might have been merely the poet whose cavalier insouciance and scorn of bourgeois prudence had led him to adopt a Bohemian way of life. He might have been merely the *vert-galant*, loving and leaving with equal elegance. He might have been the rhymster fighting shoulder to shoulder with his comrades, laying his rifle beside theirs in skirmishes with a common enemy, drinking with them in *Weinstuben* and listening intelligently to their theories without taking them too seriously. In short, he might have been an amateur in the best sense of the term. But he was more than all this, and the naturalness which caused his writings to contrast so happily with the writings of the hot-heads of his day was not a product of mere nonchalance, but the result of hard work on the part of a professional writer who fully realized the demands of his art and knew that the first of these is sincerity.

His work was impressionistic without consciously attempting to be so. Like the Goncourts, he retained only an impression of appearances, and he expressed that impression with the freshness of touch of a Monet, laying strokes of pure color side by side; but he did so with no realization that he was conforming to the tenets of any artistic school. This does not mean that he was ignorant of the artistic theories of his day, but that he considered them merely as a theoretical justification of a technique which he had discovered for himself. To him sensations meant everything. He had the lucidity with which to untangle them, the taste necessary to make a selection from among them, and the ability to express them with artistic purity. His spontaneity was no mere facility. It was the result of self-schooling on the part of a writer with a strongly developed sensibility who proclaimed the legitimacy of the senses in a milieu where their legitimacy was largely denied, but who, again in opposition to his milieu, granted them legitimacy only if they were used to achieve a higher truth and a higher beauty.

The Superman did not interest Liliencron; compared with Nietzsche he aspired merely to be the gay companion whose sallies might have brought a smile to the lips of that ascetic philosopher. Neither did the super-soul attract him. The philosophy of his day, of course, had some influence on him, but he was careful never to let it lure him out of the character he had chosen for himself— that of a man who willingly, simply, gaily renounces the desire ever to be more than a man, though he must be that insouciantly.

He has left us impressions of battle as free from false-hood as Fabrice's description of the Battle of Waterloo, but more colorful and more delicate; impressions of the huntsman, setting down his gun and stopping to smell the perfume of the blackberry blossoms and listen to the buzzing of the bees; impressions of a contemplative, solitary walker whom the solitude of the pine forest sets to thinking of the solitude of the individual, but who is neither uplifted nor depressed by the thought; reflections whose common sense does not seek to be more than com-mon sense; confessions, made in passing, which indicate a life always hospitable to pleasure, to the joys of seeing, hearing, tasting, caressing, but which is nevertheless not given over entirely to pleasure; admissions which indicate a sensibility developed to the full and yet discreet, wounded yet scorning to cry out in protest, controlled always by a rider who has his horse well in hand, an artist who has turned spontaneity into art.

Liliencron's attitude toward life was that of a gentle-man who laughs at whatever fate may bring. His friend Richard Dehmel* took the attitude of a man of the people, accepting his fate and inclined to sympathize with himself. Dehmel was the son of a Brandenburg game-

---

* RICHARD DEHMEL (1863–1920), *Gesammelte Werke*, S. Fischer Verlag (3 vol.). *Erlösungen*, 1891; *Aber die Liebe*, 1893; *Die Verwandlungen der Venus* (revision of *Aber die Liebe*); *Weib und Welt*, 1896; *Zwei Menschen*, 1903; *Der Kindergarten; Zwischen Volk und Menschheit* (Kriegstagebuch), 1919; *Ausgewählte Briefe*, 1923; *Bekenntnisse*, 1926.

keeper. Coming to Berlin first as an insurance agent, then as a littérateur, he took up the life of the common people of the suburbs. His originality lay in the fact that he remained faithful to those people, his weakness in his belief that he was magnifying them when he was in reality only broadening the outlines of their lives without changing the content, enlarging their features without modifying them. He wrote under the labels of naturalism, socialism, and finally patriotism, and though he struggled always to raise them to a higher plane, the dionysiac urge within him was never strong enough to enable him to free himself from them entirely. Afflicted with a form of nervousness which was almost epileptic and which gave him hallucinations, he claimed that he had conquered the epilepsy and at the same time had gained the power to bring on hallucinations at will. This accounts for the intensity of some of his images, which gain their strength not from the fact that they are new but from the passion with which they are perceived. They imply a taste for hyperbole; Dehmel was never satisfied that a given feeling had been sufficiently felt, or that the words in which it was expressed should not be made stronger. He was in the German tradition of the superlative.

Dehmel was an amoralist, and in 1897 had to defend his *Weib und Welt* before the Königliches Amtsgericht in Berlin. The judges were stupid enough to believe that he was attempting to subvert public morality, when he was in reality preaching a morality to the public. He had taken up the defense of a robust animality which he believed should be made a part of the morality of the normal man—for he believed, with the fervor of the reformer, in the existence of the normal man, a man conforming to a modern norm. He succeeded in shocking German public opinion in 1900 as no man had before him, with all the bluntness of a Charles Péguy, though without the peasant astuteness or the critical intelligence which served to balance the latter's mysticism. But Dehmel's religious fervor, while it stirred the social currents of his time, did not change their course. Neither the socialism whose ideas he accepted nor the religious attitude whose fervor he borrowed benefited by any modifications at his hands.

In 1914 he enthusiastically took up arms against Russia, and later, on the French front, he wrote a *Kriegstagebuch* which was filled both with generous feeling for those who had suffered invasion and with respectful admiration for the commanders of the invading armies. The reason was that he himself was invaded, at the mercy of his impulses, swept into the pathetic. He was an individualist, but he was also a humanitarian, which made him the type of revolutionist who must join an organization if he is to feel comfortable. He wanted the feeling of being elbow to elbow with the masses, whether these masses were of his own class or his race, whether they were all humanity or the nation. It was impossible for him to set up a hierarchy of feelings or of values; he thought and felt upon a single plane.

There was enough substance in him to make a lyric poet, but he lacked his friend Liliencron's gift for concrete expression. Everything he touched turned to abstractions. He thought he was ruled by his senses; he was in reality ruled by his intellect. No sooner did he have an image than it threatened to turn into an allegory. Images, ideas, feelings fused within him into a glowing ash from which he could not strike the necessary spark. He realized this himself, and after he was forty did little save rework his previous writings, which had been written with a sort of lumbering freedom of expression. The result was *Die Verwandlungen der Venus* and *Zwei Menschen*, two works of fairly broad conception.

In the first he shows the metamorphosis of woman down the ages, or rather of the conception of woman as it changed from temperament to temperament and from civilization to civilization. The sexual ethic implied in the work includes all the forms of love inspired by Venus, and fuses them with the concept of the Virgin into which Christianity, by a supreme effort of sublimation, has turned the Venus of ancient times.

In *Zwei Menschen*, successive broadenings of the ego result first, through the miracle of love, in the union of two people heretofore motivated only by the egoistic impulses of the senses, and in the resolution of the conflict between the will to justify oneself and the will to forget oneself; second, in a conception of the family whose dignity arises from the fact that two people who were only creatures become creators, rising above themselves in the process of creation; and, finally, in a conception of the social order in which race is placed above class and human society above national society.

Dehmel's lack of a selective sense hindered him greatly, but he had one lasting merit: his sympathy went out to all forms of life. The Hohenzollern civilization of his day tended to crystallize into a rigid system. Dehmel did not deny the utility of such a crystallization (his essay *Nationale Kulturpolitik* proves this), but in every manifestation of the spirit of his time or the spirit of his nation he sought the element which could serve all humanity, regardless of time or place.

Furthermore, in spite of the reservations which must be made concerning its artistic merit, Dehmel's work was extremely stimulating to his contemporaries. The revolutionary elements in it have now lost their interest. But there was a time when it was of great utility in helping to free German naturalism from the limitations which it had imposed upon itself, and from the influence of the

past, which it was fighting. Those who immediately
preceded him looked upon nature as a mechanical
force which ordered all things and pressed down upon
man with all the weight of destiny. Dehmel rediscovered
a different view of nature. He opposed the idea of organism to the idea of mechanism, inspiration to automatism.
He gave first place to the blind powers of change in a
universe which he conceived not merely as a structure
built by a great engineer, but as the creation of a great
poet. Beneath materialism he rediscovered idealism;
beneath determinism, freedom; beneath socialism, the
human personality. At least this was the direction in
which his dionysism, which resembled Nietzsche's and
was inspired by Nietzsche, tended. But he also opposed
Nietzsche—perhaps through following a little naïvely
the master's injunction to his disciples to disagree with
him—in that he discarded the intellectual and aristocratic elements in Nietzsche's individualism in favor of
an element which was democratic in an exaggeratedly
sentimental sense.

2. *Prose and Poetry in Vienna—Hofmannsthal—the Symbolist Esthetic*

Austrian poetry is one of German literature's most
delicate flowers. Vienna, the Imperial City whose post-
War aspect was so brilliantly described by the novelist
Paul Zifferer in his *Die Kaiserstadt*,* is a sheltered
capital: Viennese verse is the product not of selection
but of a thousand elements intermingled for centuries.
Asia meets Europe in the old capital of the Hapsburgs;
Slav and Latin mingle with people of Germanic blood.
Races and religions not only come face to face but fuse
together; mixed marriages are common; Catholicism and

* PAUL ZIFFERER (1879–1929), *Die Kaiserstadt*, 1923; *Der Sprung ins
Ungewisse*, 1927.

Judaism join; and the chief authors of a literature supposed to represent a Catholic civilization are Austrians in whose veins runs the blood of many diverse races.

The mental structure of Vienna is without parallel in Europe; it resembles Viennese architecture in that the sacred and the profane join hands to give pleasure to a people of highly refined sensibilities, to an audience whose eclecticism is the result of the influence of diverse civilizations. Italy lies but a step away, and Munich no farther. There is music to make a background. The whole atmosphere of this "Capua of the Mind" seems perfectly calculated for the artist's pleasure. But as the poet Grillparzer, who was born there, says, the artist's enjoyment is so great that his creative impulse is likely to suffer, for "one is enabled to feel so strongly what the intellect can only partly grasp, and one lives in a semi-poetic atmosphere which is likely to prejudice true poetry itself."

In Vienna art is no stranger to life; art dictates laws to life, colors life's smallest concrete manifestations, controls the selection of a cravat, the choice of a pose, and profoundly influences the individual's whole existence. It is only in such an atmosphere that writers like Peter Altenburg can do their best work, for to them writing is nothing, living and knowing how to live is everything. Such artists, however, run the danger of turning esthete; and the art which they produce, however exquisitely musical it may be, is likely to take on the hybrid character of a passion in which pure Mozartian fire and the Freudian libido are linked together, or to slip into harmonies which contain almost imperceptible but disturbing dissonances.

The "*Jung-Wien*" literature was a part of the general European movement usually called decadent, whose liaison agent between Vienna, Berlin, and Paris was

Hermann Bahr, the most intuitive of essayists and a prophet endowed with broad intellectual sympathies. It was a literature which consisted for the most part, as in Richard Schaukal's work, of "reactions to stimulus." But the stimuli were not always, as in Felix Dorman's case, those of the senses. They represented divergent traditions, ranging from the unalterably aristocratic and Catholic tradition of Baron Leopold Andrian to the savage terseness of biblical Judaism rediscovered by Richard Beer-Hoffmann.

Between these extremes is Arthur Schnitzler,* who has mixed modern themes in a pot-pourri calculated to please people of refined sensibilities all over Europe. Throughout a long career, during which he has produced slight play after slight play and slight novel after slight novel, he has been an outstanding representative of "pleasant naturalism"—though not without a suggestion of Freudanism only partly concealed by his even tone, a fundamental, pathological melancholy which invests mere elegant gestures with a certain gravity. The author of *Anatol* is detached, is a sceptic, but his detachment and his scepticism cost him an effort. His tragedy, *Professor Bernhardi*, and his novel, *Der Weg ins Freie*, breathe the pessimism of a man of the world who is

* ARTHUR SCHNITZLER (1862–1931), *Gesammelte Werke*, S. Fischer Verlag. *Anatol*, 1893; *Das Märchen*, 1894; *Sterben*, 1895; *Liebelei*, 1895; *Freiwild*, 1896; *Vermächtnis*, 1898; *Paracelsus, Die Gefährtin, Der grüne Kakadu*, 1899; *Reigen, Dialoge*, 1900; *Der Schleier der Beatrice*, 1900; *Leutnant Gustl*, 1901; *Bertha Garlan*, 1901; *Lebendige Stunden*, 1902; *Der einsame Weg*, 1903; *Die griechische Tänzerin*, 1904; *Zwischenspiel*, 1905; *Der Ruf des Lebens*, 1905; *Marionetten*, 1906; *Dämmerseelen*, 1907; *Der Weg ins Freie*, 1908; *Komtesse Mizzi*, 1909; *Der junge Medardus*, 1910; *Das weite Land*, 1911; *Masken und Wunder*, 1912; *Prof. Bernhardi*, 1912; *Frau Beate und ihr Sohn*, 1913; *Komödie der Worte*, 1915; *Fink und Fliederbusch*, 1917; *Doktor Graesler*, 1917; *Casanovas Heimfahrt*, 1918; *Die Schwestern*, 1919; *Komödie der Verführung*, 1924; *Fräulein Else*, 1924; *Die Frau des Richters*, 1925; *Traumnovelle*, 1925; *Der Gang zum Weiher*, 1926; *Spiel im Morgengrauen*, 1927; *Therese*, 1928; *Flucht in die Finsternis*, 1931; *Die Kleine Komödie* (Nachlass), 1932.

used to slipping lightly over the more serious problems
of life, but who, being unable to escape them entirely,
realizes that some day he must have it out with them.

Eroticism is Schnitzler's *leit-motif*, but it is an eroticism
which is neither conceived from the philosophic viewpoint
of the ordinary German writer, nor compounded of the
sensual and the metaphysical as in Dehmel's case. What
philosophy there is, is the philosophy of the man of the
world—a world which devotes its leisure to practicing
the cult of woman. Woman, whether of the bourgeoisie
or of the common people, represents luxury. She is woman
in love, woman who has abandoned herself to her femininity and yet has remained healthy in the process—
healthier, perhaps, than man, for man is only using her
as a plaything and in the end, because he is only playing,
realizes his inferiority. Man is a Don Juan who has lost
his sense of tragic illusion. He feels in his heart the
irremediable sadness of the man doomed to disillusion.
Schnitzler, the doctor, diagnoses the disease but does not
suggest a cure.

His works are popularizations, but without vulgarity
their perfection lies in the sense of playing a game which
runs through them. "No matter how great or how grave
our actions seem, we do nothing on this earth which is
not play. We are forever playing, and the wise man is he
who realizes that it is all a game." These are words of
wisdom from a voluptuary for whom even the spiritual
is voluptuous—an attitude shared also by Hofmannsthal* who wrote in his *Prolog zu dem Buch Anatol:* "So

* HUGO VON HOFMANNSTHAL (1874–1929), *Gesammelte Werke*, S. Fischer
Verlag; *Gestern*, 1891; *Der Tod des Tizian; Der Tor und der Tod, Theater in
Versen*, 1899; *Elektra*, 1903; *Victor Hugo*, 1904; *Das gerettete Venedig*, 1905;
Ödipus und die Sphinx, 1905; *Vorspiele*, 1908; *Die prosaischen Schriften*,
1907; *Gesammelte Gedichte*, 1907; *Der Rosenkavalier*, 1911; *Jedermann*, 1912;
Ariadne auf Naxos, 1912; *Prinz Eugen, der edle Ritter*, 1915; *Alkestis*, 1916;
Rodauner Nachträge, 1920; *Der Schwierige*, 1921; *Christinas Heimkehr; Die*

we shall become actors, we shall play out our own little dramas—we who are mature before our time, and tender, and sad—the dramatic comedy of our souls, the yesterday and tomorrow of our feelings, pretty formulas made up of evil things, pretty words, many-colored images, half-felt, half-dreamed things, agonies, episodes. . . . "

"He was a strange youth, now tangled in preciousness, now giving way to a heavy naïveté; proud, but winning in his pride; a child, yet in some ways frighteningly mature; fired by the slightest stimulus, but only with his intellect, for his heart remained cold; self-indulgent and a man of the world, yet terribly alone in that world and terribly sad in spite of his precocious worldliness. . . . " That was how Bahr in *Selbstbildnis* described Hofmannsthal, whom he met in 1892, at the time when *Der Tod des Tizian* and *Der Tor und der Tod* had made the Austrian poet famous at twenty.

The movement with which Hofmannsthal is usually associated goes by the name of neo-romanticism though Hofmannsthal himself denied that he was a neo-romantic. He saw in German romanticism, and particularly in Schlegel, the nostalgia of the Protestants of the North for the foreign, Catholic civilization of the South; whereas he himself was already of that southern civilization and hence felt no nostalgia for it, no desire to move. He felt that his roots were in it, and that he had merely to let the plant bloom. He was the grandson of an Italian lady and a baron of Jewish blood; he had had the good fortune to be brought up in an atmosphere of cosmopolitan culture and knowledge of the world which served

---

Frau ohne Schatten; Die Gedichte und kleinen Dramen; Florindo; Buch der Freunde, 1922; *Das Salzburger Grosse Welttheater; Reden und Aufsätze*, 1924; *Der Turm*, 1925; *Das Schrifttum als geistiger Raum der Nation*, 1928; *Buch der Freunde*, 1929; *Die Berührung der Sphären* (aus dem Nachlass), 1931.

to fuse the differing hereditary strains; and he had no
difficulty in becoming Vienna's poet *par excellence.*

Hofmannsthal's poetry is like the firefly of which he
wrote, augmenting its own flame with infinitesimal
sparks seized from the surface of things that are. The
German realists threw themselves in a frenzy upon the
world of objective reality. Hofmannsthal approached it
softly, with delicate antennæ outstretched to seize upon
relations which escaped the ordinary observer. He stood
willingly enough to watch artisans at work, but saw
their movements only in passing, as one would stand
and watch for a moment the movement of the shuttle
thrown across the warp of the universe by an invisible
weaver's hand. Standing before the forge, he saw only
the shifting flame; before the potter's wheel, he watched
only for the Eros, the nymphs, and the centaurs which
were to spring from the clay. Everything which the world
offered to his senses he clothed in illusion. His taste was
for the miraculous; he sought miracles in memories of
Greece, of the Middle Ages, of the eighteenth century.
Most of the things of his own time which others called
living seemed to him dead.

On the other hand, he felt the modern world to be
"full of other things which most people think are dead
but which are really alive." When the Viennese revolution broke out, he felt that one should be more deeply
moved by a star falling three thousand years ago than
by rifle shots beneath one's windows; when fatigue
pressed down upon his own eyelids, he felt it as the
fatigue that had come upon peoples buried beneath a
thousand years of history. To live meant to him to
resuscitate the past, after the fashion of the actors, who
won his praise. But actors are liars? Well, what need we
care for the opinions of those who cannot appreciate
the beauty of make-believe.

Hofmannsthal has not only the gift of mystification, but the will to mystify. There is a magic in the world, and it is the task of the poet, while in a half-waking, half-sleeping state, to seize upon it. He sees, he hears, but he penetrates beyond the borders of the senses and into the mystic. Here is no question of observing, of analyzing, of composing. He looks upon the most delicate associations of ideas as he would look upon colored balls tossed up and caught again upon the column of water emerging from a fountain. His only care is for the images he sees, not as they are assembled by the intelligence, but as they are suggested one by another. Everything in the universe is interrelated by a logic far more profound than our own. Poetry consists in precisely this apparent chaos, with its involuntary contrasts and its revelations of unsuspected relationships. The art of poetry is not to express these relationships, for they cannot be expressed, but to suggest them, to imply their existence.

In consequence, "a being, a dream, a thing, are one and the same." According to Hofmannsthal's esthetic, as formulated in *Die Prosaischen Schriften* and in particular in the *Letter from Lord Chandos*, the poet is dispossessed of himself. "Not because he ceases to turn his thought upon the things of the universe, but because they also turn their thought upon him, because they are in him, because they dominate him." His soul is invaded; it is like a dovecot which harbors carrier pigeons going to and coming from the beyond. He feels it to be foreign to him, an empty stage upon which is played a drama whose very strangeness gives him pleasure. His ego takes on the color of "the things it touches," and these things have for him a fascination such as his Senator Crassus felt before the eel with inexpressive eyes. His function becomes the purely impersonal one of registering at a distance, like a seismograph, the slightest tremors from the outside world.

The poet's ego, however, is not entirely suppressed. It is present, but diffused among the things of the objective world, which become symbols. Instead of seeking within to find himself, the poet turns to the outside world, finds himself in the coolness of a fountain, in the reflection of the setting sun upon a pond, in the thousand and one details of the objective world upon which the world within depends. The powerful destiny which stands in the background and controls his movements finds expression in his poetry, but not that exact expression which answers the need of the seeker after truth. The inexplicable resists explanation; we can feel only a vague contact with it. The art of the poet lies not in answers to questions, but in exclamations, and in the lyric line.

No doubt there is a certain grandeur in this confused perception of an unknown which is nevertheless a portion of experience, in this voluntary effacing of the ego in order to permit the poet vaguely to sense the presence of something greater than himself. But there is nothing new in the relation of the individual to the universe which this implies. Novalis rediscovered it through the philosophers of antiquity, with their belief that evil lay in individuation, and good in abandoning oneself without resistance to the flow of the universe. Hofmannsthal's symbolism is in a way a part of German pantheism, but with an odd overlay of Catholic humility. Werther and Faust aspired to a knowledge of the universe, and saw as tragic its resistance to comprehension. In Hofmannsthal this aspiration to knowledge of the universe becomes a religious acceptance of the universe, and religion instead of carrying with it the uncertainty of a founder brings the certainty of the priest who is satisfied that his ordination gives him the right to accept miracles without question. Hofmannsthal does not attempt to explain life or to modify men's actions. The bourgeois in him has too much respect for the ordered movements of an existence which is not of his own conception; his femininity leads him to embrace a harmony which is not of his making but of which he feels that he is the extension and the most delicate echo.

"*Écho sonore.*" But Hugo, whom Hofmannsthal took as the subject of his doctoral thesis, was something more as well.

> *Tous les objets créés, feu qui luit, mer qui tremble,*
> *Ne savent qu'à demi le grand nom du Très-Haut.*
> *Ils jettent vaguement des noms que seul j'assemble.*
> *Chacun dit sa syllabe, et moi je dis le mot,*

> (All things created, gleaming fire and shifting sea,
> Have but half-knowledge of the Most High's name.
> They murmur names which I and I alone assemble.
> Each says its syllable, but I alone the word.)

Hofmannsthal never says that word. He borrows from God, but never dares to speak with God face to face. His self-effacement is of the same character as the self-effacement of the naturalists before the forces that control a determinist world. The difference between the naturalists and Hofmannsthal is that he juxtaposes the external world which they rediscovered and the internal world of which he took soundings. But the internal world reflected in Hofmannsthal's symbols is not that of a Mallarmé. It is the internal world of a Maeterlinck, of little Yniold caught in the "traps of destiny": "Ah! Ah! Oh! Oh! It is too dark. . . . I want to say something to someone. . . . "

In surrounding his images with flattering shadows, in achieving a powerful charm of expression, Hofmannsthal took expert advantage of the richness of the German language in impersonal modes of speech, and of the ease with which in German every infinitive may be turned into a noun. There never was a more conscious artist than this poet of the unconscious, a less naïve writer than this professor of the naïve. Incapable of Novalis' bursts of feeling, or of the intoxication of a Verlaine "choosing his words a little disdainfully," he maintained the expectant coldness of a precocious youth who knows exactly what he is doing and what effect it will have upon his audience; he never lets anything but his imagination catch fire. That imagination deals less with his own experience than with motifs created by others; his aim is not so much to mold the findings of his senses into a personal and original poetic form, as to show how poetic the poetry of life can be.

In spite of the conscious artistry of Hofmannsthal's work, however, both his prose and his verse have a musicality which distinguishes them from other writings in the German language. No one before him had ever drawn such soft sonorities from the German tongue. Just as Shakespeare played with human destinies abstracted from historical reality and ended with an impression not of chaos but of a skein woven by genius, so Hofmannsthal juggles with the elements of a living language and draws delightful melody from their combinations. The senses draw the intellect after them in a seductive adventure. A thousand passions are suggested by the music; in the distance one hears the violins of Hungary. It was only a step from this kind of writing to the *Rosenkavalier* and the other lyrics which Hofmannsthal wrote for Strauss.

For a long while Hofmannsthal stifled the question that was within him, postponed the answer, maintained the sense of mystery. Because the things of the external world were superimposed upon his thinking, and not his thinking upon the things of the external world, the answer finally came from that world, from the symbols of Catholicism and the institutions of the society in which he lived. The diffused ego of the poet was merely the nimbus of the social ego ordered by tradition and standing firm despite literary effusions. Hofmannsthal found himself at last. Confronted with the threat of bolshevism, he realized that he had a task to which he had already unconsciously sworn himself. His ardor was a conserving, not a consuming, ardor.

At fifty he had found his mission, and his mysticism lost its troubled quality to become the mysticism of mystery plays given on cathedral porches. In *Jedermann* and *Das Salzburger Grosse Welttheater*, staged by Reinhardt in ecclesiastical Salzburg, he glorifies a Providence to whom we may confidently entrust ourselves. Hofmannsthal admired the works of Paul Claudel, but, unlike him, sought deep peace without the necessity of passing through great storms. In his efforts to save the Catholic order in Austria he comes very close to Henri Ghéon.

Above all a man of the world, Hofmannsthal in the end begged the fundamental questions, believing that they would be answered in due course by an impersonal wisdom—a smiling wisdom, whose most attractive manifestation is to be found in his comedy *Der Schwierige*. That play gains its distinction rather from the milieu which it represents than from the author's individual achievement. The difficulty which confronts Hofmannsthal's "difficult" hero is how to reconcile the conflicting forces which permit decency and license to exist side by side in the world of polite society. His conversation sparkles as brilliantly as a proverb of Musset, but there is in him nothing of the *enfant terrible* who, in spite of all his grace of movement, upsets bourgeois conventions right and left. The obstacles which beset his path are obstacles to be overcome by experience rather than by distinction of mind or heart; for he lives in a world in which the wise rule of life is that of the abandoned mistress of the *Rosenkavalier:* "Not too much seriousness—light hearts, light hands—take and hold, hold and leave. . . . "

Hofmannsthal, when all is said and done, represents a blind alley—a blind alley filled with music and light and shadow, to be sure, but a blind alley nevertheless. His poetry lacks poetry's greatest virtue—the creative quality. It becomes a game for esthetes, concerning which Gundolf said in his *George:* "This newly fashionable estheticism had this advantage over academism and naturalism, that it had at its disposal more varied and more intense modes of expression and a more brilliant technique, as well as eyes which naturalism had taught to see the objective world in concrete detail and a sense of touch which had learned to recognize the fiber and the grain of matter. Furthermore it was less cramped than naturalism, not restricted to the immediate incidents of daily life, and therefore able to make effective use of distances in time and space. It had the whole world from which to choose, and had as well the ability to make a choice—in other words, a sense of taste. But it was less honest than either academism or naturalism.

"The academists and the naturalists believed in what they were saying; the esthete is interested only in its effect. Estheticism is but one more step along the path that leads to absolute worthlessness of content in literature, to complete falsehood. It has become a mere game, an unnecessary lie, a lie for the sake of lying. It is no mere coincidence that the growth of estheticism in literature has been accompanied by an epidemic of 'pseudologia phantastica.' The esthetes have made use of a language capable of giving a sense of knowledge, of emotion, of distance, but they have used it like actors whose only interest is to move their audience—emptying the words of their spiritual content, cutting them off from their roots, depriving them of the spirit which alone makes them what they are. Because he had invented and taught this new language, George was considered the founder of estheticism, whereas its true leader, and he in whom it found its most perfect expression, was Hugo von Hofmannsthal."

This opinion from a German critic, severe as it is, is worth quoting, if only as a warning against being too liberal in our eulogies and thereby running the risk of sinning against true greatness.

3. *Rainer Maria Rilke—Orphic Lyricism*

Rainer Maria Rilke* was poor, solitary, frightened by the world and by the fanfares of fame, happy only when he was allowed to love in his own sensitive fashion. He reminds one of a modern Saint Francis of Assisi. Luckily, he had friends, attracted by his very sensitiveness, who served as intermediaries between the poet and the public.

In his earliest works—*Aufzeichnungen des Malte Laurids Brigge* and *Geschichten vom lieben Gott*—he had hardly begun to free himself from the influence of the

---

* RAINER MARIA RILKE (1875–1926), *Gesammelte Werke*, Insel Verlag. *Leben und Lieder*, 1894; *Larenopfer*, 1896; *Traumgekrönt*, 1897; *Frühfrost*, 1897; *Advent*, 1898; *Am Leben hin*, 1898; *Zwei Präger Geschichten*, 1899; *Mir zur Feier*, 1899; *Vom lieben Gott und andere Geschichten*, 1900; *Das tägliche Leben*, 1902; *Das Buch der Bilder*, 1902; *Aug. Rodin*, 1903; *Das Stundenbuch*, 1906; *Die Weise von Liebe und Tod des Cornets Christoph Rilke*, 1906; *Neue Gedichte*, 1907; *Requiem*, 1909; *Aufzeichnungen des Malte Laurids Brigge*, 1910; *Das Marienleben*, 1913; *Erste Gedichte*, 1913; *Die Sonette an Orpheus*, 1923; *Duineser Elegien*, 1923; *Briefe*, 1931.

romanticists and neo-romanticists. Later on, he left
Maeterlinck and Hofmannsthal far behind, late representatives of the line of Novalis. His roots were in a
dozen nations; he reached beyond what was a mere
literary fashion, a merely local way of thinking and
feeling; his great object was a search for God in which
the whole intelligence and all the sensibilities are brought
into play, and whose nobility lies in the fact that the
seeker does not desire an end to his quest, refuses ever
to admit that God has been found.

Rilke defined God as "the direction in which love is
turned, not love's object." His love has an intellectual
virility unexpected in so delicate a personality. His
hands were extended toward God in a gesture of will to
discover the direction which alone seemed important to
him, and of exquisite prayer that he might find it. His
hesitations and his inspirations are accounted for by his
realization that he must not seek God along an unswerv-
ing line, but by a courageous effort of the intelligence
orient himself from many shifting angles.

Rilke was Czech by birth, Austrian by education. He
knew the works of the Dane, Jacobsen; he underwent
influences from Russia, Italy, Spain, and France; he
lived in each of these countries for a time. He was
influenced by Dostoievski, by Rodin, later by André
Gide and Paul Valéry, of several of whose works he made
excellent German translations; toward the end of his life
he even wrote poems in French. The result was a Rilke
broadly European. His death proved to be what he
thought death should be—a further growth, the continued flowering of something which had been only
temporarily embodied in him and which he knew was
greater than himself, the triumph of the infinite being
over the finite individual. He taught that death's
triumph over individual life is a triumph of nobility

over pettiness; he felt the infinity of a world which is continually deepening. These are the things which in the last analysis he preached, and they are the finest elements in his work. His lyricism might be called an Orphic lyricism; from the very beginning it led toward the wisdom which found its full expression in *Die Sonette an Orpheus*. It is there, beneath the surface of myth, that the true Rilke is to be sought.

Set up no funeral monument to Orpheus: the divine singer is not dead. Wherever we turn our eyes we see him in his manifold aspects. Everywhere rises his song. His voice thrills in every stone. A rose trembles; it is the god who has passed, present but invisible. He is the ceaseless throbbing of ceaseless life. Where life seems to be dying, it is really only being born again. Its ends are all beginnings. The rhythm of the universe is a thrust continued secretly, and infinitely renewed, in spite of all outward opposition.

To sense this rhythm, to harmonize the lift and fall of his own breast with the movement of forces which are forever halting, forever rushing on again greater than before—this is the poet's task. To become greater than oneself, this is the law by which we are all controlled, whether we are conscious of it or not. Ah, let us accept it, let us yield to it as gladly as Orpheus! He too suffers because he must continually leave one place for another, continually change his form. But he is willing, he is joyous. He is here, and yet he is no longer here; he is detached from the present, for the sole virtue of the present is its promise of the future.

Must we then push on to the utmost confines of uneasiness? Yes, for it is there that uneasiness changes to happiness, to unbounded, endless delight. Orpheus had to be torn to pieces by the Mænads in order that he might escape from the flesh, in order that his song be no longer bound to the strings of a lyre.

The essence of Rilke's lyricism is this deeply felt uneasiness. In his poetry is the trembling harmony of the sadness and delight which rush alternately through his being like contrary winds across the sky. He is double, divided within himself; he finds his fondest images in the interplay of those winds as they sweep from obstacle to obstacle, dividing space among them, thrusting against it until they have enlarged its boundaries. So breathes the poet. His lips, now closed while he savors silence, now open as inspiration jets from them, are like some antique sarcophagus whose lid has slipped off to give vent to the sudden buzzing of a hive of bees. The song is the more powerful because it emerges from lips which know silence, and more profound because it springs from a tomb.

The objective universe has no absolute reality. For us the only reality lies in change, in metamorphosis. The spirit, the god who has seized the earth, "loves nothing in an upward-thrusting line so much as the point at which it changes direction." If in our pride we attempt to press the winged world to change its course, we only disturb its activity. To participate in divinity we must free ourselves of weight, dignify the ephemeral, float upon the universal current. True being consists in pushing beyond the boundaries of one's individual being. Only through a deep forgetfulness of self, only through incessant interchange with the universal, can the individual ego, divided, diffused, achieve a kind of unity, not in matter but in movement. The true object is not so much to identify oneself with the universe as to sense its harmonies.

This is a task for delicate ears. Rilke's pantheism is infinitely more subtle than the pantheism of his predecessors, who abandoned themselves to crude ecstasy. Rilke's lyricism does not consist, like theirs, in mere sentimental effusions. It assumes the ability to orchestrate, like a composer, the fragments of melody given out by trees and brooks. As in Mallarmé's formula, spontaneity is subject to disciplinary forces supplied by the intelligence.

Perhaps the harmony which we manage to establish between the warring elements in our nature is illusory. It is like the harmony of horse and rider. Both are carried along in the same rhythm, and, for the length of the race, are one; then, when the race is over, they find themselves separated again. But there is beauty in their unanimity of effort, and in the pride of the rider who, though carried away by his mount, nevertheless controls his direction.

Rilke's acceptance of the universe was more subtle, contained more intellectual elements, than the ordinary sense of acceptance which has always been a strong German characteristic and which the Hohenzollern Empire systematically cultivated. The intellectual elements in Rilke were not so broad as in Goethe, but they helped him nevertheless to break away from the childish philosophy which Maeterlinck, in childish imitation of Novalis, had made fashionable. Rilke grew impatient with the wringing of hands of an Aglavaine confronted by the mystery which is to engulf us all, and with the naïve self-effacement which made his character Malte Laurids Brigge say: "I am frightened, but after the fashion of a man confronted by tremendous things. Once, I remember, when I was about to write, I felt such things moving within me. Now it is not I who write, but I who shall be written. I am the impression which is being expressed. And oh! I am so close to understanding everything, accepting everything at last!"

Rilke indeed still saw life as a mystery, a miracle, and his "boundless" heart still "sought to identify itself with the great heart of the indistinct universe." But the intellect was beginning to take its rightful place again. Mallarmé, Stefan George, Gide, and Valéry were representatives of the same change.

Rilke's art bears many similarities to the art of the esthetes who preceded him, but it is animated by a fervor which makes it something far warmer than mere art for art's sake. Indeed there is sometimes nobility in his very delicacy. Whatever pleasure he gains from his suffering comes as a result of severe inner restraints. He is apparently changeable, volatile, but his volatility represents an effort of the will, his changeability is a result of effort, and he forces himself to glory in the flame in which his individuality is being destroyed.

He is like a ringing crystal which sounds only when it breaks; he loves the blow which breaks it for the single musical note which will result. Deprived of his desire, he writes: "Sing, O my heart, of the gardens which thou shalt never see—O my heart, show that they are not gone from thee—Let those who say there is such a thing as privation be proven wrong." He conquers through renunciation; he enriches himself by giving. He is not the victim of the flame which is consuming him; it is he who feeds that flame and makes it flare the higher. Divinity is destined constantly to grow; he gives of his substance that it may be nourished. "Die and live again through change. Who shall say what brings the greater suffering? If the drink is bitter, turn thyself into wine. . . . And if the world forget thee, say to the unmoving earth, 'Thus do I move,' and to the flowing water, 'I flow with thee.'"

No doubt Rilke's art is closer to chamber music than to the tradition of Goethe and Nietzsche. But his very preciosity and his conception of beauty are significant. His taste was perhaps too exquisite, and he chose gems which appeal to those of highly refined taste rather than the crude stones of rushing everyday life. But it was just this taste for the rare and exquisite which at the time was threatened with extinction. Rilke fought shy of the forces of mere expansion, and in so doing helped those who speak the German language to save a part of their spiritual heritage. Through his efforts the clear waters of a crystal spring were enabled to filter through the stones of the massive Germanic edifice. At a time when all other eyes were turned toward the utilitarian, he with André Gide rediscovered the gratuitous, which is a form of idealism, and with Paul Valéry pointed out values which lie beyond the horizon of the ordinary man.

4. Stefan George*—Aristocratic Individualism and Inner Style

Stefan George began publishing the periodical *Die Blätter für die Kunst* in 1892. The twelve series which were brought out between that date and 1919 represented the growth of an artistic movement which is by far the most interesting of any that have influenced the thought and feeling of the Germans of our day. The journal, originally addressed to "a strictly limited group of selected people," seemed at first the undertaking of a small group of worshippers at a shrine. Today they must be compared to the builders of cathedrals. It was no mere affectation on the part of the editors when they decided to keep all contributions anonymous. While they knew that the veil of anonymity could easily be pierced, they wished to show that they considered the work itself more important than the workman. Even the work itself they did not conceive

---

* STEFAN GEORGE (1868–1933). Note especially, *Das Jahr der Seele* (1897), *Der Teppich des Lebens und die Lieder von Traum und Tod* (1899), *Der Siebente Ring* (1907), *Das Neue Reich* (1928).

as standing alone in isolated perfection, but as part of a larger whole. They were building a temple, establishing a cult. Its significance was to lie in its breadth of conception; its beauty not in the perfection of a single statue but in the inspiration which pervaded it. Unlike the church makers of the Middle Ages, the builders were not borne on a wave of faith. They had cut themselves off from their people in order to work out a new body of law; in the early days they turned the hills of the Rhineland into their own little Sinai.

At first it did not look as if a religion with so high a standard could ever achieve popularity. They sent out no evangelists, and they themselves did not believe that the time had yet come when "words of noble passion, or even words of reason" could affect the great mass of neo-Europeans, who were "victims of crime." Nevertheless they attracted to themselves an élite which represented the deepest spiritual forces of Germany and which set to work to give those forces fresh strength. A new spirituality was born, involving a difficult choice from among the various aspirations of the community and the elimination of those which were no more than communal. Its objective was to raise humanity to a nobler plane.

The first few poems, essays, and critical works* were enough to indicate the broad poetic structure for which these men were striving, and gave clear evidence of the powerful force which motivated them. This motivating force, escaping from the hermetically closed group in which it had its origin, gradually reached a large number of other writers who also felt the need of

* In addition to *Die Blätter für die Kunst*, see FRIEDRICH GUNDOLF (1880–1931), *Zwiegespräche*, 1905; *Shakespeare und der deutsche Geist*, 1911; *Hölderlins Archipelagus*, 1911; *Goethe*, 1916; *George*, 1920; *Dichter und Helden*, 1921; *Heinrich von Kleist*, 1922; *Caesar*, 1924; and ERNST BERTRAM (b. 1884), *Nietzsche*, 1918.

achieving an artistic style suited to a changed inner life.
It helped to give direction to the taste of a cultivated
public, and so found many devotees. A secret communion
of spirit arose among men who had theretofore been
strangers. They all had this in common, that they felt
the necessity of breaking with the complacent way of
life, of putting the human personality through a process
of change which should have not only the absolute
nature of a revolution but the artistic character of a
creation. A set of intellectual and moral values, which
George's followers did not so much invent as swear
loyalty to were gaining force. They could not fail to
gain acceptance among the noble of spirit, or to trouble
even those who were not, for the latter realized that they
had at their disposal only the currency of a civilization
of yesterday, a currency which they secretly knew had
lost its worth.

The Hohenzollern monarchy brought about the political
unification of Germany, but left the country completely
lacking in spiritual unity. George inherited something
of the spiritual sovereignty of the age of Goethe, and
while he lacked the support of a court, he had the backing
of a tradition which was no longer diffuse. The genius
of Goethe, of Hölderlin, and of Jean-Paul played no
small part in stimulating the fervor of George and his
disciples.

Stefan George and his followers represent the permanent demand for a style—something not unusual in
Germany, where, because the Germans feel that their
self-realization is still incomplete, such demands are
heard continuously. The classicism of Weimar seemed
to the mass of German writers like some beautiful park
which they visited on Sundays and holidays; but they
spent their weekdays in their native forest, both because

it seemed natural to them and because they feared the academism into which they had seen others fall. Many still did not believe that plastic form was a proper vehicle for the spirit. There had been, of course, the musical drama which Wagner believed would give birth to a German style, an integrated style which would represent a synthesis of all the arts and the rich life which those arts were attempting to express. But that synthesis turned out to be nothing more than a mixture of art forms and artistic genres, contrary in spirit to a natural artistic evolution which was tending toward increasing differentiation in the arts.

Even Wagner's music, which sought to express the German inspiration in its totality but exerted instead a dissolving influence upon it, failed to express it with anything like the clarity which the idea of style implies. Wagner did not succeed in breathing form into life; he left life at the point where it was still mere desire. He stimulated sensuality, bridged the gap between the soul and the senses not by the spirit but by desire, complicated the problem rather than set it on the way toward solution. The effect of such an art was to excite rather than to uplift. There was still a chasm between man and the musician.

When the Wagnerian conception failed, experiments were made in another direction. In 1890 the publication of Langbehn's book caused the appearance of the *Rembrandtdeutsche*, who conceived the true German style to bear the same relation to French style that Rembrandt's bears to Poussin's: atmosphere in place of line, and, beyond the familiar three dimensions, the unknown, the indefiniteness of chiaroscuro. But this fantasy of excited theoreticians failed to produce Rembrandts. The problem of style remained to be solved.

Neither the realists nor the symbolists had provided
a solution. The symbolism of Hofmannsthal and the
neo-romantics was merely another step down the slope
of the indeterminate, a final slipping back into medieval
allegory. As for the realists, they indeed came close
to creating a style, but it was only the style of the
Hohenzollern era. Conditioned by matter and by
technique, born of the demands of the present and the
real rather than of an inventive force responsive to
deeper desires, it produced engineers rather than artists.
Not that these engineers lacked creative faculties,
or that the civilization which they expressed failed to
inspire poetry. But their temples opened upon empty
heavens.

The significance of George's work, coming after
Nietzsche's, was that it re-peopled those heavens.
The phase of the reversal of values had passed. A reform-
ing genius had first to upset the established order, deny
its validity. Only then were George and his followers
free to give body to a liberated inspiration, set themselves
up as "*Bildner,*" become formers rather than reformers.

This movement to which Stefan George gave direction
is usually called aristocratic individualism. The term
is roughly accurate. Its inspiration was indeed both
aristocratic and individualist. But we must remember
that it was an individualism and an aristocracy which
were not without a strong sense of obligation to the
community. George's aristocracy has little to do with
inherited advantages. Indeed the very idea of advantage
becomes meaningless in a hierarchy of values which
corresponds to nothing objective in society. George's
community lies within time and space, but it denies a
standard of values imposed by particular time or place.

The basis of the movement is to be found in a reaction
against the contemporary denial of the things of the

spirit in favor of the things of the senses. Humanity had become matter, responding to the same laws as matter. The man who sought salvation must flee the herd, but is not necessarily to flee life, as George has sometimes been accused of doing. The first attack was against naturalism. George and his followers admitted that the naturalists were an improvement over the academists in that they were more honest and were endowed with a greater ability to perceive sensible reality, but deplored the fact that the naturalists' preoccupation with complete detail rendered a truly great style impossible. The enemy, however, was a Hydra with more than one head. Contemporary mediocrity, in all its changing aspects, must be overcome.*

* Gundolf in his book on *George* analyzes it thus: "One bond unites them all: an incapacity to choose between stimuli, a confusion of values, and a misconstruction, either unintentional or voluntary, of the ranks and degrees of humanity. It is not by chance that some of them make an apology for carrion, that others picture themselves as vermin, and that all think for themselves in the form of material objects. The greater part of them revel in planes of existence sometimes sub-human, sometimes superhuman; they are obsessed by an animal delight in matter and a romantic intoxication with machinism *à l'Americaine* or by the need to embrace abstract humanity. Nothing but irresponsible stimulation, complete abandon cries into emptiness. All of them make an effort to escape the specific human figure which moves in a conditional space, but which has its unconditional law. They know no will except in the form of an impulse or a program, no love except as slack pity, regardless of its object, or as lubricity, or as Utopia. They confuse passion with nervous tension or fanaticism, respect with infatuation, piety with swooning emotionalism. In general they desire happiness, that is to say, the nullification of destiny by one pleasure succeeding another, or regulation of the common welfare; they do not aspire to work, the fulfillment of a destiny which demands to be, to create, to shape. Of all forms of existence only one excites their hatred: that of the heroic man; they cannot conceive of him except under the aspect of an invalid or a promoter. At the same time they have a special cult for woman, for sorrowful flesh, for that consecrated thing, the pure soul—here and there a human door opening upon realms beyond human experience, either in the direction of the chaos before man or the Nirvana after him."

George did not deem it sufficient to set an aristocratic hauteur against the prevalent democratic effusiveness, or coldness against the intoxication of patriotism. He had rediscovered a conception of the masses different from and broader than either the social or the national conception. He reached out to those masses with all his will to nobility, scorning only one means of identifying himself with them, a means available to all classes and to all nations—vulgarity.

The word "*Volkheit*" signifies the eternal part of itself which a people should strive never to lose. George believed that it could be saved only by setting up a type of community which he insists should be entirely masculine and which is a sort of ideal freemasonry, an ideal church in which respect for symbols and strict observance of rites, as in Goethe's case, lend majesty to the development of an ego perpetually growing and perpetually anxious to bring itself into conformity with the law of nature. A refusal to expose oneself to the world is then not a refusal to take the communion of the church; it is merely to choose not to commune except in one's own special fashion. Retirement from the world is to take part in the world through prayer. The artist has a mission, and this mission is to think on a higher plane than the unintelligent masses, to discover for the masses the mysterious meaning of the life which flows within them. This meaning is revealed only to the elect, and to them only in moments of grace; it does not always correspond to their desire. To discover it requires an heroic effort; to express it requires another. There is no use attempting to shout it in public places. It can only be transferred by affinity, by a process of preparing, step by step, souls worthy of being initiated into it. Society places no limit upon its spread; it finds its only obstacles in the lack of culture of the individual. As culture increases, slowly as the centuries, man is delivered from the mass of men. But nowhere, at no time, has man been so delivered save for a precarious moment. Even in the community of George's disciples there are impure elements.* The disciples love the faith, but they can betray it also. Merely to reflect it passively is tantamount to betrayal. The true human value is in the individual ego, solitary and alone. Even the ego must fight against itself. It gains its vitality from the perishable things around it, and must therefore strive to retain only their essence, strive to become the essence of the universe rather than the emanation of objective society which the subjective ego must remain. It must shun the complacent attitude of a romanticism concerned with preserving the social order. It must represent that in man which is striving to rise above itself, the soul-to-be toward which, through and beyond itself, the soul aspires.

This is a Nietzschean reaching toward a beyond not divorced from this earth or postponed until after death. Eternity is contained in the present, the whole universe in the here, and all humanity in the individual. Greatness lies in that which strives to rise above the object in which it is manifested. Let a man say, this is being, idea, act of faith, and do not scorn him; but all these things can achieve dignity only through the will to surpass one's being, through thinking which rises above itself, through faith which is greater than act of faith. The spiritual history of humanity is made up of successive sublimations, each accomplished only to begin again. To live passionately is to raise human understanding to a higher power, discover for the apparently divided ego the one

* *Die Blätter für die Kunst* welcomed contributors of varying race, religion, and nationality. But it is carefully pointed out that not all who took part in the activity of the circle could lay claim to its inspiration.

law in which the individual and the cosmos, the finite and the infinite, the perishable and the eternal are linked.

George is more than a miniature Goethe, an affected Nietzsche. His inheritance from both Goethe and Nietzsche has been modified by an inspiration of his own. The fact that he was born near Bingen on the Rhine, and loved that river as something which unites two lands rather than divides them, together with his visits to France, during which he liked to think of himself as the Frank returning to "*France dulce terre*," helped him to see the relation between problems which cannot well be attacked singly. Paganism, the messianism of Germany, Europeanism, all the inner attitudes of the West which represent feeling rather than thought, met within him and were fused. He saw the ancient Porta Negra of Treves among Roman towers and Gothic spires, and learned to despise the modern traffic which flowed against its sides. The new is colossal, but the old is great. Not that the present has not its own greatness, which cannot be found in that of the past. A return to antique or early Christian civilization, if it were no more than a mere return, could only cloud the modern's view of his own world. Myths have been necessary to all eras, but each era should produce its own. Proteus must be more than mere change, Pantheus more than mere acceptance of nature, Prometheus more than mere revolt. That life must destroy itself in order to be reborn, this is the law in which life's higher meaning lies. The pantheist's instinct leads him to yield to that law; the Christian conceives of the law as opposed to instinct; the thinker feels the complexity of the law; the artist attempts to express it; but only he who can fuse within himself the inspirations of all ages—poetry, mysticism, and thought —can serve the law entirely.

George did not have to struggle like Goethe and Nietzsche with a tremendous demoniac, dionysiac power. Seeking a conception of order in the universe, he reached a more eclectic one than that of the classicists. In spite of its severity, it left room for escapes into the obscure. His paganism differs from the paganism of Olympus in that it contains an element of asceticism—an asceticism which like Nietzsche's is tempered with evangelical gentleness and with a touch of the pontifical as well. George goes beyond church and throne to find true majesty in the life of a man like Leo XIII, lived beautifully and serving as a lesson that "the salvation to come is in the love to come."

George has both the mystic love of the Rosicrucian—"the Rose is our youthful passion, our carnal desire, the flame within us; the Cross is our ability to bear our burdens and to suffer proudly"—and the militant love of the Templar. Renunciation of the world does not mean abdication of sovereignty over the world; the very act of renunciation is a proof of sovereignty and lends it its sovereign quality. The leader rules severely over the "Ring," the followers who are grouped about him in an order which reflects the internal hierarchy of values he imposes upon himself.

There is set up a rhythm of domination and submission which is the rhythm of man in his relation to nature. The individual neither attempts to rise wholly above nature, after the fashion of the Christian or the rationalist, nor does he entirely abandon himself to nature like the pantheist or the determinist. On the contrary, he proves his mastery over nature by yielding to it, for only thus can there be dignity in his yielding.

"When great Nature, refusing in her anger—To bow to Man—One night when the world is veiled—Comes, weary and worn, to knock at Man's door—Then only he who has learned to fight her and to overcome her—And who has never obeyed her law—Can touch her hand, stroke her hair—And send her submissive away to take up her work again—Set her to making the body divine, and to giving body to divinity."

George's whole teaching is summed up in that precept: Make the body divine, and give body to divinity. The great error of Christianity was that it rejected the body, when the mere concept of divine incarnation should have sufficed to sanctify it. The equally great error of the moderns is that though they have rediscovered the body, they have rid it of God. In the one case, evil lies in the failure to exercise a selective sense on the part of him who gives himself up to the play of his instincts, regardless of what those instincts may be or of the nature of the pleasure. In the other, evil lies in the false choice made by the saint who, in order to fuse his ego with God, abolishes that ego by denying the senses.

This false choice implies a dissociation which prevents being, instead of perfecting being in the image of divine perfection. Every time a man achieves individuality, becomes *Gestalt*, a being unique yet partaking of the universal, ephemeral yet linked to the eternal, he has taken one more step toward that divine perfection. Life itself contains the essence of the style which Stefan George sought—a style which by no means robs life of its character of ceaseless becoming, but merely assumes that each phase of becoming shall give the appearance of completion.

To reëstablish the rights of the ego implies something to strive against. The world is both pleasure and opposition. Opposition and pleasure are part of a law superior to the ego. Thus what in George and his followers seemed a rigidity resulting from esthetic fancy, in reality resulted from the requirements of conscious being, an inner style which controlled the carriage of the head and the gestures of the hands—a style which did not permit sloppiness in bodily things, for sloppiness in bodily things means sloppiness of the soul. A civilization's greatest glory is the individual in whom culture, joining with nature, carries the latter to a higher plane. In him reside all culture and all nature; they are he, and at the same time they overflow him in their radiance. He must not only be, but through this radiant power he must be great. This radiance implies a sublimation of the conscious being which makes greater and greater demands as it increases in breadth. The noble style rejects overloading, rejects ornamentation which conceals line. Its spiritual as well as its plastic beauty is achieved through relentless rejection.

This severity is reflected in George's writing as well as in his ideology and in his life. An inner demand works changes in German syntax, whose rigid exterior held softnesses hidden beneath. George uses ellipses to express a type of thought which is as much concerned with conciseness as with precision. Alternately elaborating and rejecting, he shows the false grandeur of the epithet. Language ceases merely to reproduce that which already exists, becomes again thought in motion. It breathes life, individual life, into elements still trembling in the mystery of an unending beginning.

There is no doubt that Mallarmé influenced George,* but George's work does more than stimulate in Mallarmé's fashion. In his desire for only the quintessence of life, George may seem to withdraw from life; but no matter how refined that quintessence is, it is still alive

---

* Besides Mallarmé, Stefan George's translations into German include selections from the poems of Verhaeren, Verlaine, Rimbaud, Baudelaire, d'Annunzio, Dante, Jacobsen, Rossetti, Swinburne, Dowson and Shakespeare's *Sonnets*.

and charged with power. A musician's soul sets aquiver the hierarchical boundaries enclosing it.

One can feel this quivering in George's work, in spite of its remnants of preciosity and obscurity. The danger is that his disciples, incapable of breaking wholly away from the mental habits that bind them, will betray him, and that the followers of the new religion will slip suddenly back into the old ways of thought. Another danger lies in too much critical interpretation of George's work. It may well be analyzed, but the chief thing is that it should be felt. Indeed George's poetry needs no exegesis. It is full of naïve elements; one of the liveliest sources of its inspiration is simplest nature, the gardens and the fields of the Rhenish country. Their rural freshness gives added delicacy to an intellect that demands both of itself and of the objective world the greatest possible exquisiteness.

CHAPTER III

The Novel

1. *Heinrich Mann and Thomas Mann—The Social Novel and the Novel of the Artist-Ego*

A KNOWLEDGE of a writer's nationality, ancestry, and milieu helps us to understand him, but it does not completely explain him. There remains the mysterious question of personality, the unknown through which, out of a thousand possible combinations of known elements, a particular combination is chosen which resembles no other. The rationalist biographers of Taine's school might well be given pause by the case of Heinrich and Thomas Mann. Here were two brothers, of the same parentage, with the same education, leading approximately the same kind of life in the same city, Munich, and achieving equal success, though with different publics. Yet the talents which fell to them equally are entirely distinct one from the other.

The brothers Mann were born in Lübeck, of a family of Hanseatic patricians. Generations of Manns sitting in the Senate of Lübeck bequeathed to these two descendants a political tradition and a sense of autonomy which led them early to embrace the idea of a republican Germany. But they differed in their conceptions of the form which the German Republic should take. Heinrich Mann, the elder, was drawn toward rationalism; Thomas, the younger, toward a vital empiricism. Yet on this point as on many others the two brothers had this in common; the attitudes of both were conditioned by the fact that they were descendants of a patrician class which had survived the tidal wave of industrialism. Beneath their artist exterior is the hauteur, the rigidity of the North-erner; a life in other respects open to the demands of desire still has a Protestant conscience at its axis.

In the case of the brothers Mann, that desire early took artistic form. They did not approach literature by the by-path of ideas. They began by writing novels—not by discussing theories, like most of the German writers of their day. They were responsible for the return, about 1900, of a spontaneity of which Fontane and Liliencron had theretofore been almost the sole examples. Not that their novels contain no ideas. Ideas came gradually as the result of experience. But the original motivating force was the need for self-expression of a being which feels that it can realize itself only through a work of art.

Both brothers were born with the sense of play, a gift doubtless inherited from their mother. She was musical and emotional, the daughter of a Brazilian mother of Portuguese origin, and she had introduced Latin elements into a family in which, until then, passion, and even music, had been but vaguely felt. Another ancestor had come to Lübeck from the French-speaking part of Switzer-land, to establish himself as grain merchant to the armies of Napoleon. Thus the sense of initiative and the habit of authority were allied in the descendants with the boldness and fantasy of strong sensibilities, and served to control those sensibilities. Northern coldness tempered the ardor of the South; a Roman sense of form, a South-ern taste for plastic conception brought to a Northern imagination a mistrust of its own tumbled luxuriance, and taught born stylists to fill in their outlines with only enough softness to maintain the sense of mystery.

In neither of the Mann brothers is there any trace of literary pantheism. They do not feel the desire to be constantly a part of the cosmos. Nature is almost entirely absent from their work—at least that type of nature which threw other writers into ecstasies of description. The nature that interests them is that which man bears within himself. They see a whole cosmos in society, in a family, in an individual. In this respect they approach the French tradition, but they diverge from it again in that their view of man is far less abstract. As psychologists they are interested in the soul, but in their view the life of the soul, if it is ever to be made clear, must be conceived in relation to the sensible world which their intelligence apprehends all about them. This desire for lucidity, however, does not exclude a certain musicality of thought, even if the presence of this musical element sometimes complicates their problem.

Heinrich and Thomas Mann think for the common people even more paternally than the Buddenbrooks family, struggling in 1848 to preserve their patriarchal authority. But they do not think from the point of view of the common people, as for instance Dehmel did. Heinrich Mann, when he mingles with the crowds in an Italian city or when he describes the poor, attacks social questions as an enlightened bourgeois, a French bourgeois of the eighteenth century. The novel which the Mann brothers gave to Germany—a novel which borrowed nothing save stimuli from abroad—was, by the very nature of the two writers, bound to be a social novel, or a novel of the bourgeoisie, or both at once. It was also a novel of the ego. Both brothers were artists and psychologists; both knew how to combine the two types of novel; but the result was different in the case of each.

The ego seems at first glance to be entirely excluded from Heinrich's work; there is scarcely any reference to the author's memories or the author's personal feelings in *Zwischen den Rassen, Die Göttinnen, Der Kopf*. Heinrich Mann is an observer, and his characters have been snatched from the whirlpool of contemporary life. They have an existence in actuality, they exist for others than himself, and they are not himself. Yet it is through him that their existence is what it is. His ardor, the intensity of his feeling, the multiplicity of his experiences, though they are never presented as his own, are nevertheless continually inflaming, animating, and driving to action characters which without him would be sorry creatures indeed. To him they owe the fact that they are really alive, though he shifts to them the responsibility for their acts.

Thomas Mann, on the other hand, seems at first glance a subjective writer. All his works without exception are built around his own ego. One speaks of his egoism as one speaks of Barrès' egoism—a process in which the ego, born and reborn in successive novels, is linked to the bourgeois whole by means different from those of Heinrich. Thomas Mann's is an artistic ego, but the ego of an artist who feels the need of his family, his class, and his nation as a setting and a support rather than as a source of material to work upon.

Doubtless their mixed heredity contributed to keeping the Mann brothers in that "state of dialogue" to which André Gide attributes some of his own talent. Each brother had to question himself to determine what rôle art should play in his life. In this respect their personal problem was identical with one of the great problems of contemporary German culture. Both for them and for German culture this problem of art was only a particular aspect of a far greater problem, namely, whether the victory should go to instinct or intellect, feeling or reason, tradition or revolution, and, further, whether

either the tradition or the revolution should be essentially
Latin or German or European, and whether the inevitable
evolution should have as its objective the social, national
being or the human personality expanded and developed
to its highest point. Within the mind and soul of the
Mann brothers was the same battle which was shaking
Europe, a battle in which the antagonists were Wagner,
Nietzsche, Tolstoy, Dostoievski, Zola, Flaubert, Balzac,
Stendhal, Goethe, and Napoleon. Their good fortune lay
in the fact that they could expose themselves to all these
diverse influences without attempting to arrive at a
systematic solution of their contradictions, without
ever asking more than: "How, through all this welter,
shall I achieve my fullest stature?" Even when their
success later brought them into public life they carried
with them not a system of philosophy, but a personal
wisdom which was the result of ceaseless self-correction.

Heinrich Mann*

Heinrich Mann has lived much abroad. He spent his
youth in Italy, where he had for guides not archaeologists,
but Italians absorbed in the passions of small city life,
and Stendhal, who had shared that life many years
before. He has a great fondness for France—not alone
the France of Paris, but the France of the Midi, with
its soil and its sky, and the France of literature. He speaks
and writes French beautifully. From France he has
learned much to which his technique and his thinking
bear witness. Is such a writer, of mixed blood and
divided sympathies, truly representative of Germany?
This is the question which some of the admirers of his
Italian stories asked when Heinrich Mann went on to
satirize contemporary German society. But there can

* HEINRICH MANN (1871–   ). For bibliography, see p. 309.

be no doubt that Heinrich Mann is a German, just as Thomas Mann is. Nature, by the same strange caprice which made Thomas, the younger, dark and slim and Latin complexioned, made Heinrich, the elder, the tall, blond type which is supposed to be typically German. Of course his Germanic nature is not restricted to stature and coloring. His characters may have some of the fire of the South in them, but they are nevertheless Northerners. The truculence of his humor, the sensual and nervous violence of his most exaggerated heroes, have no place save in German realism. Only there is a little more sunshine than usual in his work; and though he draws laugh-provoking caricatures *à la* Daumier, his cruelty has much of the character of a modern Simplicissimus, who has none of the good humor of the seventeenth century.

That good humor, which was sympathetic and sister to tears, is lost to the moderns. Thomas Mann has substituted for it a pointed smile, but not Heinrich. His humor is more the maliciousness of a Til Eulenspiegel, the verve of a Rabelais, had these two figures been present at the close of the nineteenth century. In an age of illusions and blissful optimism, he was a disillusionist, seeking to sharpen the senses of his public. Yet his criticism does not exclude generosity; his bitterness is that of conviction mingled with sympathy. His thinking, in spite of its severity, has flashes of passion. One example is the reproach, in *Schauspielerin*, to the uncertain lover who could never express "his final word, his truest thought." Like his favorite heroine, Heinrich Mann has a hot scorn for the lukewarm, the tepid. His is an art of hyperbole; he avoids subtleties; his passionate logic shuns distinctions which are merely relative. He strips his material bare, with a hurried, clean, direct movement. His mood is always imperative, even when he is reserved or persuasive. His satire is accompanied by panegyrics. For everything he destroys he has a substitute ready, piping hot. Destructive or constructive, he is always radical. His is the vehemence of over-lively sensibilities, of a mind which sees too clearly, knows too much and cannot withhold it. At least he makes no effort to withhold it. He is at once a Schiller—with all the pathos of *Die Räuber* and *Don Carlos*, though without the dreamy quality; colorful; taking his themes as willingly from the French Revolution as from modern Berlin—and a Roman senator. He instinctively seeks out the public of the forum. Literature offers him not a pulpit from which to philosophize, but a tribune from which to impose his ideas upon the people—ideas not alone political but esthetic, psychological, moral as well.

Heinrich Mann was destined to give Germany the social novel which neither Gutzkov nor Freitag nor Spielhagen had succeeded in creating. He is passionately desirous of asserting himself, scornful of mere self-reminiscence or egoism and even of introspection. His inmost thought is turned outward; his whole work is oriented toward contemporary society. His chief function, he believes, is to seek out the springs of power in that society. It may be added that he seeks also to introduce into that society power in another, the spiritual, form.

His first conception of that power was that it sprang from the dynamism of the individual. The ego is power. He felt this power in all the characters with which he filled his novels—bourgeois, artists, poor worthless wretches as well as exceptional personalities. He thus broke with the tradition of the novel of individual development and attached himself to the naturalist tradition, substituting for the single hero the numberless mass, for the author's ego the thousand egos of contemporary reality. At the same time he cast off the German habit of turning the novel into lyric effusions and descriptions. No more of those confidences in which the author pours out his soul, those "confidences of a noble spirit." Heinrich Mann's objectivity recalls both that of the experimental novel of Zola and that of the *Wahlverwandtschaften*. He looks upon individuals as so many objects with which to experiment. But he surpasses the observation of the naturalists, does more than express exterior states. He attempts also to seize upon and to express the reactions which take place within the individual, to uncover the properties of each element which goes to make up that individual, emphatically rejecting the complacencies of a dishonest psychology.

Even in the most mediocre of his characters he discovers an astonishing dynamism of instinct. He carried his investigations into the least known regions of sensibility and sensuality. "One must unlearn modesty before one can learn life," says Jean Guignol in *Die Göttinnen*. During his Italian period Heinrich Mann reintroduced sensuality into Protestant literature; but at the same time he overcame what there was in him of the d'Annunzio type of estheticism. His was the task of the amoral moralist who must himself remain cold if he is to comprehend the human soul. Then forced optimism ceases; man wherever he appears is a beast of prey and pleasure, sometimes bursting civilization open, sometimes turning civilization into a lie. In every adventurer there is a bourgeois who ultimately recognizes himself; in every bourgeois there is an adventurer who is unconscious of his own existence. In every man there is a demon which alternately sleeps and wakes, and it is the activity of this demon which Heinrich Mann describes. His Professor Unrat is merely one of the types of ecstatic philistines whom he sets up as a contrast to the deceiving tameness of the camomile-tea version of the same man.

Heinrich Mann attracted disciples, and Sternheim's heroes are inspired by his. The fury of passion in which they live is not pathological; Heinrich Mann is not depicting a morbid state. Here is no influence of the Russian novel, but rather a dissection, in the French tradition, of men whose lusts, however base or strange they may be, are nevertheless, though carried to unusual intensity, the lusts of the normal human being. These men are adventurers, but their adventures are not poetic, not cosmic—for this reason they reach beyond the outdated German romantic tradition; they are realistic, social. The adventurers live their adventures not outstretched and dreaming, but upright and on their two feet, and either take the maximum of gratification from the society in which they live, or combat that society in an effort to find gratifications other than those which it has to offer.

From this last distinction there arise two classes of characters. In one the adventure is comic, in the other, tragic. In the first are people whose instincts are unleashed, but who have not yet freed themselves from conventional restraints. The contrast between their passions and their inhibitions renders them grotesque. The body and soul which the idealists considered as separate are in them united, or rather set side by side, to form a *diable au corps* which is different from the familiar, sentimental Kobold of the romanticists. It boils in Unrat, it sings in a Fleurissoier or a Profitendieu. To discover it, to point it out, is to do a moralist's work.

In the second class of character, the adventure is tragic. *Branzilla*, *Schauspielerin*, Terra in *Der Kopf*, Cassini in *Das gastliche Haus*, *Mutter Marie*, Bonaparte in *Der Weg zur Macht*, are adventurers in the grand style.

Nature has given them blanket freedom from the moral principles of a society on whose borders they move at ease, whether they succeed in subjugating it to their ambitions or not. It is interesting to note that the women come off rather better than the men. Heinrich Mann has given a preferred place to woman in the German novel, where formerly she had to be content with a secondary rôle; he has stripped women as well as men of the sentimental and endowed them with great energies.

In Heinrich Mann, as in his friend Wedekind, the individual no longer deals passively with the anonymous forces of nature and society. Before he has submitted to the discipline of the spirit, he is the instinctive being turned loose in the group. He encounters other beings of instinct and carnal passion. A conflict arises. The novel is worked out in terms of appetites and in terms of conventions. In *Zwischen den Rassen* Mann deals with a foreign woman caught in the race problem. In *Schlaraffenland* a Berlin Bel Ami takes part in the rush of parvenus to Cockaigne. In *Novellen* and *Die Göttinnen* a plethora of artists which recalls the Renaissance brings about a situation in which the individual aspect of life becomes more important than the social aspect; but in *Die Kleine Stadt* the foreground is occupied by the whole life of an Italian city, embracing all the passions of individuals and families and political parties.

At this point in his career Heinrich Mann's perspective of space and time, his political sense as a citizen of Lübeck, his curiosity concerning history, particularly French history, his reading of Stendhal and of Zola, and the memory of the fact that he once wanted to be a painter, all led him to embark upon a work conceived as a sweeping fresco of the Germany of William II. The power whose source he had sought in the individual he was now to find in synthesized form in groups, each of which was to have its own novel—the bourgeois, the poor, the ruling classes. Hence he wrote the trilogy *Der Untertan*, *Die Armen*, and *Der Kopf*. Since that trilogy he has returned to quieter themes. In *Liliane und Paul* and *Mutter Marie*, as in *Das gastliche Haus*, has set out merely to depict the manners and customs of post-War society. It is too early to say that his political period is over, but it may at least be pointed out that its high point coincided with the crisis in German political history.

Der Untertan was going through the press in July of 1914. It is a satire upon the "subjects" of the Hohenzollern Empire, conceived by a mind which has the faculty of discovering the defects of a society or régime at the very moment when that society seems to have achieved its fullest flower, that régime its apogee. In this book Heinrich Mann laid bare the being of Diedrich Hessling, upstart and subject of the Empire, and drew a dark picture of the vices of climbing and of subjection. German patriots objected to the caricature, as if Mann had invented the vices which he was merely denouncing. Yet if one believes in the efficacy of self-criticism, drawing that caricature was an act of merit, for Heinrich Mann made the position of the "subject" as morally indefensible in Germany as Flaubert had made that of Monsieur Homais in France. Perhaps the German people in Heinrich Mann's trilogy are only the German people in the sense that Zola represented the French people in his story of the Rougon-Macquart. In the work of this German Zola the picture of the German masses lacks the nuances, the shades which are essentially German.

Nevertheless Heinrich Mann succeeded in dissipating the fog which German dealers in literary opiates had maintained around this *Gemüt* in order that it might be taken for depth of soul, and which was itself harmful

to that very profundity. The path of the true idealist
was clearly to let in light and air, even if he were to
shock the people in the process. The critical rationalism
of the literary revolutionists seemed destructive; actually
it stripped away only the parasitic cells clustered about
an organism that was of itself already well on the way to
regaining its normal health. Events aided the process.
Heinrich Mann, however, is one of those who not only
accept the assistance of events but help to bring them
about; and it was no mere coincidence that his own
idealism was closely allied to that of the German Revolution of 1918. When he wrote of the stupefying effects of
power—whether of *Realpolitik* or of contemporary
Wagnerism—he was following in the path of Nietzsche,
and himself became a moving force. Germany had had
no Encyclopedists, no Revolution, no Dreyfus Case;
in that Germany Heinrich Mann stirred up a conflict of
the soul in search of justice, the mind in search of
autonomy. To *Macht* he opposed *Mensch*, and in so
doing he was not only defending man against might,
but mind against the machine.

Another of his formulas—*Geist und Tat*—inflamed
the youth of 1910 and in certain intellectual groups
aroused passions which were to be useful in the coming
change of régime. Heinrich Mann urged mind to action—
perhaps not directly to revolutionary action, but at
least to the kind of action represented by Voltaire and
Rousseau, the kind of action which prepares a people
for a revolution of the soul. Just as Heinrich Mann
was militant, he wanted reason itself to become militant,
and introduced it into German public life as a full-
armed power. And it was to this mind that he wished to
give hegemony when he later wrote *Diktatur der Vernunft*.

The intellectual movement for which he was responsible reached its peak just after 1918. Since then,

Heinrich Mann's work, and German literature in general until very recently, has tended to leave politics aside. The thrust of mind is ephemeral if it is restricted to political forms, is permanent only if it frees the mind of bondage to the accidental.

Obviously Heinrich Mann did not completely succeed in his effort so to free the mind. The type of individual represented in his books is filled with contradictory passions superimposed one upon the other. There is an apparently insoluble conflict between the concept of a reasonable humanity and the concept of a demonism ever brooding in its depths. Heinrich Mann's originality lies in the fact that he does not attempt to eliminate the one in order to strengthen the other, but accepts the coexistence of forces of order and forces of destruction in the human soul, seeing in their antagonism the true mystery of life. Victory for Heinrich Mann would not be a victory in which the opposing armies are destroyed and the field of battle cleared; he comprehends the opposing forces, but for him the conflict never ends. It gives us power enough that we should understand it.

Mann is more than the *"Zivilisationsliterat"* which he has sometimes been called. He is more than the defender of a strictly rationalist Latin civilization which many claim the Latins themselves would never recognize. His concept of the true European includes both the Baltic and the Mediterranean. His concept of reason is not merely *Verstand* but *Vernunft*, a higher form of reason that contains elements of dynamism and growth. His concept of the ego is not, like that of the realists, a concept of the self abandoned to the magic influences of milieu, from which the realists expected all things, even to the rise of great individual personalities. Heinrich Mann's concept is that of the self imposing itself upon its milieu, expanding as it fights against political, social, or intellectual automatism. The fact that these struggles against adversaries within and without never cease, are never settled, makes them more fruitful than would be a precarious peace.

From the literary point of view Heinrich Mann's art may not be pleasing; it may shock and obviously enjoy shocking; but it undeniably represents an astounding creative force. Unrat drunk with tyrannical power, Hessling drunk with his condition as a subject of the Empire, Kobes drunk with organization, are all drawn on Balzacian lines. The violence of a character like Kobes is the expression of a violent age. The one dictatorship that can quell its anarchy is the dictatorship of *Wirtschaft*, of Economics—a dictatorship, as Heinrich Mann points out, beside which the dictatorship of Mussolini or the Soviets seems pale and wan. The grandeur of Kobes' character lies in the fact that he is two things in one: the ambitious man of all times (he would once have been called Richelieu or Mazarin); and the leader of the future, whose ambition takes forms totally unsuspected by the enslaved masses.

The life into which Heinrich Mann thrusts his characters exceeds the limitations of the novel. It is a whirlpool which can be rendered only in terms of the drama, for it is itself a drama of individuals struggling against events. Therefore Heinrich Mann has evolved a style in accordance with his requirements, a style which has the thrust of dramatic writing but is at the same time not too thin; loaded when circumstances demand it, and yet direct and spare when expressing the rhythm of a bare, hard existence. It is because he absorbed this latter rhythm that Heinrich Mann became the father of expressionism. His is a style which is still evolving in other writers, and evolving in accordance with a genius which is neither typically Northern nor typically Southern. Its qualities spring from no one region, from no one people. They are the qualities of a Europe in process of rebirth, a Europe whose tradition has always remained basically one. When we observe its extreme manifestations, we are struck by the contrast. But when, as in Heinrich Mann, the extremes are joined, we are impressed by its potential unity. And this unity is not merely an artistic unity; it is the unity of a collective soul, guided by the moralists in its evolution and prevented from going astray in the chaos of events.

Eugénie oder die Kaiserzeit is an intermezzo. In it Heinrich Mann evoked with quiet imaginativeness the period of his grandmother, the period of a bourgeoisie still flourishing but already conscious of its approaching end. After this, in *Die grosse Sache*, he again took up his teaching rôle. He depicts contemporary youth at grips with a disorganized world, struggling to overcome its difficulties through family connections, through speculation, through murder; and he offers a solution— labor, and faith in creative effort. This is a wisdom which he has learned during his own lifetime—partly from the great Frenchmen whom he studied in *Geist und Tat*, partly from the events of 1921–1928, in which he was both audience and actor. He has a great rôle to play in the chaos which is still far from its end: to inspire and to teach.

Thomas Mann*

Thomas Mann is not an imaginative writer. His books grow out of events, and the source of his material is his own experience. Looked at as a whole, his writings are a continuous novel of the development of the author

* Thomas Mann (1875–   ). For bibliography, see p. 310.

and his times. Nevertheless his standard of selection has this distinctive feature, that he invariably takes life at a point where it seems about to degenerate, to struggle against destruction, to seek a discipline. The plot of every one of his novels concerns an organism whose vitality is threatened; one can never be sure whether the crisis will end ineluctably in death or whether it is not instead the critical point in a rebirth. In *Buddenbrooks* he has chosen as his subject a family which represents the Hanseatic bourgeoisie taken at the point where it is threatened by the various forces of decadence of the nineteenth century—social changes, moral revolutions, rise of the musical and artistic spirit. In *Tristan*, the equilibrium of a bourgeois family is again threatened through the illness of the heroine, through Wagnerian romanticism and the attractions of love and death. In *Königliche Hoheit* the reigning family of a small principality is threatened with extinction unless an American woman supplies new blood and new money. *Der Tod in Venedig* depicts the problem of the intellectual who, believing that he has organized his existence on a rational basis, finds that carefully organized existence breaking up under the onslaught of demons and abandons himself to dissolving passions. *Tonio Kröger* is an anti-romantic story of the poet who stumbles into the labyrinthine passions of an artistic community and is overcome by a nostalgia for the lost paradise of his bourgeois youth. Even the wartime essays—*Friedrich und die grosse Koalition* and *Betrachtungen eines Un-politischen*—are the work of an uneasy German who, watching his nation in a crisis, is seeking first a sign of vitality in the crisis itself by considering that crisis as an explosion of German demonism; second, through the example of Frederick II, a discipline capable of channeling that demonism effectively. The big post-War novel, *Der Zauberberg*, is again the story of an organism passing through a crisis. It concerns the inhabitants of a sanatorium in Davos, come from every corner of the world; and the illness against which they are fighting is the illness of Europe struggling to regain her strength.

Whereas Heinrich Mann set out to seek the sources of power in contemporary society, one might almost say that Thomas Mann set out to seek the sources of weakness. But curiously enough, although they differed in the objects of their search, each found what he was seeking in the same place. Where Heinrich Mann sees a "*Befreiung*," a liberation of vital dynamism, Thomas Mann sees the appearance of the forces of break-up and decline. Heinrich is considered a revolutionary, Thomas a conservative. But these are untrustworthy formulas. Thomas Mann is a revolutionary also; he does not preach violent revolution, but he lives in a state of instinctive revolt, a state in which the obscure forces of the soul are so freed that he feels it necessary to seek a "*Bindung*," a restraint, to hold them in check. For a long while the great difference between the two brothers was that Heinrich felt that that restraint would be found in reason, and hence demanded a dictatorship of reason; whereas Thomas Mann, like Luther, saw in reason a disturbing force, and felt that instinct offers not only a source of disorder but a source of restraint as well. Finally they met on common ground: the conception that *Geist* and *Musik*, the spirit of lucidity and the spirit of musicality, should not be considered as separate, but should be united in a higher form of reason and perform a work of both construction and destruction.

Heinrich Mann's novels give the impression of social pessimism; Thomas Mann's of national optimism. As a matter of fact in both cases the two are united, and both writers finally embrace an optimism of pessimism. In

Heinrich Mann it is the optimism of a sturdy nature which does not hesitate to cut open a wound; in Thomas Mann it is the optimism of a sensitive personality fearful of interfering and leaning rather upon man's faculties of adaptation, man's ability to overcome evil by skirting it.

It is easy to be misled by Thomas Mann's apparent facility. His smile is agreeable, but it illuminates features twisted by effort, and represents a continual struggle. He has taken health and normality as his ideals, but he has done so precisely because neither health nor normality is natural to him. He is a troubled artist who feels an original sin deep within him, senses the threat of destructive forces which he must prepare to oppose; and for this reason he has tried to evade the vast and the dreary, and constantly to rebuild a tissue of sensibility which forever tends to tear itself to shreds.

Less direct than his brother, he has attained his own particular heights of optimism only with difficulty, by circuitous paths, by dint of insinuation, by counterbalancing. The virtue of his art is in the fact that he has been able to dissimulate the effort and leave only an impression of sensual enjoyment. His artistic talent seems compounded of facility and compliance; as a matter of fact it is the result of much labor. Those who have compared him to René Bazin have been deceived by appearances. Those who have called him a German Barrès have been misled by a certain similarity of preoccupations between the two writers. The faith, the scepticism, the egoism, the patriotism of Barrès are made of a different stuff from the faith and scepticism and egoism and patriotism of Thomas Mann. It was not the German writer's task, as it was the Frenchman's, to develop a novel of national energy; on the contrary, in Thomas Mann's case, Germany's national energy seemed already to have reached its peak, and the observer's task was rather to show its deficiencies. Thomas Mann has a greater frankness than Barrès, together with more irony and greater emancipation of spirit.

Heinrich Mann sets up a conflict between the individual taken as a whole and a unified society desirous of change. Thomas Mann places the conflict within himself and expresses it in a conflict between the artist ego, tending to escape from the forms imposed upon it, and the social ego, tending to hold the artist ego within the formal limits of tradition. His distrust of his art is by his own admission the distrust which the universal bourgeois feels for the implications of boldness, license, and indecency contained in all art. But it has other bases as well. It is a Protestant distrust both of Catholicism, which canalizes sensuality, and of Luther, who transposes sensuality into popular sentimentality. To bend the Protestant conscience, the Protestant morality, to the ends of enjoyment is to play with fire. Conscience and morality make him distrust the very play of the senses as if there were something essentially reprehensible in sensual enjoyment, even when it takes a non-religious or an esthetic form. Thomas Mann is of course too clever not to make this censure a matter of degree. He does not conceive the artistic temperament as always following the same model, and he has varied his characters accordingly: Christian Buddenbrook, the mere mimic; Gerda, his sister-in-law, the dilettante; Johann, one of her sons, a consumptive; Tonio Kröger, a hybrid whose two sets of desires destine him to compromise; Spinell, the ecstatic; Aschenbach, the cold demoniacal type, whose demon ultimately melts his icy crust; Felix Krull, the virtuoso of simulation. In his ironical condemnation of Krull, Thomas Mann is also condemning the essential sham in all art.

Thomas Mann feels that the artistic urge calls forth a whole gamut of poisons. But though like Mithridates he fears them, like Mithridates also he makes no effort to flee them. He introduces them into his system, and thanks to his eclecticism finds a certain charm in the very threat of danger which their introduction carries with it. His intellect and his sensibilities are so active that we cannot tell whether it is tragedy or pleasure for him to half-open the door upon events, to live at once a whole life and a measured one, to feel madness seep into his mind and soul without ever losing his reason, and, like the quinquagenarian in *Unordnung und frühes Leid*, to live in sympathy with both the spirit of life and the spirit of death.

Underneath the masterfully arranged exterior broods a somber passion. This passion has no definite object; it is rather the attraction of the abyss. Music stirs it or accompanies it; it is always allied to music; it is music. Now an air from *Carmen* played on the sanatorium phonograph, now the song of the Tilleul in the *Battle of Verdun*, now the mad aria of a wandering singer in Venice, now a movement from *Tristan*, ally themselves with the soul in tumult, raise moving problems of the moral universe. A big book and a fine book could be made by collecting the writings in which Thomas Mann describes musical emotion. Music for him is like the cathedral organ for Gretchen: it brings to the surface deep hidden thoughts which would otherwise never reach the point of expression; it permits forebodings to take form in consciousness. The whole forms a symphonic tragedy in which the music is a perpetual prelude to death. But it is a death in the Holbein manner, a dance of death, which draws into its wild movement beings who are living at their greatest intensity, caught at a moment when life surpasses itself, and which tends toward its own destruction—the condition which precedes metamorphosis.

Strangely, but in accordance with a profound logic, the theme of love and the theme of death are indissolubly allied. To love is to wish to die; this theme recurs in successive novels. Johann Buddenbrook, the heroine of his *Tristan*, Aschenbach, Hans Castorp are all condemned to die. They are awaiting destruction, and music turns the period of waiting into ecstasy. They see and feel while rapt in a wild dream like that of Aschenbach when the plague breaks out in Venice, in the midst of the swarming activity of nature—a constant, intoxicating process by which bodies are returned to their elements and new bodies formed from the elements again. It is the theme of death looked upon as the annunciation of divine resurrection—a theme within the traditions of both paganism and Germanism, and at the same time in the tradition of Christianity, which gave subtlety to the Oriental idea of redemption.

It is likewise in the Wagnerian tradition. Music for Thomas Mann means above all the music of Bayreuth. Wagner represents one pole of his existence. The artist ego which he distrusts is the ego which tends to yield to the spell of Wagnerian music. And it is this ego which is dearest to him, this ego which he was combating most strongly when in *Der Tod in Venedig* he said: "As poets we can be neither wise nor worthy, we are fated to go astray and be destroyed. Mastery of style is a snare and a delusion. Education through art is a risky undertaking which should be forbidden. For of what use in education is a thing which by its very nature tends irresistibly toward the abyss?"

The other pole of Thomas Mann's existence is the bourgeois tradition, a fact which is true less because he is conservative in mind than because he is conservative by instinct. He does not merely, like Thomas Budden-brook, feel the desire to be correct; he feels an organic necessity to unite himself with the mass of that which exists, to partake of its stability. In the life of good bourgeois society there is poetry also, a poetry diametrically opposed to the romanticism of passion. This poetry has a rhythm dictated by events listed in the bourgeois calendar or consecrated by a rational tradition. Ritual festivals, picnics, baptisms, birthdays, weddings, funerals, fill the forty years of *Buddenbrooks* with a majestic sweeping rhythm. As in Proust, but with none of Proust's Bergsonism, Time is the principal hero.

The other important hero is the bourgeois family. Thomas Mann has dealt chiefly with the old bourgeoisie. Families like the Grünlichs and the Permanenders are considered mésalliances and remain in the background. The Hanseatic families represent a patrician class pure in its dignity, equally removed from the business bourgeoisie, which lacks the sense of honor and the class consciousness of the Buddenbrooks, and from the philistines, who attempt to deny their pettiness by masking it beneath a confusion of stars and blossoms.

The entry of this old German bourgeoisie into German literature is a new phenomenon. Even Goethe in *Hermann und Dorothea* did not achieve it, for he took an attitude of condescension toward his characters, and, though he hid his smile, the gravity which he gave them left them without true pride and greatness. Tony Buddenbrook, on the contrary, is a woman obviously proud of her bourgeois condition. As in any aristocracy of race, she takes pride in the feeling that in her is embodied a whole greater than herself. That whole is both family and function in society, the honor of the one dependent upon the honor of the other. Everything is a part of it: the firm with its grain vessels, its offices, its employees, its credit with the banks, as well as ancestors and the elder members of the family, brothers, husbands, cousins, and the family's reputation in the city. The desires, the renunciations, the whole existence of the heroine depend upon the concept of an indivisible heritage. Tony comes unsoiled through mésalliances, divorces, disappointments; no matter what happens she still represents all the beings and things included in that rich plural—the Buddenbrooks. From the family she acquires a sort of impersonal dignity so great that her virtues and vices no longer seem to her to be her own, but those of her family itself.

Thomas Mann, like the naturalists, depended for his material upon experience of reality. But he differs from the naturalists in that he does not approach the problems of his time systematically or from without. His was a single problem; it was born in him, he lived it within himself, he watched it take every possible form— individual, family, social, national. A single spiritual destiny, seen from different viewpoints, was at stake, threatened by what was called the decadence of the times. Did Thomas Mann ever entirely believe in that decadence? Probably not, no more than he believed absolutely in the virtue of the tradition which he said he embraced. When he set out to depict a bourgeoisie at once so proud and so seriously undermined, a caustic touch crept into the work. He never entirely lost the "*schweres Blut*," a drop of which mixes well with humor. But there is champagne sparkling in his veins also, and a malicious twinkle in his eye. He brought to German literature the bantering note which it had previously lacked. Banter is his mode of criticism. He does not engage in open satire of the customs and institutions of the German nation. His is an art of understatement rather than an art of hyperbole. Where his brother employs

sharps, he uses flats. He marks the point at which the
German novel began to free itself of the excess of emotionalism with which it was overloaded. The tremendous desires
and the tremendous hungers of the individual are often
scaled down in Thomas Mann's work to the dimensions
of the gluttonous pastor who was served a Lenten meal
by an irritated housewife, or to little Thilda, the poor
relation who took pleasure in mocking idealism by
exhibiting before the assembled family the fruits of her
questionable activities. Thomas Buddenbrook, deranged
by Schopenhauer, dies of an abscessed tooth; his son,
wasted away by musical ecstasy, is finally carried off by a
commonplace attack of typhoid fever. Thomas Mann
pretends to show such an excessive reverence for authority that his mocking detachment becomes obvious, as
when Miss Poelman jostles the guardsman in front of
the royal castle at the sacred moment when the guard
is to be changed. Delicately, in his own fashion, he has
attacked the remaining evidences of feudalism in the
social and political structure.

Although he early discovered in art a natural ferment
dangerous to morality, Thomas Mann was quick to see
in it the germ of a new grandeur. The bourgeois class
which he was depicting no longer included all the basic
conceptions of contemporary society, and this may have
accounted for its decline. It had grown greater only just
so long as a will to growth was allied with its desire to
conserve. Initiative, the taste for innovation, and a
sense if not of revolution at least of necessary evolution,
had all been part of the true bourgeois tradition. But
that tradition was now threatened by the introduction
of artistic elements. Every thrust of the artistic is a
revolutionary thrust. The question was whether the
disrupting influence of the artistic was not itself a demand
for change, was not preparing the way for a transposition

of the bourgeoisie to a higher plane. Thomas Mann, as his career has progressed, has tended more and more to answer this question in the affirmative.

Just as in his own life Thomas Mann tends toward conformity, so in his literary style he seems to make an effort to avoid originality. He is a stylist, but his style is not a creation bearing new promise, nor is it likely to undergo any sudden evolution. It represents rather the highest mastery in the utilization of already existing means of expression—all means of expression. He combines the resources of Latin logical composition with a German capacity for musical composition. The plot of *Der Tod in Venedig* is developed on a musical theme of death, just as Marguerite's tragedy is developed around a theme of fidelity. After a Wagnerian overture, the theme which has been stated reappears, flows out, swells to a tragic finale. In others of his novels part of the charm even of secondary characters lies in the fact that their interior life progresses like a melody whose rhythm is marked by the recurrence of a favorite phrase: Hans Castorp's "little bourgeois still wet behind the ears;" Tony's "I'm no longer a stupid goose;" Christian's "My nerves are too short on the left side." This is a curious psychology, but it fits to perfection characters who never analyze themselves, who live their lives like a song, who take up the refrain again in every reincarnation.

Indeed Thomas Mann's is a complex art. He respects tradition, but conceives of it as being in process of evolution, capable of assimilating heterogeneous elements from outside itself. In it are joined culture and nature, conservation and revolution, the individual and the social, music and reason. In Thomas Mann's thinking the influence of Nietzsche counterbalances that of Wagner, and on a plane above either is the inspiration of Goethe. The conception of art as suspect has been replaced by the

conception of a great art which does not parody nature,
or attempt to modify nature's law, but which seeks out
nature at living founts and imposes upon it restraints
which are at once esthetic and moral. In this conception
the spirit of music is no longer a purely German attribute,
nor the spirit of lucidity a purely Latin one. With *Rede
und Antwort* and *Der Zauberberg*, that encyclopedia of
the present, Thomas Mann achieved a truly European
outlook. While he does not attempt to show how a
Europe on the way to dissolution should be rebuilt, he
maintains within himself that condition of passionate
questioning which was common to the German élite even
throughout the period of the Hohenzollern Empire.

Bemühungen and *Die Forderung des Tages* are essays
for the times. Although he avoids the rôle of *praeceptor
Germaniae*, Thomas Mann is nevertheless, like his brother,
one of the great who draw their inspiration from reason.
In Germany, which, unlike France in the eighteenth
century, had no encyclopedists to clarify the opinions
of the people; in which Lessing's voice was drowned by
the clamor of romanticism; in which even Goethe did
not wield the influence that was his due, Thomas Mann
has come increasingly to feel that he partakes of Goethe's
tradition. His growing prestige has allowed him to address
to a German public, deluded by the obscurantism of
the National Socialists, that *Appell an die Vernunft* of
which all nations as well as Germany stand in need. The
strength and nobility of the views which he expresses in
that document make it far more than an appeal to
ideologues. He has stated the commanding ideas to which
we must turn if we hope to find an effective solution of
the present universal spiritual crisis.

Fascism, which Thomas Mann satirizes so neatly in
Mario und der Zauberer; dictatorships which hold things
together temporarily—these are solutions which are

powerless to create the new order which the world demands. During the twenty centuries of the Christian era the bourgeoisie, whose bankruptcy is everywhere proclaimed, has steadily manifested a creative energy whose products subsist today in what we call Western civilization. There is no question but that that creative energy has now become wholly conservative, that that civilization demands fresh inspiration and new forms. But no new civilization can be created unless we maintain the concept of order, enriching it with new elements from the present. Thomas Mann is on the side of those who are working for this metamorphosis of the old traditions. He is the last bourgeois of the past, and at the same time the first prescriber of a future which shall also have its order, though the name by which that order shall be called is as yet unspoken.

2. *Jakob Wassermann*—*The Romantic Novel*

It is useless to try to place Jakob Wassermann in relation to literary trends, or even in a geographical milieu. Because he was born in Franconia, because he wrote *Die Juden von Zirndorf*, or because he depicted the antique interiors of Nuremberg, he has been called the novelist of Franconia. Because he later withdrew to Styria, he has been considered an Austrian. In actual fact no place existed where he could not give rein to his marvelous Oriental imagination. He belongs to farther places than either Germany or Austria; he is the descendant of Jews who established a very ancient colony in Franconia and have never fused with their new milieu. Yet he is also in a sense a renegade from this

---

* JOKOB WASSERMANN (1873–1934). Note especially *Geschichte der Jungen Renate Fuchs* (1900), *Caspar Hauser* (1908), *Das Gänsemännchen* (1915), *Christian Wahnschaffe* (1919), *Der Fall Maurizius* (1928), among almost a score of his widely read works.

race, or at least from those social habits which might have made him merely the representative of a tribe. He does not gloss over the failings of the victims of anti-Semitism, any more than he minimizes the failings of their race-conscious persecutors. He took up their problems, which are much more serious in Germany than in France, in *Mein Weg als Deutscher und Jude*.

The Jews have played a notable part in the intellectual life of Berlin and Vienna;* they stimulate the processes of assimilation and rejection; they are the means of modifying a culture which would otherwise tend to feed upon itself, not always with resultant growth. Some may consider the messianism of the Jews useful, some may consider it harmful; some may feel that their revolutionary uneasiness is destructive, others that their critical activity helps the individual genius to evolve. However this may be, it is undeniable that the Germans themselves once recognized the importance of this non-German inspiration which is to be found in a good deal more than half their literature.

Wassermann was born for adventure, and fate willed that he was to live his adventures before he wrote of them. He avoided the automatism which threatened other young men of his generation. He belonged to the German bourgeoisie neither by birth nor by education, and at an age when others were sitting at the feet of the great and building elaborate theories, he was wandering in the open, far from the Universities, where he appeared only as a bird of passage; far from the social machine, which caught him up only for a passing moment; unamenable to the discipline of the army or of business or of normal society. He was at once naïve, like his Caspar Hauser, and cunning; he learned in the school

* For a picture of the Israelite community of pre-war Berlin, see Georg Hermann's novel *Jettchen Gebert*, 1906.

of the highroad, slept in the open; he told stories that thrilled his younger brother and the farm children round about, and these were his first audience. To live a novel, and, as he lived it, each day to reconceive it with a changed moral significance, this was his destiny.

Even after his miraculous popular success, he kept himself free of entanglements which might otherwise have paralyzed his fantasy. The richest reality represents to him no more than a springboard from which to leap once again into the realm of imagination. He had chosen to live far from the big cities, and came to them only occasionally for inspiration. He lived by the Aussee, not as the respectable gentleman who retains his city habits in spite of his retirement to the country, but as a visionary who carries on commerce with a mystic world in a setting of trees and mountains and rushing water. As a result, his characters take on a naïve and elementary freshness.

All this does not mean that Wassermann has no social sense. Indeed, in novels like *Der Wendekreis* and *Der Fall Maurizius*, he has attempted a Balzacian picture of contemporary German society. But his conception of social intercourse is different from that of the French. The groups which form about him form more from reasons of taste than from reasons of social convention. Ideas are not discussed in the usual spirit of conversation. Here are no social beings pooling that which is common to them all, but solitary creatures set face to face and trying to express the most incommunicable part of themselves. This makes it difficult for a writer to make use of a tradition, other than that gained through books and museums. He has no daily contact with the organism whose life he might then merely express or interpret. He is confronted by a culture which contains too much specialization, too many divisions to be able easily to sense its unity. This has the advantage of leaving the individual more open to cosmopolitan influences, a situation of which Wassermann took good advantage.

He made Dickens and Dostoievski his masters as well as Balzac; and, like some of the best French story-tellers, he did not scorn to learn from Eugène Sue. He read the memoirs of Vidocq as well as those of the Cardinal de Retz; he was not ashamed to browse in the scandal columns of the newspapers. He was a novelist who had faith in his métier, who knew that it must be learned; and he worked out its requirements in several essays which clearly explain his technique and his ambitions. (*Die Kunst der Erzählung, Der Literat als Psycholog, Imaginäre Brücken, Gestalt und Humanität*.) He fused his own experience with that of the elder masters, but always in his own work he let instinct prevail. He knew his own temperament, and while he kept control of it he trusted everything to it.

By 1900, when Wassermann began to gain recognition, personality and imagination had been all but banished from the novel by the naturalists. But with the younger writers, who cared little for literary laboratory researches, imagination and personality were again to come into their own. These men approached literature simply with a desire to express their spontaneous feelings. They were not concerned with nature conceived according to the laws of chemistry or physiology; each gave ear to his own special nature, and, while he took advantage of what had been done before him, expressed himself in a form corresponding to the gifts with which he had been born.

Wassermann's was the gift of Scheherezade. He filled the real with fantasy and wrought it into a Thousand And

One Nights. Judea, with its sudden passions and its sudden returns to indifference, was in him reborn. He brought a brilliant new illumination to traditional German fantasy. The conflict between light and shadow was heightened; the poetry of action took the place of the poetry of emotion. Yet his novels retain the atmosphere which gives German novels their originality. In *Caspar Hauser* and *Das Gänsemännchen* there is that singing, poetic something which fascinates a Latin mind; whereas at the same time, in a book like *Oberlins drei Stufen*, in addition to an interesting psychological study of German youth trying to find itself, there is the very kind of rigorous composition which is essentially Latin.

Wassermann took his material from the newspapers, from underworld chronicles, from his own rich experience. Although he mingled fact and fiction willy-nilly, employed all the ingredients of cheap newspaper fiction, tried every available formula, nevertheless, thanks to the very richness of flow in his writing, thanks to the contagious intoxication of an imagination that was content to run unbridled, to leap from fantasy to fantasy, he managed to achieve a certain unity. The goal he sets himself is scarcely more than a pretext; the pleasure lies in the act of moving toward it.

The individual, kept bound in chains by the naturalists, reappeared in Wassermann's work not only as a creature of flesh and blood but as mind, action, caprice. Wassermann conceives of a novel first in terms of a character who overpowers the author—"*die Gestalt*," the individual who is glimpsed in the mass and who fires the imagination of the observer. The author watches through half-closed eyes, and as the character takes on color and relief, begins to move and live, so the novel is born and the plot gets under way. The novelist is carried along by the character he has created, never knows exactly where he is being led, finally discovers that the story has been told by the character rather than by himself. This sort of hallucination probably accounts for the intensity of Wassermann's characters. Even when their actions are banal and the plot is obviously over-complicated or over-ingenious, the story moves astonishingly, seizes the reader's interest, and flaws are overlooked.

This does not mean that Wassermann neglects the effort to achieve psychological unity. The point is that where others would conceive of the novel as a picture of the evolution of an individual, he conceives of it as the history of the spasmodic advances which the individual makes in the course of that evolution. For him the interesting moment in the life of an individual is the moment when *"die Wandlung"* takes place, when there is a sudden metamorphosis in an apparently stable ego behind which abruptly and inexplicably appears a new and different ego. He used this idea of psychological discontinuity in *Ulrike Woytich*, in *Oberlins drei Stufen*, in *Faber*, in *Laudin und die Seinen;* it borrows something from Freud, but is not to be confused with the theory of inhibition. We harbor within us, according to Wassermann, a whole series of coexistent selves, which substitute themselves one for the other under the pressure of events, or which come to the surface through accident. These events, these accidents, become the material of the novel which, instead of containing drab uniformity, deals with the brilliant instant, the momentary evolutionary burst, and consists entirely of clear images.

There is little doubt that Wassermann learned this process of selection from the French novelists, but he does not write as they write. While his novels tend toward a fixed architectural form, their chief virtue lies in the unpredictability of what happens, in a plot which unfolds

in arabesques. The author follows his instinct like a
hunting-dog set on a scent that he is mad with eagerness
to pursue. At the same time, however, Wassermann has
a certain formula that he follows. This is to keep his
characters purposely cloaked in mystery during the first
chapters of the novel in order to hold the reader in suspense, in order to give his hero a romantic halo. It is the
technique of "*Entschleierung*," which consists in keeping
curiosity aroused by letting the veils of mystery fall
slowly one by one. This is a revival of the methods of
the cheap newspaper writers, but Jakob Wassermann
handles it with a master's hand. He is a story-teller whose
chief charm lies in the quickness of his inventive faculties;
and it is when he pretends to no more than story-telling
that he reaches a certain perfection of his own.

But in some cases he conceives of himself as more than
a story-teller. *Der Fall Maurizius* in particular treats of
one of Germany's great present-day problems—the
problem of justice. After the revolution there developed
a new ideology which tended to destroy the old submission to existing conditions. Numerous cases of error,
many judicial crimes awoke the passions of the public.
The case of Judge Andergast, who was convinced that
he had condemned an innocent man to prison, but who
could not find the strength to redeem the wrong done,
and the opposition of the Judge's son, both to his father
and to the monstrous authority which the elder Andergast was defending, were characteristic of a division
of opinion which inflamed the passions of the public in
somewhat the same way as the Dreyfus Case in France.
Etzel Andergast, the sequel in which Wassermann follows
the career of the son, is the story of a younger generation
devoured by uncertainties, inflamed by the problems of
a period of primarily spiritual chaos, looking for teachers

without knowing where to turn for them, and temporarily incapable of self-discipline.

Imagination, even if it is imitative more often than inventive, still constitutes the principal strength of the German novel. The sense of fantasy which Hoffmann revealed to France is still a source of inspiration to German writers. Among them should be mentioned Gustav Meyrink. His curious novel *Der Golem* deserved the success it achieved if only because of its unusually powerful evocation of the atmosphere of the ghetto in Prague. The character of the Golem is more than a lay figure animated by the Cabala; almost without the author being conscious of it, the Golem personifies the modern automaton into whom civilization breathes a soul foreign to him. This accounts for the tragic misunderstanding implicit in gestures which he has not willed but makes with painful severity.

In their novels of travel and adventure and in their descriptions of nature at home and abroad, Bernhard Kellermann* and Waldemar Bonsels† have shown high ability as story-tellers, but they have done nothing which Wells and Kipling have not done better. They appeal to a public which is still satisfied with the simple virtues of faith, hope, and charity. Max Dauthendey in some of his work has given better expression than they to the sense of being placed in strange surroundings; his descriptions of Japan have a particularly delicate charm. Herbert Eulenberg‡ has an imagination which does not require the stimulus of travel. As dramatist and novelist he has attempted to achieve a Shakespearian freedom of invention. Shakespearianism without Shakespeare would

---

* BERNHARD KELLERMANN (1879–   ). For bibliography see p. 305.
† WALDEMAR BONSELS (1881–   ). For bibliography see p. 288.
‡ HERBERT EULENBERG (1876–   ). For bibliography see p. 292.

amount to little did not this Rhenish writer also have a highly developed sense of the grotesque. His inventions are often amusing satires on contemporary society.

3. The Tradition of the Little Masters—Realism and Sentiment

A tradition of little masters which has no equivalent in France has been steadily carried on in Northern Europe, outside the reach of any but minor influences from world literature in general. The work of these writers has an earthy savor, but it is more than mere regional literature. It contains dashes of universal humanity—a humanity hemmed in by conditions which it cannot overcome, forced to develop within given limits. The result is that it gains in depth what it is forced to give up in breadth. Danes like Jacobsen and Hermann Bang are good examples, and Rilke was not alone in profiting by their powerful inspiration. It is a double tradition: realism based upon limited material, in striking contrast with a feeling of the infinite horizons which literature opens to the man who lives alone and apart. Other good representatives of the tradition are Hermann Hesse, Emil Strauss, Jakob Schaffner, and Oskar Loerke.

Hermann Hesse,* after he wrote *Peter Camenzind* and *Unterm Rad*, broke out of the narrow field of Swabian youth repressed by parental and professorial authority. Nevertheless he remains in revolt against the tutelage to which society subjects the individual—a tutelage which he considers particularly ineffectual in the midst of the confusion of the present time, when youth needs more help than ever. His *Demian* appealed to that youth because the younger generation recognized their own uneasiness in its pages—a childhood empty of romance,

* HERMANN HESSE (1877–   ). For bibliography see p. 302.

a hot sensuality at first repressed and then at last
bursting forth into flame. When Hesse wrote *Siddharta*
he was yielding to the spirit of his time, seeking a
sedative in India. He then realized that the way out of
the chaos of the present lay not in the Orient but within
that chaos itself. By the time he wrote *Steppenwolf* he
had come to believe that a lasting harmony between
nature and spirit requires a profound reëxamination of
both nature and spirit. Perhaps it is not impossible to
bridge the chasm between the wolf-man and domesti-
cated, civilized beings. A higher humanity might fuse
primitive energy with spirituality—provided that the
conception of a self divided into enemy halves be
renounced and that of poly-individualism accepted in
its stead; provided, in other words, that the moral personality accept primitive forces as sources of dynamism
and impress its own unity upon them. Hesse is allied
with the mysticism of Buddha and of Zarathustra,
with the Goethe of the dialogue between God and
Mephistopheles, with the authors of *The Marriage of
Heaven and Hell, The Brothers Karamazov,* and *The
Counterfeiters.*

Another Swabian, Emil Strauss,* has written novels
much like Hesse's. With melancholy charm he depicts
the evolution of personalities like that of the student
Freund Hein, whose sensitiveness finally results in suicide, or of other characters whose uneasiness leads to
error and who stumble along the path of purification.
Jakob Schaffner,† who was born in Basle and who, like
Gottfried Keller, inherited the vigor of the Swiss, believes
in the reconstruction of a European humanity through
faith and love—a faith without dogma, a love which

---

* Emil Strauss (1866–   ). For bibliography see p. 319.
† Jakob Schaffner (1875–   ). For bibliography see p. 317.

shall rise above beliefs and nations to reach a biblical purity. Oskar Loerke* is a novelist and poet who depicts unimportant events in original tones whose subtlety lends a certain halo to life.

Hans Carossa† is a follower of the tradition of Stifter's *Nachsommer*. Writing in a period when youth is upsetting all values, Carossa draws upon his own youth for stories breathing a simple piety, a love of family, the school, the human atmosphere, the villages, the towns, and the Bavarian countryside in which he lived. He is neither a destroyer nor an innovator; he is a preserver. And the most precious of the gifts which he preserves is the gift of sympathy for every form of life which he encounters on his path. Whether he is writing a *Confessions of Doctor Bürger* or a *Roumanian Diary*, the doctor in him is allied with the poet, watching over suffering and drawing from it deep inspiration. He has the power of abstracting from all life an element of goodness and an element of beauty as well.

Robert Musil‡ has received tardy recognition. In *Die Verwirrungen des Zöglings Törless*, published in 1906, he examined the romanesque uneasiness of puberty with rare subtlety and restraint, and at last that book was recognized for what it is: the work of a writer who has great promise. That promise has been kept in *Der Mann ohne Eigenschaften* (1931), in which Musil has achieved true mastery of his art. It is a long book—there are a thousand pages in the first part alone; the second part is equally long—and it is slow-moving, but it is a great novel. Against a background of the Austrian monarchy of 1913 appear the problems of all Europe, all

* Oskar Loerke (1884–   ). Note especially *Der Turmbau*, 1910 (nov.); *Gedichte*, 1916; *Der Oger*, 1921 (nov.); *Der längste Tag*, 1926 (poetry). For bibliography see p. 308.

† Hans Carossa (1878–   ). For bibliography see p. 291.

‡ Robert Musil (1880–   ). For bibliography see p. 314.

he problems of more than Europe—little problems and
big problems. Musil's brilliance lies in his gift for seeing
what is big in little things, what is petty in the big. Each
thought is carefully weighed. His irony is not merely
destructive; it is the irony of a thinker who knows how
to distinguish between good money and bad. In a period
which was rationalizing in the manner of Rathenau and
at the same time demanding freedom for the uncontrolled impulses of the soul, there was need for this lucid
mind to synthesize what is worthy of survival both in
the mechanical organization of civilization and in the
élan vital that is working toward the separation of
mechanism from that civilization.

PART III

The Quest for Fresh Orientations

CHAPTER I

From Impressionism to Expressionism—the Transition between Generations

A LITERARY movement is not easily separated from a corresponding philosophical movement. The writers of any period are always conscious of the new views of men and the world appearing upon the horizon. This close connection between literature and philosophy is not peculiar to Germany. Great writers, if only by instinct, are inclined to take a definite stand toward the great problems of their time, just as Gide and Barrès did. In Germany, however, there has for a long while been a peculiarly close and conscious relation between literature and philosophic thought. Always, behind a novel or a play or a poem, can be sensed the system to which the author gives his allegiance. The naturalist movement in literature sprang from Darwin and Marx; symbolism was a reflection of determinist philosophical thinking.

Thus between 1890 and 1914 there occurred among truly creative writers a transformation parallel to that which was taking place in philosophy. The period of systematic philosophy was over. Nietzsche and his aphorisms were the sign of a general desire to win free from systems too rigid. First metaphysics had been denied as being foreign to reality; now came the denial of the philosophy which had replaced metaphysics and had set reality up as a tyrant. Husserl discovered afresh that thought was itself a part of reality, and in doing this, consecrated its right to an independent existence. Slavery to reality ceased with him, with Nietzsche, Dilthey, Simmel, Max Weber, Ernst Troeltsch. The idea of value was rediscovered and began to become a part of an ego which owed its philosophy to changing experience and not to any impersonal, immutable view of the world. The individual regained his autonomy. Thought, escaping from the dogmas of the scientific, once more took on the character of movement. This was true even in the Germany of William II, for the closed circle was already virtually broken at the very moment when it seemed most firm.

It would therefore be an error to suppose that the quest for fresh orientations in Germany began only with the War. On the contrary, long before 1914, writers and philosophers were already actively engaged in bringing about a revolution far more profound than the political revolution of 1918. The latter, indeed, profited almost as much from these preliminary subterranean activities as it did from the circumstances of the War. And when it was finally accomplished there arose a legion of popular philosophers who came over to the new ideas merely through pressure of circumstance. The student must be careful to make a distinction between them and the true innovators. They represent only a sort of rearguard, and the spirit in which they took over the new philosophic ideas was merely the old spirit of adaptation. Chief among them are Spengler and Keyserling.

Spengler* revived the ancient theme of the *Götter-dämmerung*, always dear to the popular imagination, and called it the Decline of the West. This idea of catastrophe befalling the civilizations of the West as the result

---

* OSWALD SPENGLER (1880–   ), *Untergang des Abendlandes*, 1918–1922; *Preussentum und Sozialismus*, 1920. For bibliography see p. 319.

of the infinite extension of local failures has the double appeal of satisfying the public need for cosmic views and of soothing wounded sensibilities. Its manner of presentation, with all the documents of all the libraries of the world used to justify the impression of engulfing chaos, is pleasing to the very young and to the general public, who fail to realize the staleness of these Spenglerian revelations. National feeling was once more flattered with an "*Oberlehrer*" ideology, just as it had been with H. S. Chamberlain and with Langbehn, author of *Rembrandt als Erzieher*, thirty years before. Spengler, in *Preussentum und Sozialismus*, offered the same panacea—the fusion of Prussianism and socialism—toward which public sentiment in the Reich had long been sympathetic, and which Hermann Conradi saw reason to denounce at the enthronement of William II as the greatest danger to his reign.

Walther Rathenau* had earlier proposed an ideology of an entirely different nature. His views on the rationalization of economic life are still far from having lost their interest. It was not only economic life which was evolving in the direction that Rathenau urged. In every field there was progress toward the idea of necessity, which is the foundation of Rathenau's thinking. This notion does not necessarily imply a decadence of liberty. It is possible to conceive of the soul increasing in proportion to the very restraints to which it submits, of the individual assuring his liberty by a sacrifice of his convenience—a sacrifice through which that liberty becomes a virtue instead of mere indulgence. Rathenau's weakness was that in arguing against the machine in favor of the soul,

* Walther Rathenau (1867-1922), *Gesammelte Werke*, among others: *Zur Kritik der Zeit; Zur Mechanik des Geistes; Von Kommenden Dingen; Die neue Wirtschaft; Der Kaiser; Der neue Staat; Kritik der dreifachen Revolution; Die neue Gesellschaft.*

he conceived of the soul as merely superimposed upon the machine, which continued brazenly on its way. However interesting to society his economic gospel may be, it remains no more than a morality of production.

Count Hermann Keyserling* might well have been able to bring back from the Orient a set of ideas through which Europe could have been turned aside from making the machine its ultimate end. But the author of *The Travel Diary of a Philosopher*, too anxious to trim his sails to the prevailing wind, was no man to set up a new philosophical current. He contented himself with proposing a mixture of spiritual values with either nationalism or industrialism—a process against which the War should have been sufficient warning. Which is he, Hamann or Cagliostro? This was the question the Germans asked themselves when the Baltic Baron first broke into print. They answered it with the same good sense as Paul Souday. Keyserling is a sage, a cure-worker; his only virtue is an ability to maneuver cleverly between opposing currents. The founder of the Darmstadt School of Wisdom is a dilettante with the odor of the philosophers about him; the kind of support he brings to the new philosophic ideas in Germany is the kind of support the rope offers to the hanged. Indeed there is as much or more to be learned from the works left by the novelist of the same name, Eduard von Keyserling.† At least the latter's novels of Baltic aristocracy do not pretend to be anything but novels, and even judged in comparison with the work of Fontane can be enjoyed for their subtle irony and their resignation.

---

* HERMANN VON KEYSERLING (1880–   ). For bibliography see p. 306.

† EDUARD VON KEYSERLING (1855–1918), *Gesammelte Erzählungen*, S. Fischer Verlag; *Beate und Mareile; Wellen; Bunte Herzen; Abendliche Häuser; Schwüle Tage.*

The changes which the thinking of Max Scheler*
underwent, however, were no mere accommodations to
the spirit of the times. Scheler's will to comprehend the
necessary changes in the world leaves no room for sus-
picion of camouflage. He has an astonishingly mobile
intelligence, and while following the movement of change,
is able to discriminate among the phenomena presented
to him. In Scheler's recent short essays will be found the
clearest available statement of the revision of values
which had been going forward in Germany. The idea of
"*Kultur*" had been replaced by the idea of "*Bildung*,"
which is an approach to the conception of the "gentleman" in all that is most human in the latter, and recalls
Nietzsche's single admiration for that culture which
became one with "action, flesh, instinct." Culture was
no longer conceived as knowledge, but as a mode of
being of the individual, who has the quality of unique-
ness. Society gains its character from the interplay of
individuals, whom it should leave free and merely draw
together in a synthesis. Society is the macrocosm; the
individual is the microcosm. There is no ideal except
that of the individual, who grows in dignity as he becomes
more and more wholly human. Scheler's conception of the
"whole man" may be eclectic, but it at least serves to
prepare the establishment of a hierarchy of values accept-
able to the European mind. The important thing is that
in the integral humanism which he upholds, it is the mind
which assumes the power of orientation.

In general the result of the tendency to join literature
and philosophy was that philosophy spoiled literature
and literature spoiled philosophy. Few writers could
achieve, like Goethe, Schopenhauer, and Nietzsche, a

* MAX SCHELER (1875–1928), *Vom Ewigen im Menschen; Vom Umsturz der
Werte*, coll. ess. 1919–1921; *Moralia*, 1923; *Probleme einer Soziologie des
Wissens*, 1924 (in *Versuche zu einer Soziologie des Wissens*); *Die Formen des
Wissens und die Bildung*, 1925.

perfect fusion of the two. In recent years, however, an effort has been made to have proper recognition given in Germany to a type of philosophico-literary writing which is bastard only when it is left in mediocre hands: the essay, which has been approaching a place of honor among German writers.

The demand of *Die Blätter für die Kunst* for a short prose form was not formulated in vain. Alfred Kerr, Franz Blei, Heinrich and Thomas Mann, Hofmannsthal, Alfred Polgar, and the disciples of Stefan George, among whom Gundolf with his *Goethe* and his *George* and Bertram with his *Nietzsche* are outstanding, have all given examples of the perfection to which this type of writing can be brought. It represents a reaction against the effacement of the subjective by the objective which was the fashion at the end of the nineteenth century. Just as in pure literature we have seen the personality of the writer resisting invasion by impressions from without, and becoming creative again, so in this case we see a stiffening of the seeker against the object of his search—and the search profits thereby. The essay becomes a work of art. Its purpose is no longer merely to register facts, only to be crushed beneath their weight; its object is to attain through attention to style the maximum of honesty while keeping the facts always in view, and never committing the sins of ignorance and superficiality committed by the improvisations of former days and the novelized biographies of today. Not merely the predilection of these essayists for great subjects and great men, but the spirit which they brought to their study, is clear evidence that criticism was regaining a sense of values.

Indeed that sense of values had never been entirely lost. The work of Alfred Kerr,* whose reputation dates

* ALFRED KERR (1867–   ). For bibliography see p. 305.

from the naturalist period, evidences such vigorous faculties of discrimination that it deserves permanent popularity. The books which he praised when they appeared all have a chance of lasting, and for the very merits which he then proclaimed. His critical diagnoses owe much of their sureness to intelligence and taste, but much also to a cosmopolitan culture which has become just as indispensable to literary criticism as to artistic criticism. It was this latter quality that made Brandes a greater man than either Brunetière or Lemaître.

There are other modern German critics who, because they are essentially European, command an audience in France—Hermann Bahr,* Franz Blei,† Rudolf Kassner. In the field of art-criticism, those who followed Walter von Seydlitz—Max Lehrs, Meier-Graefe, Wölfflin, and Karl Scheffler—can also attract a French audience, for the same reason. The merit of these alert intellects is that instead of merely offering dogmas and impressions they state problems in their full amplitude. This is why they were of such assistance in keeping alive in Germany an art and a literature which threatened to waste away within the limits of strict nationalism.

Indeed Alfred Kerr attempted to do even more than this. The texts with which he dealt were often "pretexts." "My writing," he said, "is not an essay on, but an essay suggested by"; and he added that "the true critic is always a poet, a creator." This desire to achieve the status of artist sometimes led Kerr into the temptation of shining at his victim's expense, and one may also criticize in his work a certain seeking after the musical and an obvious pleasure in sticking darts into his victims' flesh. Nevertheless he is never merely coquettish. Al-

---

* HERMANN BAHR (1863–1934). Among the very numerous works of Bahr, note especially *Das Hermann Bahr-Buch*, 1913; *Selbstbildnis*, 1923.

† FRANZ BLEI (1871–   ). For bibliography see p. 287.

though he has no system of his own, he helps the thinkers to build their systems. His aphoristic manner is never a mannerism; it represents a splendid style placed at the service of a mind seeking freedom, and the result is definitely the work of a writer who, rather than being inspired by others, is himself inspiring.

Franz Blei should have known Watteau and should have lived in the time of Choderlos de Laclos, Voltaire and Chamfort. But if he had, he would have been deprived of the intense pleasure he has taken in serving as a connecting link between two *fins de siècle*, and, while keeping all that was exquisite in their abandon, at the same time never abandoning himself. He has a marvelously sharp intellect which even during the War prevented him from falling a prey to mass psychology; the writing he did at that time (*Menschliche Betrachtungen*) when read today gives evidence of a striking sang-froid which still preserves the human touch. Intelligence, in his view, is a virtue, and if the bitterness of his satire is a little frightening, he saves his bitterness for works whose inspiration is false, and is indulgent toward those which show originality. He has also been accused of being too much attracted by exquisiteness of form, without always making certain that there is living flesh and fibre beneath the outer covering. The truth is that his judgment is good precisely because it is the judgment of a connoisseur never misled either by the false richness of basic materials or by the attractions of surface ornament. He said "no" to many things, which in itself was a great merit at a time when everyone was only too ready to say "yes" to anything; and in addition he had the gift of saying it in Lucian's manner.

The Austrian Alfred Polgar,* discovered late in his

---

* ALFRED POLGAR (1875–   ), *Gestern und heute; An den Rand geschrieben; Orchester von oben; Ja und nein; Ich bin Zeuge*, 1928. For bibliography see p. 315.

life, makes no pretense to pontifical judgments. But his work serves to prove once again that the short essay form, to which he gave his greatest care, can inspire the reader to look between the lines. There is much finesse and a subtle sense of values in his playing with great men and great emotions.

Although critical periodicals are less numerous in Germany than in France, and, because the public is less interested in literary battles, do not command so wide an audience, they still played their part in the new literary movement. With consistent eclecticism, *Die Neue Rundschau*, founded in the period when naturalism and symbolism were struggling for precedence, could be counted upon to accord recognition to the various literary currents as fast as they reached the point where it became clear that they were more than ephemeral. Rudolf Kayser, the editor, was as much interested in new developments outside Germany as within, and his review therefore preserved a certain balance between youthfulness and conservatism. But other than *Die neue Rundschau* and *Das Inselschiff*, a journal characterized by a sort of classic European eclecticism, there was nothing to occupy the position previously held by *Pan* (1894–1901) *Die Blätter für die Kunst*, and *Das Jahrbuch für geistige Bewegung*.

Hofmannsthal's *Neue Deutsche Beiträge* served merely to emphasize the lack of critical periodicals aiding the cause of intellectual audacity. Efraim Frisch* ceased publishing *Der neue Merkur* rather than fit his views to the requirements of his readers, and turned his intellectualism and his critical activity into the channels of the novel. *Die Zukunft* owed its success as much to the fact that its readers could count upon a new scandal every week as to its editor's talent. Harden,† the editor, favored

---

* Efraim Frisch (1873–   ). For bibliography see p. 297.
† Maximilian Harden (1861–1927).

the younger writers, but chiefly because of a love of the new and a taste for paradox. He was endowed with more taste than judgment, which meant that he committed fewer errors in literature than in politics, in which latter field he served the worst causes as often as the best. By turns flaying and flattering his audience, he played upon their instincts rather than oriented them. He was as theatrical as William II himself, and presented a picture of the Reich on a changing film with an eye perpetually on the public's response.

What Harden lacked—character and a style—is to be found in Karl Kraus,* who has edited *Die Fackel* in Vienna since 1899. He is a journalist who is prepared to attack journalism itself; his polemic reaches beyond the adversary of the moment to strike at a mass prejudice, to denounce a political, social, or poetic lie. The formal perfection of his prose and his verse is merely a sign of his intellectual integrity.

Wilhelm Herzog,† taking both politics and literature as his field, had waged in *Das Forum* for many years, and with particular courage during the War, a struggle against established power which did not cease with the fall of the Austrian monarchy. A similar revolutionary activity, though expressed more on the literary side, had been maintained by *Die weissen Blätter*, whose editor, René Schickele, was driven out of Germany into Switzerland by the censor. Pfemfert's *Die Aktion* and Herwarth Walden's *Der Sturm* were organs of the *avant-garde* of painters, supporting futurism and cubism. The *Europäische Revue*, organ of the "*Kulturbund*" or Intellectual Union, a medium for propaganda, looked toward the organization of an élite—an élite of salons conceived as places in which may be brought together the ideas and

* KARL KRAUS (1874–   ). For bibliography see p. 306.
† WILHELM HERZOG (1884–   ). For bibliography see p. 301.

interests of all the European nations, whose very conflict has disposed them toward such exchanges of views. *Nord und Süd* maintained a diplomatic effort to establish non-German contacts. The Zurich *Neue Schweitzer Rundschau*, under Max Rychner, had become one of the best literary reviews in the German language. *Die Literatur* filled the need for an informational journal of encyclopedic nature.

Besides the great newspapers such as the *Frankfurter Zeitung*, the *Berliner Tageblatt*, the *Vossische Zeitung*, and the *Börsen-Courier*, all of which gave a good deal of space to worthwhile literary criticism, there were two lively weeklies—*Die Weltbühne*, edited by Peter Panter (Tucholsky), successor to Siegfried Jacobsen, and *Das Tagebuch*, conducted by Stefan Grossmann. They placed politics and literature on an equal plane, and treated both briefly. Their articles were biting, but not entirely given over to satire; they were written by polemists who, although fighting reaction in all its forms, were nevertheless careful not to be entirely anti-something. Without themselves being internationalists, they surveyed a Europe in which thought was awakening in response to the call of an international system of ethics.

Willy Haas, in *Die Literarische Welt*, was carrying out a formula similar to that of the *Nouvelles Littéraires*, to the benefit of writers not all of whom expected to be honored by the Preussische Akademie. It is too bad that two other reviews, *Der Zwiebelfisch* and *Das fünfte Rad*, did not develop further than they did. Wedderkopp's *Querschnitt*, together with *Das Stachelschwein*, set a new style in periodicals—the *magazine piquant*. There was some snobbishness in them, but not so much as to spoil their intellectual value. The *Revue d'Allemagne* and the *Deutsch-Französische Rundschau*, both founded in 1927, have undertaken parallel tasks in providing information in France and in Germany about the other country for a public that had seen the necessity of combating the prejudices which threaten Franco-German intellectual relations.

At least some mention of the work of the German book publishers should be made at this point. Particularly in the last quarter of the nineteenth century their activities were closely associated with the *Kulturpolitik*. In some cases, such as that of Diedrichs in Jena, their interest was restricted to that of raising the level of German culture; others, such as S. Fischer in Berlin, managed to escape the limitations of a narrow patriotism. This latter house, besides publishing the naturalists and the symbolists, became the pioneer in the movement toward a culture that was truly European but which at the same time did not forget the virtues of the home-land. Toward this end Fischer contributed greatly by his translations from French, Russian, and especially from the Scandinavian languages, as well as by the publication of a group of German authors who represent values recognized in every European country, and by his undertaking of the *Neue Rundschau*. The Insel-Verlag in Leipzig had been working toward the same end, forming the taste of the public by publishing only choice books well presented.

In addition, firms such as Bruno Cassirer, Paul Cassirer, Kurt Wolff, who first published the expressionists; Rowohlt, Kiepenheuer, Ullstein, Spaeth, Zsolnay, Die Schmiede, Albert Langen, and the Malik Verlag, dropped the pre-War type of *Kulturpolitik* and took up the movement toward a renewal of ideas and forms which even carried along with it the old established firms such as Die Deutsche Verlagsanstalt. This changed attitude of the publishers represented neither the old type of hyper-organization, designed to regiment ideas along with everything else, nor a mere revolutionary negation of the past. It was a coöperative effort of publishers and authors to carry through the transition from the Hohenzollern idea of Germany, which was gradually being relegated to the provinces, to the idea of a Germany open to the influences of both West and East.

The "Manifesto of the Intellectuals" was designed to make people believe that the Reich, in going into the War, had the support of every representative of German thought, and it succeeded only too well. But how many of its ninety-three signatories represented anything more than an abandonment of the spiritual for the temporal— a "treason of the intellectuals"—which had really been consummated long before? Dehmel represented only a cautious *Sozialdemokratie* which had lost its revolutionary directing force and had incorporated itself into a régime that had granted it social insurance. Gerhart Hauptmann was surprised into signing, for only a year earlier, in the heat of the Centenary of 1813, he had caused a scandal by consigning Blücher's sword to the scrap-heap. Names which would have carried much weight did not appear at all, among them Stefan George, Heinrich Mann, Thomas Mann. In July of 1914 Heinrich Mann's satire, *Der Untertan*, was actually in course of publication. For twenty years Stefan George had been proclaiming his disdain for the vulgarity of the Hohenzollern régime. That régime, and not merely the political régime but the spiritual régime as well, had already developed within itself the enemies which Nietzsche had hoped for and inspired.

In addition to the opposition elements in the generation which was approaching fifty, those who were born in the eighties began to make their appearance. Their appointed rôle seemed to be to serve as intermediaries between the generation preceding the War and the generation following it; their task to accomplish the transition. The explosion of 1918 surprised them as much as it favored them, as through their thirties they worked upon the beginnings of their organized struggle against the established authority. Among this latter group were such critics and polemists as René Schickele, Sternheim, Stefan Zweig, Karl Kraus, and Wilhelm Herzog. Heinrich Mann's manifesto, *Geist und Tat*, published in 1910, marked the turning point, evidenced the new will to change the established relations between "mind" and "action."

The intellectual habit of the times had been to place the mind at the service of a stated activity whose object in every case was the greater power of the German nation, that nation being conceived only in terms of the then existing Reich. The appointed ideal was an ideal of expansion within the already existent. Germany had had neither her encyclopedists nor her revolution. An endemic romanticism had kept her in a state of hypnotic subservience to authority. Philosophy, poetry, and political thought were fused into a religion of the State. That religion, which had a touch of the Gothic in it, and only one aspect of which was revealed in the Hegelian religion, made intellectual subservience seem desirable. The bliss of communion robbed the mind of the idea of autonomy.

It was in this atmosphere that the liberalism of Young Germany had been shipwrecked. Heine's persiflage went in one ear and out the other. This hyper-esthesia continued until the middle of the World War. The type of brain which was considered worthy of organized Germany contained a series of beautifully arranged compartments, but each was so full that nothing new could enter in. Hermann Conradi, who realized as Nietzsche did the necessity for a sweeping revision of values, died crushed and isolated in 1890. The naturalists, who had made the cry for social justice fashionable, lacked intellectual force. Their ideology was elementary, as was their sensibility. It is easy to understand why the silliness of some of their cries for pity exasperated Nietzsche. Even forebodings, such as were movingly presented in Hauptmann's work, were no substitute for effective intellectual activity. It was just this effective intellectual activity, then, which, when the signal was given by some of the older generation, was reborn in 1910 among the younger writers. Mind was to be turned to effective action, freed from its servitude to the power that was.

The activity into which these writers entered was directed as much toward a liberation from the restraints of determinism as from the restraints of pan-Germanism. They had the courage to attack Hohenzollern society at a time when it seemed a very Pantheon, and to deny that the grandeur of that civilization was the only desirable or possible grandeur. Their movement had been mapped out before their time, but it was they who made it frankly one of national self-criticism. In doing so, they owed a part of their inspiration to French literature past and contemporary. And they went beyond the political field. They represented the evolution of a rationalism that was again to oppose in Germany a romanticism that was already fully evolved and indeed overstuffed with nourishment. Thought began to take its proper place again, on a plane superior to magnified reality. Intellectual independence was reintroduced into a literature which until that time had too often been dominated by contemporary reality.

The inspiration for all this came not only from Germans, all the way from Nietzsche to Heinrich Mann, but in part from the West; and it is worth noting that many of those responsible were Jews. Whatever may have been the reaction of the Germans to the introduction of this Jewish element—shock to mental structure, shock to race sensibilities, defense reaction against foreign ideas—there is no doubt that the introduction of Jewish vigor into German thinking was of exceptional importance.

Carl Sternheim* represents everything that is sharpest in the intellect, as well as vigor and sensibility. He lacks the fluidity in which these elements might bathe, the ability to create a figure with life in it. His work is typical of a period shot through with high-tension currents which now and then discharge in sparks that light brief but interesting fires.

Sternheim would still have been Sternheim if he had written nothing more than such essays as *Berlin oder Juste Milieu*. Social satire conceived as he there conceives it is true comedy of manners. These essays have the brutal and caustic humor for which the people of Berlin are famous, though indeed it would have taken an unusually gifted Berliner to write them. Not a single section of the understructure of society escapes the probing searchlight. Sternheim is like an examining magistrate exhilarated by the conviction that he is right. The defendant is guilty from the beginning, and the prosecutor takes the greatest pleasure in making a psychological analysis of the crime. In taking the existing German régime as defendant, Sternheim assured himself of an interesting trial. The chief criminals were obvious: the folly of confusing number with greatness and of substituting quantity for quality; the mechanization of the "subject" for the benefit of a State considered divine but in fact become itself an automaton, driven on by the

* CARL STERNHEIM (1878-   .) Note especially *Die Hose* (1911), *Die Kassette* and *Bürger Schippel* (1912), *Der Snob* (1913), *Berlin oder Juste Milieu* (1920), *Die Schule von Uznach* (1926).

humming motors of instinct; and the intoxication of producing and enjoying with no control over either production or enjoyment.

Although there were others, from Nietzsche to Heine, who started him on his way, Sternheim's critical examination of contemporary Germany is not without its own merit. It represents a recapitulation that has the virtue of brevity and is gathered into formulas of unusual compactness. *Berlin oder Juste Milieu* is a chapter, written by a historian-psychologist, which ought to be smuggled into the great tomes of Sombart and Lamprecht, who lacked Sternheim's masterly ability with the examining surgeon's scalpel. Sternheim's mastery, of course, has its easily discernible limits, for it was relatively easy to lance the abscesses of a society which had laid itself absolutely bare to the observer. Its immense naïveté would have made a superb target for a Saint-Simon, a Voltaire, or a Montesquieu.

Sternheim, in other words, has sufficient malice and sufficient cleverness to take the machine which he has before him to pieces; but he has neither that lightness of touch which gives literary charm to satire, nor that depth of understanding which permits us to foresee Montesquieu's *Esprit des Lois* in his *Lettres Persanes*. The picture he paints is exact only in so far as Hohenzollern Germany partook of the nature of an automaton. The structure of his thinking has a curious rigidity; it contains only what can be abstracted and desicsated. The complexity of life is not in it, nor, perhaps, the essential unity of life. Marianne says to Christian in *Der Snob:* "You have the gift of lending plasticity to individuals." And Christian replies: "Let us call it rather the faculty of forming concepts." This from the alert intelligence of a satirist who knows the limits of his own talents and thus forestalls criticism.

Sternheim's intelligence is biting, but it lacks breadth. Sternheim's comedies, though they are in the best tradition, are works of cerebration only. Unable to grasp the living, he deals in algebraic terms. He is a psychologist who, in his effort to define groups, is condemned to making generalizations, with everything that is strongest and weakest in generalizations. Besides, the only milieu which he studies is that of the *petite bourgeoisie*, which limits his comic effects. In *Bürger Schippel* an English or a French audience would find much that is instructive and amusing about contemporary history, but it is not at all certain that they would laugh very loudly. Sternheim lacks broad contact with the universal tragic and the universal comic. Not that he disregarded Molière or even Goethe; indeed he follows them both methodically. But his characters are somehow not whole characters; they cannot create the sympathy upon which laughter must always depend.

When Sternheim is at his best he approaches the Molière of *Scapin* rather than the Molière of *Tartuffe;* and even though some of his scenes recall the truculence of Faust, all the milieux of all his plays make up a universe from which Faust himself would be excluded. What remains? Poor grotesque wretches like the Philistines in an Easter play: Theobald Maske thrilling to dangers which are far removed from him as he reads his newspaper, and in one breath ordering his wife to pray to God, water the tulips, watch the roast, and to stop losing her drawers in public; Dame Martha, become Gertrud Deuter, matchmaker and soothsayer; the students in the tavern at Auerbach, turned into husbands and heroes of the bourgeois comedy; and finally there is Mephistopheles—Sternheim himself, jiggling the strings that make these poor devils dance. He is a little like La Bruyère in the way he notes scattered characteristics, pulls them all together into a character to which he gives a name, such as Bürger Schippel, or (in the trilogy *Die Hose*, *Der Snob*, and *1913*) first the elder Maske, then his son. But the character is always at bottom the same: the provincial bourgeois, with his romanticism compounded of quartets and chorals, his outmoded loyalist reverence for petty princes, who nevertheless yields to the violence of the plebeian Schippel and is dominated by parvenus like the Maskes, gradually acquiring, from father to son, the attributes of civilization.

Sternheim, however, by no means represents mere negation. He has a corrosive tongue, a pen dipped in vitriol, and he spares neither Germany nor Europe; but this in itself shows a passion that is not negative, a passion that has a positive object which it is frantically seeking. Superficially this object might seem to be justice, meted out with all the absence of feeling of a nihilist and all the savage fire of ancient Judaism. Actually, however, it is basically a savage defense of the individual's right to be himself.

Sternheim thinks that that liberty is the right even of the dissolute, of even those whose instincts are mediocre. The social mechanism, indeed, has forced their vital energy into ridiculous manifestations. But that vital energy exists, with its obscure founts, its own ends in view, even its own modes of being. The individual who is generally considered enslaved by society, emasculated, appears to Sternheim as a man possessed, seeking to find issue for the demoniacal force that is in him. "The lesson I am trying to teach," he says in the preface to his comedies, "is that no living force is ever lost, that the individual should never be content with merely repeating a refrain, that he should listen to no other voice but his own and should not allow himself to be disturbed at the names which the bourgeois calls his often crude and brutal song."

Sternheim himself spares us none of the brutality which his own demon supplies. The characters who speak for him are all distinguished by the fact that they defer to no one. Their cynicism brings out in them a gross and unrefined dynamic power which seems almost a virtue in contrast to the hypocrisy Sternheim is fighting. The cook Napoleon, the policeman Busekov, and the musician Schuhlin in his stories, like Schippel and Maske in his plays, were right in scorning the society in which they lived, though they were not always right in considering its stupidity an opportunity for personal profit. The insolence of their bearing is unpleasantly similar to that of the hero of Paul Adam's *Serpent Noir;* as in Schuhlin's case their speech has a stale sub-Nietzschean odor which would have offended the nostrils of the real Nietzsche. But, like Shaw's characters, had they not existed we should have missed them. And one is more than amused at their sallies. The portraits, like Georg Grosz's caricatures, are not entirely lacking in resemblance to the original. They have a certain unity, a sort of style, which is due to Sternheim's own personality.

This unity is all the more obvious since the author, unlike the naturalists, makes them all speak his own language, with no attempt at verisimilitude, and that language is as scornful of grammatical conventions as Sternheim is of social conventions. You cannot help feeling the man's aggressive strength; a hail of shot is showered upon us, and more than accomplishes its object.

Sternheim, then, has a distinct and easily recognizable manner, but one can hardly call it a style. He has reacted so strongly against the excesses of intellectual and sentimental naïveté that he has gone too far in the other direction. In opposition to a mechanized society he has set up a mechanized individual. His characters may be exact, but they lack atmosphere; he is so dry that he does not permit himself even the artistic artifices that gave a certain good humor to Anatole France. Instead of the irony of a M. Bergeret, we have only direct sarcasm. Hauptmann retained the optimism of a religious nature; there is in Wedekind a certain cheerfulness, melancholy, perhaps, but nevertheless the cheerfulness of a sensual being who feels that "the flesh has its own mind." Compared with them Sternheim seems stripped bare, reduced to a mere skeleton of brain and sensory organs. He pretends that their free play is all he wants. But his apparent contentment with his freedom hides an underlying pessimism. His thinking is positive and direct, but he must realize that life cannot be forced into the lines he has laid out for it. He has freed himself, but on one plane only, and on this plane he has set himself up as an explosive power. That explosive power is his only resemblance to Nietzsche.

The drama is for Sternheim only a brilliant form of polemic. Georg Kaiser,* on the other hand, obeyed a necessity of his own nature in writing for the theatre. He sees and thinks in terms of the drama; and thanks to him the drama is freed of the prolixity and lyric languor with which the naturalists and symbolists had saddled it. He might be compared to Wedekind and Strindberg did he not have such a special talent: he is like an expert clock-maker, bringing a strong inventive spirit to the business of presenting dramatic action.

That dramatic action, no matter where or when laid, is invariably compact, spare, and vigorous—the kind of dramatic action that is part of war or revolution. This affects the dialogue, which smacks of the soldier, the

* Georg Kaiser (1878–   ). For bibliography see p. 303.

revolutionary, and the business executive upon whose shoulders great tasks weigh: orders barked out over the telephone, statements condensed into the form in which they would appear in a report written for a general or an employer. No time for sentimentality: a situation, and the need for getting out of it. Few abstract considerations: reality demands speedy action, and thought must be pragmatic.

Kaiser's coldness is not the coldness of a Stendhal; it is not designed to permit a disinterested analysis of psychological problems, but to distinguish clearly between the means available to an individual or a group by which a specific end may be gained. There is also a certain affectation which accounts for a tendency toward stylization in the dialogue: articles left out, short speeches, one word used instead of a sentence, and monosyllables rather than long words. Kaiser pays no attention to subordinates and relatives; he has other things to worry about, other restrictions to throw off more important than the grammatical.

Such dialogue is as much a reflection of modern life as it is a means of introducing new meaning into it; and Georg Kaiser puts it to clever use in the drama. He has an unusually good sense of theatre, of what is effective with a public used to the cinema. He approaches that public as a technician familiar with all the tricks of his trade, rather than as an inspired poet. The subjects which seem to him important are those which lend themselves readily to dramatic presentation and offer opportunity for the expression of the type of idea which can successfully be brought out in the drama. He has often sought them in history, as in *Der Bürger von Calais*, *Gilles und Jeanne*, *Frauenopfer* (from the Napoleonic period); and a sensational scandal, such as that of the Bonapartist Lavalette freed from prison as a result of his wife offering her body to his jailers is sure game. (What will be the feelings of the Count when he has once more close to him the lovely body which was sacrificed to free him?) In *Kolportage*, Kaiser put into melodramatic form the theme of the substitution of a guttersnipe for the legitimate heir to a great fortune and a great name. In *Nebeneinander* he went for his inspiration to the compartmented drama of the romanticists and presented three dramas in one, with alternating scenes from each; instead of a unified story, a simple juxtaposition of scenes such as is used in the films.

Such *tours de force*, of course, should not be made to seem more important than they are. They are attractive to the German public, whose appetite for theatrical innovations is more jaded than that of Parisians; indeed the latter refused their favor to *Der Brand im Opernhaus* as much out of conservative indifference and annoyance with the difficult as they did out of good judgment. Kaiser's true talent lies in his ability to simplify and to condense his material into violent contrasts. In *Von Morgens bis Mitternachts* he concentrates into one day of the life of a cashier, who has embezzled his employer's funds, a whole existence of dissipation that reaches the point of disgust. He handles such subjects better than when he tries to set up a philosophy of matter opposed to mind as he did in *David und Goliath* and *Der gerettete Alkibiades*, or of the innocence of primitive humanity opposed to the sins of capitalism as in *Hölle, Weg, Erde*.

Kaiser's greatest achievement is his depiction, in *Gas*, of the fundamental conflict in present-day society: on the one hand the machine and on the other a humanity in revolt against the machine and clinging to its natural instincts, good and bad. It is a conflict broader in conception than that of the strike in *Germinal* or *Die Weber;* and it represents the birth of an art which is more synthetic, more spontaneous than naturalism. There is true vigor in the conflict of the ideas Force, Law, and a Kingdom-which-is-not-of-this-World, and in that of the symbolic characters of the Chief Engineer, the Billionaire Worker, and the Figures in Yellow. The play contains many old formulas, but they are turned to fresh account —formulas that have the merit of being concerned not alone with questions of stage setting, which in Germany tend to absorb the drama itself, but which also affect the play and its characters. Those characters are representatives of a topsy-turvy society; the problem was to make clear the internal disorder which accompanies such upsets, and to show the vital force springing forth in spite of everything, ready to be turned to a definite end by those capable of giving it direction.

It is this feeling of the flow of vital force that Alfred Döblin's* novels give with unusual intensity. Döblin is a Jew, a Berliner by adoption, a practicing doctor, a psychologist, and a poet: in him a whole cataract of personalities stimulate and complement each other. He makes no effort to separate them; he lets them all burst forth at once. They fill all his books with explosive life; their combined power bursts from every smallest sentence. There is no novelist of his generation who is more variously gifted than Alfred Döblin.

He conceives of himself not merely as a writer, but as a human being whose allegiance is first to his function as a well balanced personality, then to his profession as physician, and to whom literature—being merely the supreme pleasure of expression after experience—does not come until these two are served. From the age of twenty until he was thirty-five he postponed writing for media other than the medical journals. The power that

* ALFRED DÖBLIN (1878–   ). For bibliography see p. 291.

was thus dammed up within him exploded suddenly in 1915 with *Die Drei Sprünge des Wang-Lun*, which brought him immediate fame. Döblin had written it without changing his mode of life in the least, living in the slums of Berlin, surrounded by his patients, his books, his laboratory work, and the activity before his door. For can one not make the most marvelous journey imaginable in a trolley running from the suburbs to the city, and were not ten Chinese poems, an ethnographic museum, and a miniature garden enough to evoke the tremendous swarming Asia of *Wang-Lun?*

Döblin thinks with his imagination, which does not mean that he thinks in images, but that his thinking is fed by the imagination. For him the ear and the eye are organs of thought. The smallest fragment of life he treats like a cutting placed in the field of vision of his laboratory microscope. His eye observes something living, something swarming with a life that he can see and render, in things which would not even arrest our glance. In that swarming of life Döblin divines and brings about order. Once he finds a place for his imagination to take hold, he explores that place completely, intoxicates himself with the multiplication of surfaces and depths; and this intoxication is creative.

Döblin's danger lay in the possibility that his creative power might fail to achieve a clear orientation, might remain merely an affirmation of a prolific energy. *Wang-Lun, Wallenstein, Berge, Meere und Giganten,* and *Manas* all leave the reader with an impression of a chaos in which thought is struggling toward the light like a tropical flower still tangled in a mass of over-luxuriant vegetation. That vegetation combines the characteristics of the Hindu nature, the Germanic nature, and of Judaism. But the ego remains unsmothered, even by a pantheism in which Orient and Occident are mingled.

Fantasy and sensibility in Döblin are allied with too strong a critical spirit and too much trenchant will, to permit him to remain permanently enslaved by the evocations of his imagination. He has an instinct which warns him that grandeur lies in order, not in mass, and in the ego which creates that order rather than in organic nature itself, which merely furnishes the elements with which the ordering ego works.

Nevertheless the myth idea exercised a powerful and primitive attraction over him. He was not merely yielding to current fashion when in the China of *Wang-Lun* and the India of *Manas* he sought the religious emotion through which the individual finds communion with the universe; he was following the tradition of the Germany of Goethe and Schopenhauer, who felt no barriers between them and the Orient. It was natural that the German spirit, irked by the machine, should once more bathe itself in the Ganges, seeking forgetfulness of an over-praised and faltering civilization. The Asia of Döblin's imagination again represented merely one Germany seeking to free itself from the other. Thirty years earlier, the naturalists, the "moderns," had set out to combat the tendency to define Germany in terms of the German past. During the years of the World War and the Revolution, the expressionists came forward in revolt against the tendency to define Germany in terms of the existing Reich. The temporal and spiritual limitations which that Germany implied were being broken. There was a growing feeling of the need to redissolve its elements in the universal flood.

The danger of this course was the possibility of falling into the undetermined, the uncertain. In his three incarnations Wang-Lun, the Chinese leader of secret societies, asks himself successively three questions. First, is violence the only means of protesting against an ill-constructed society? Second, does not the true revolution consist in non-resistance, in uncontrolled abandon to love? Finally, violence and love having both proved ineffectual, a last question: "Is it then possible not to resist, not to speak out"? Döblin anticipated what was to happen in his own country; gradually, one by one, he saw the problems that he raised arising all about him. Neither he nor anyone else found their solution. That solution is not to be found in the forgetfulness of self which Manas sought, any more than in the futuristic vision of humanity frightened by the machine but ultimately adjusting itself to it, while seeking regeneration through contact with the mountains, the sea, and the vast universe.

Gradually, yielding to the changing atmosphere about him, Döblin returned to Occidental forms of thinking. Little by little he tended to set up the ego in opposition to nature; an ego conceived as greater than nature and not to be mingled with it. A trip to Poland showed him the power of mind to liberate itself from accidental circumstance; the Jewish community had lived in Poland for many generations as a purely moral organism, without frontiers or territory or political status or social order, and yet through war and revolution and persecution had manifested an amazing grandeur of spirit. Here was an example which argued that Germany should free herself from the set of values which had held sway in the Hohenzollern era, should set spiritual values above them. By a circuitous route, Döblin was arriving at a philosophy somewhat in common with Nietzsche, George, and the Mann brothers.

Döblin's evolution is not yet complete. His recent efforts mark one phase of it—the ego raising itself above nature, with nature conceived as including the whole apparatus of modern civilization, which should be neither scorned nor overpraised. The individual is involved in the complexities of societies and cultures, Chinese, Hindu, or European; but though he may share their destiny he also has the power to undo it. The struggle for knowledge is a tragic struggle, but it leads to a progressive self-deliverance. As the individual destiny becomes more and more internal, less and less dependent on things outside itself, it reaches closer and closer harmony with the universal destiny. It need not yield to the infinite, for it is itself potentially infinite, endowed with an unlimited power of expansion. And not merely a power of expansion, but also a power of orientation. It is here, in the question of orientation, that the intervention of the lucid mind is implied; and it is for this lucidity of mind that Döblin, among others in Germany, appeals. His effort to seek contact with Mediterranean culture represents a following of the movement toward the introduction of an element of intellectualism into German thinking.

Thought must be defended against the intoxication of mass action. In his open letter to German youth, Döblin warns against the temptations of the appeal to action for action's sake—unconsidered action, a yielding to the instincts and to political passions, a blind faith in violence. Against this revival of an old German madness he sets the clarity of thought "which is itself action, the finest and most difficult kind of action." And he goes on to try to discover to what degree reason demands approval of collective forms of human activity such as have been adopted in Russia, and on the other hand to what extent we should attempt to preserve those individual values without which humanity runs the danger of becoming a mere sum of zeros; the danger of dragging civilization down to mediocrity, of stripping it of its greatest spiritual values.

Those spiritual values exist, in a latent state, within the meanest soul. It is the obligation of a democracy to extract them from the vein in which they lie. In *Berlin— Alexanderplatz*, thus far Döblin's greatest novel, the hero is the anonymous masses inhabiting the workmen's sections of the capital, whom the author, in his capacity as doctor to the poor, has had opportunity to examine closely in his consulting room. He has examined bodies crawling with lice and covered with ulcers, he has discovered a thousand secret sores and secret miseries. Beneath all this he finds a strong vitality, often undirected, but demanding to be delivered from evil.

The book states a moral as well as a psychological problem. Does not the lack of moral sense, the lack of "*Gewissen*," among the poor arise from a mere lack of psychological awareness, a lack of "*Bewusstsein*"? Goethe opened this same question when he showed Gretchen turned corrupt through naïveté, love, and good will. Döblin's Franz Biberkopf steals and lets women support him, but the reason he steals is that he is tired of being a bullied bully. He is by nature a hard worker; but an ill-constructed society disgusts him with work. And, in his capacity as lover, since his women are not countesses it is explicable that he should treat them a little roughly. Unconsciously he is an apache; but though he is not aware of his strength and cannot control it, he nevertheless has his scruples. Likewise, although he cannot recognize justice beneath the green uniform of the *Schupo*, he nevertheless has a sense of equity.

Döblin's characters do not have logical minds like the characters created by the old-fashioned psychologists. They are simple, but not without emotional complexities. They are incoherent, shifting from lyricism to humor and endowed with the biting common sense of the Berliner; but their disordered existence retains an organic coher-

ence. For the first time in Europe a novel of the masses
has the true popular accent—the language of the people,
reproduced with the fidelity of a phonograph recording
the hum of the city crowd. Such faithful documentation,
such eyewitness authenticity, make *Berlin–Alexanderplatz* an extremely valuable document. Apart from this
however, the book is still no more than a splendid monster in which the elements of a new esthetic are confused
in the author's mind in a bubbling mass of everything
from Joyce to the inspired messianism of the Old Testament. But sheer massive power gives the work value, as
well as the scalpel strokes with which the author lays
bare hitherto hidden fibers in the tissue of man.

In Theodor Däubler,* the same interpenetration of
North and South which we have noted beginning in
Döblin was long ago accomplished. Däubler was born in
Trieste, and represents a tradition and a civilization
which are in no sense local. His inspiration comes to him
from two poles, between which he attempts to set up a
permanent relation. Like Döblin, he has a sense of the
cosmos. An innate religiosity leads him to conceive of
the universe as full of mysterious forces, to think with the
aid of myths. He differs from Wagner in that he is not
content with presenting gods and heroes with a blare of
trumpets; nor does he present them like a modern
psychologist. He reconstructs a cosmogony of his own
with all the freedom of fancy of a Spitteler in *Olympische
Frühlung* or a Döblin in *Manas*.

Something has here occurred in German literature
which would be inconceivable anywhere else in Europe:
poets who are fully of their times, and who know those
times from profound experience, are expressing that

* Theodor Däubler (1876–1934). Note especially *Das Nordlicht* (1910)
Wir wollen nicht verweilen (1914), *Das Sternenkind* (1917).

experience in a kind of epic into which all mythologies and all civilizations are drawn. Here are pantheism and cosmopolitanism united in an appeal to all the divinities of Europe and of Asia; here is the faith of all the peoples of the earth mingled with the thinking of every age. Even history takes on the aspect of mythology—in Däubler's work the song of Pan is mingled with the song of the Italian city-states of the Renaissance, of the chivalry of the Middle Ages, of Egypt, of India, of Judea, bringing about a vision of mingled chaos and order which induces a sensuous and metaphysical intoxication.

His epic *Nordlicht* is dedicated to the glory of the South. But Southern light is not enough. There is a yearning beyond toward the Nordic shadow, toward the pleasure of penetrating within that shadow. One plays upon the other, and from their interplay emerges an unexploited richness for art to seize upon. The sleeping Pan needs awakening from his torpor at the hands of Orpheus, and the spirit awakened by Orpheus strives to outreach Orpheus just as Orpheus outreached Pan.

In *Die Treppe zum Nordlicht*, Däubler, who has often shown an intelligent sympathy toward French culture, delivers himself of the sally: "*Fast riefe ich: Franzosen, rettet einen Dichter.*" But he realizes that his salvation is secure, regardless of France, regardless of the Berlin Academy on whose rolls his name appears. The abstruse sections of his work will disappear. The handful of stories that he wrote will give no true idea of the breadth of his talent. But the poems and the lyric fragments in which greatness of desire threatens to shatter the outlines of the design will live long after him. Here are images which are at once plastic and full of atmosphere, lit with a light which might be that of Florence or that of Paris, but which extends into a vaporous beyond like the light in Dresden or the Rhenish countryside.

Däubler's poetry, in its quiet portions, is like a Puvis de Chavannes fresco: it opens the door to dreams, and the mind of the reader is drawn through that door gently, gradually, never wrenched from the real. It is not surprising therefore that in *Sainte Geneviève* and *The Sinner* Däubler was able to reveal a France of different aspect from the France that appears in the endlessly repeated reportorial descriptions of Montmartre and Montparnasse. He was prepared to understand. The very thing which he had sought in philosophic chaos he saw confronting him in the frescoes of the Pantheon, in Fouquet's and Clouet's portraits, in the churches and landscapes of the Île-de-France: a humanity fitting exactly and naturally into the space it occupies, and with great simplicity reaching beyond the confines of that space through a religiosity which, instead of making ceaseless appeal to the cosmos, accomplishes its ends entirely through the commonplace gestures of daily life.

René Schickele* is a journalist who has turned to the novel, and he happens to be an Alsatian as well. He might very conceivably have written only journalistic novels from a provincial viewpoint. What might have been a danger in a writer who was less an artist, however, constitutes Schickele's greatest richness. His training in journalism, which he approached as psychologist and sociologist, and his Alsatian origin, led him to make comparisons between the spirit of the peoples on either side of the Rhine, and to conceive of the Rhine as a river uniting two civilizations rather than dividing them. Barrès, whose activities he consciously opposed, called him "uprooted"; in actual fact he was transplanted rather, with roots in more than one soil. During the War he continued the publication of his journal *Weisse*

* RENÉ SCHICKELE (1883–   ). For bibliography see p. 318.

Blätter in Switzerland; and in its files the historians of the new-born European culture will find many precious documents.

In *Hans im Schnakenloch*, "who has everything he wants, but wants nothing he has," Schickele, himself of an old Alsatian family, sets out with great finesse and honesty to discover the psychological basis of the Alsatian problem. The trilogy *Das Erbe am Rhein*, made up of *Maria Capponi*, *Blick auf die Vogesen*, and *Der Wolf in der Hürde*, constitutes the great novel of Alsace.

From the heights of the Black Forest Schickele looks out upon the two slopes of Occidental culture and sees things no longer as a political writer, from without, but as a simple human being, from within. The drama of the individual caught between groups, divided against himself by national passions, is the drama of his own life; it has the moving quality of true experience, the experience of an individual's flesh and heart and brain. It gains breadth from the fact that it is also the drama of an ethnic group and of the post-War German and Frenchman as well. Can that drama reach a solution? "No," is the answer of those who follow a favorite French habit of thought, which consists in choosing between two alternatives, deciding upon one possibility to the exclusion of all other possibilities. "Yes," is the secret hope of Schickele, who believes that to absorb antagonistic elements within oneself aids the growth of the individual, whereas to divide oneself into two opposing egos can only end in destroying the universal tissue.

A true conservative instinct has warned Schickele to avoid the categories set up by bourgeois nationalism. At the same time he is too human and too much the artist to fall into the equally narrow categories set up by abstract internationalism. He states the problems of present-day Europe not as an ideologue or a reasoner, but as a sensitive, intelligent, independent Alsatian. The fact that he is an Alsatian, the heterogeneity of his nature, help him to envisage these problems in all their complexity. Fortunately he does not pretend that he has found their solution; but he serves as an example of how anyone can so conduct himself as to bring that solution closer.

His recent writings are those of a man completely disengaged from political and esthetic ideology, who serves the cause of peace between two nations all the better because the only way he will serve it is by letting the two extreme attitudes fuse spontaneously within him. There is no fruitless pathos in *Das Erbe am Rhein;* and the same streak of humor which appeared in *Hans im Schnakenloch,* and which has always tended to save the Alsatian from sentimentalism, infuses a certain gaiety into its dark background. This is a plastic and a sensuous art, bathed in the clear atmosphere of Nice, but nevertheless flooded also with the dreamy mists of the gardens and woods of the Black Forest. In it the German language, without losing its harmonic richness, takes on the nervous precision which is usually reserved to the French.

Otto Flake* is another of the transplanted. The hero of his first novel, *Freitagskind,* is a German immigrant's son in whom Lorraine awakes sympathies wider than those of patriotism. In later writings—chronicles, essays, novels—Flake has steadily sought nourishment for those sympathies. He came to literature at a time of intellectual crisis, and had assumed the task of following the manifestations of that crisis in a cosmopolitan Germany open to European and extra-European currents of thought. His ambition was, by depicting a society as Balzac did,

* OTTO FLAKE (1882–   ). See p. 295 for bibliography.

to help bring about the rebirth of that society, to insist upon the modifications in intellectual life which must precede changes of social custom.

He has proved himself an excellent chronicler, describing in detail the people who serve as points of contact between Germany and Switzerland, Italy, Russia, France, and the United States. The background is reminiscent of Paul Morand; but instead of giving each scene an imaginative finality, and then packing up for a fresh trip, Flake, using the novel as a higher type of reporting, struggles to follow the fluctuations of contemporary ideology, to analyze its contradictions as in *Nein und Ja*. He is a cosmopolitan personality capable of bearing with those contradictions, if not of dominating them.

The elements of shock and nervous tension in Flake are softened in Stefan Zweig.* To the new cosmopolitanism he brings a softness of aspect such as the European capitals might have after they had undergone a strong Austrian influence. Zweig senses the direction in which the new intellectual currents are tending, and in which progress therefore will be possible; he does his best to accelerate that progress. From Salzburg, through his critical writings, he has made reputations, oriented hesitant writers, served as intermediary between countries and literatures little known to each other, made clear the bond between living authors and dead, and made the latter live for the benefit of the former. He introduced Verhaeren to German-language readers in an excellent translation; he assisted in the diffusion of the writings of Baudelaire; since then, with conscious versatility, he has brought the German public closer to

---

* STEFAN ZWEIG (1881–   ). See p. 325 for bibliography.

such varied writers as Balzac, Dickens, Dostoievski, Hölderlin, Kleist, and Nietzsche.

Stefan Zweig's effectiveness as an essayist arises from his ability to make clear in a dead writer those elements which can still appeal to the sensibilities of the present. His Balzac, his Hölderlin, his Nietzsche are not Balzac and Hölderlin and Nietzsche seen in the absolute, but the Balzac, Hölderlin, and Nietzsche who have something to offer to the post-War German. In his novels he uses his psychological gifts to follow the most delicate subtleties of passion and employs backgrounds from the East as well as from the West. The style, like that of his essays, belongs to a writer who is a master of his craft.

On the edge of the *Blätter für die Kunst* circle, like the ring of lighter tint which spreads around a spot of water-color, is a confused mixture of Judaism, Catholicism, and nationalism. In this twilight zone we find Rudolf Borchardt.* He had the stuff of an elegiac poet, but hardened himself in an effort to model his style on George, and in believing that he was called upon to define German inspiration in its purest form misjudged his own vocation. He is an esthete, and by the introduction of pedantic borrowings from Gothic stiffness and from Dante he has bastardized the literary forms he imitated. The language which he developed has archaisms built into it in an ingenious mosaic, but it is a dead language. His is a talent which has lost much through trying to force itself.

Rudolf Alexander Schröder† belongs to the spiritual family of Hofmannsthal; he created a universe apart from specific time and specific place. In him an essen-

---

* RUDOLF BORCHARDT (1877–   ). See p. 289 for bibliography.
† RUDOLF ALEXANDER SCHRÖDER (1878–   ). See p. 319 for bibliography.

tially demonic force brings about the development of an ego dependent on more distant laws than those of the accidental evolution of present reality. He retained, however, a secret ambition to influence the world in which he lived, to shape its destiny—not by intervention in its daily affairs, but by the creation of a higher spirituality through the magic of language and form.

A frank and outspoken Judaism is responsible for a number of books, some of which have artistic interest as well as authenticity. Gustav Meyrink, Max Brod, Franz Kafka, Franz Werfel, have, like Jean-Richard Bloch in France, been attracted to a type of thinking neither wholly national nor wholly Occidental. All four are Czechs who have lived in Prague. It is difficult to tell whether they have reached the new position they occupy between Austrian and German literature because they have lived in that Czech island of resistance to Germanism, or merely because they are Jews. In any case, their style has distinctive qualities: a moving directness in Kafka; in Werfel a musical softness shot through with Levite ardor.

Max Brod's* chief virtues are his alert narrative sense and the limpidity of his style. *Die Jüdinnen* is a curious contribution to the psychology of his race, and *Das grosse Wagnis* contains touches of ecstatic expressionism; but in general Brod has limited himself to stories which can be made graceful and piquant. In *Tycho Brahes Weg zu Gott*, however, he hit upon a great theme; the novel appeared in 1915 and was, with *Der Golem* and *Die Drei Sprünge des Wang-Lun*, one of the popular books of the year. Tycho Brahe the astrologer is placed in contrast with Kepler the astronomer, metaphysics in contrast with physics, mysticism in contrast with mathematics.

* Max Brod (1884–   ). See p. 290 for bibliography.

Tycho Brahe, swept on by fantasy and sensibility, seems a tremendous figure compared to Kepler, who is reduced to the stature of an admirably functioning brain. Even Tycho Brahe's follies contribute to his grandeur; they are the follies of a passionately human man in conflict with the angels, and they were received sympathetically in a period when the peoples of Europe were engaged in a struggle whose outcome was still unknown. Tycho Brahe brought back a little of the optimism of Goethe, who saw purification in suffering, and in error a necessary step on the road that leads toward God.

Not the least of Max Brod's merits is his activity as literary executor for his friend Kafka,* who died a premature death. Kafka's dying request that the manuscripts of the three novels, *Der Prozess*, *Das Schloss*, and *Amerika*, be destroyed evidenced an obsession with perfection that almost reached the point of self-torment. His was an exigent soul, and he never felt that he had found the form that answered his requirements.

Stories like *Die Verwandlung* afford some notion of what Kafka was seeking, but they are likely to give too simplified an image of him. He is an artist of astonishing intensity. He is an etcher, perhaps; a little master like the fifteenth-century Germans whose work hangs in the Basle Museum; he is a poet, like Hoffmann and Poe, subject to hallucinations in broad daylight. An ultra-modern psychologist of the obscure, he seeks out its subtleties with a passion for clarity that is Slav or Jewish or perhaps even French. One can say all these things about Kafka, and still not explain why the Czech novelist reveals such stimulating possibilities.

* FRANZ KAFKA (1883–1924), *Ein Landarzt; In der Strafkolonie; Das Urteil; Die Verwandlung*, 1917; *Der Heizer* (reprinted in *Amerika*); *Ein Hungerkünstler* (*Erstes Leid; Eine kleine Frau; Ein Hungerkünstler; Josefine, die Sängerin*), 1924; *Der Prozess*, 1925; *Das Schloss*, 1926; *Amerika*, 1927; *Beim Bau der Chinesischen Mauer*, 1931.

In *Die Verwandlung* a man discovers, on awakening, that he has been changed into a loathsome insect; and yet the reader still feels himself on the level ground of reality. Here is a situation which might have been treated *à la* Hoffmann. The novelty of Kafka's treatment lies in the absence of "literature"; in the setting of the fantastic on the plane of psychiatry; in the rigor and subtlety of the means of expression, which outstrip the efforts of Meyrink in *Der Golem* and of Däubler in *Der Werwolf*. Kafka's monster bears no resemblance to the monster that Saint Anthony saw; it is an interior monster; the individual is not merely possessed of definite, objective demons, nor merely the victim of a *Seelenschwängerung*, a soul prevented from being itself by a parasite soul. With Kafka the restricted ego retains its unity; the factors limiting that ego in its search for the divine are in human nature itself. Gregor Samsa's thoughts are always those of a common-sense human being, but his feelings are those of a monster, imprisoned by sensations as a cockroach is imprisoned by his shell; driven mad by the horror with which he increasingly inspires his mother, his father, his sister, and himself.

The symbol is a powerful one: that of the madman who retains his own lucidity of thought, and whose madness is increased by that very lucidity. We are lucid ourselves, yet all our passions go to nourish a madness that perverts our normal being—if one believes in a normal being and rejects the plurality of the self, inhabited, possessed, in all its emotional states, by powers which paralyze it, render it inarticulate, inhuman.

Kafka's characters perform only the simplest acts. The scenes he depicts take place against the most usual sort of background. There is not a single motivation that is not taken from the commonest experience. The action is the action of ordinary existence. The words which carry it forward are as colorless as a police report. Here is a writer whose effort is not to stimulate the reader's imagination, but to keep it down to earth. K, the hero of *Der Prozess*, talks business in his bank, telephones, makes love to questionable women with gusto, argues with his judges; his existence seems identical with that of his neighbors, and yet over it hovers something inexplicable. He is on trial; yet what he is accused of no one knows. He does not know, nor does he ask. He has judges, but they wear no robes; he goes to court, but he does not know where the court is—in a garret, in public opinion, in his own conscience, in Heaven. K is executed, and he desires his execution at the same time that he desires his acquittal. The details of the story are so plastically realistic that they haunt you, and yet the more plastic they become, the more oppressive becomes the sense of mystery. A metaphysic penetrates the real, finds unsuspected depths in its interstices.

It can perhaps be said without bias that Kafka is inspired not merely by the desire for a revolutionary ethic, like so many of his Jewish fellows, but also by an Old Testament thirst for justice. His anonymous character K represents not merely a monomaniac suffering from a persecution complex, which is how an alienist would diagnose him, admitting that Kafka had depicted the symptoms with astonishing accuracy. He is also the original man, eternally athirst for the Law. This Law is not the written law; it is diffused in society; our slightest gesture follows its dictates. An unformulated accusation weighs perpetually upon us. A court made up of all society is sitting in judgment upon us everywhere, always, accusing, condemning. We feel vaguely that we are under its jurisdiction. Unfortunately we try to escape judgment, "try not to attract attention," drag the case out as long as possible, postpone it until death, until the Last Judgment, through fear of our own fear. K, however, is not afraid, or at least he believes in controlling his fear, in trying to understand. He defies his judges, and his judges vanish beyond his grasp. He seeks to know "the Law"; he waits, just as the fanatic in the curious symbolic episode in *Vor dem Gesetz* waited for twenty years outside the portals of the Law whose guardian refused him entry.

That guardian is human society. Society does not understand or recognize the Law, but defends it nevertheless. The knowledge to which society pretends is in reality reserved to the higher, the inaccessible judge. But the yearning for that knowledge is strong enough to devour K. Joseph K is conscience in the form of man— a man whose life is spent in attempting to achieve a full realization of his strangeness on this earth, and who aspires (in *Das Schloss* and *Amerika*) to grace and to deliverance from himself through justice.

Kafka's sense of the fantastic arises not from mere formulas, but from a fanatical love of the truth hidden in humble things, behind gestures which we think we can explain. Our explanations, indeed, are lies; our logic is deluded. Our reality is an evasion of the true reality, and both realities a madness which is nevertheless reasonable, and whose internal laws need always to be made clear. To that task Franz Kafka devoted himself in the spirit of a geometrist. There is no German writing in which pure reason is more obviously in control, which takes so linear a form, with straight lines running off to meet at a point infinitely distant.

Readers of Kafka's novels may find themselves disconcerted by the contrast between excessive soberness of presentation and a metaphysical content which escapes these sober bounds. They will not find in his work the sense of familiar humanity which in the English novel, for example, spontaneously attracts us. In Kafka's work even madmen, as one German has said, are so natural that we are embarrassed and ashamed that we also are not mad, although at the same time we cannot help feeling that the characters are somehow removed from the humanity that we know. Kafka makes us feel that we have been removed from that humanity by some mysterious trick. But it is a trick which marks the creative artist—that slight twist of axis characteristic of the artists and the mystics for whom reality is not all that exists, nor the existing order the only order possible.

These writers whom we have seen collaborating in the transition between two ages are isolated figures. They have nothing in common save their struggle against a surrounding state of mind that tends to permit invasion by determinist notions. Each of them in his own way has revolted against the gregarious modes of existence, has tried to escape from the national machine, the social machine that was turning out individuals, like coins, in the same mold. They all sought values arising not from the mold, but from the metal itself; personality was rebelling against being stamped in any mold, was rediscovering its elasticity.

The rebound toward disorder foretold expressionism; but there was as yet no general movement. The writers who provoked the expressionist revolt—men in their forties—had no illusions about it. They remembered too much of the pre-War period, of the nineteenth century and its views toward the world and toward men—a philosophy, an esthetics, an ethical system whose demolition required such effort of them that they were too exhausted to abandon themselves to the intoxication of the new freedom.

That intoxication was to be enjoyed only by the next generation, born around 1890, for whom the past was destroyed by force of events. The servitude that this new generation remembered was only in childhood, in school. It was a past that had little weight in comparison with the chaotic world into which these twenty-year-olds found themselves thrown. Circumstances permitted an unrestrained expansion. The term expressionism meant the transition, this time as a group, to freer ways of thinking and feeling; and the now generalized movement was rather a flowering than a revolt. Lyricism was to burst forth again in a literature which still remained a combative literature, but to which the younger writers were to add the bursts of a sensibility yielding to the passions which their elders had avoided. The final result was not merely an awakening of spirit in opposition to the condemned régime, with its accompanying individual demands, but a crisis of the German spirit and a collective insistence upon a new régime, although no one could say exactly what should constitute its newness.

CHAPTER II

The Writers of the Period of Conflict—From Expressionism to Dispassionate Order

T O DEFINE is to restrict. The young Germans at the beginning of the twentieth century felt that previous generations had been so excessively anxious for definition that they had ended in over-restriction. In twenty years the concept of essential Germanity, which the generation of 1880 had demanded be revealed in its full extent and profundity, had failed to achieve its highest manifestation; but it had unquestionably undergone definite changes. It had emerged from the uncertainties of birth and had definitely established itself in existing reality; it had borrowed specific attributes from that reality; achieved a fixed form, and determined upon a field of action within the confines of the Reich.

The term *"Kultur"* came to represent a vigorous combination of forces whose effectiveness was undeniable. Poetry and thinking collaborated with the political, the economic, and the technical in organizing a concept of Germanity that was no longer being defined in terms of the past or in terms of legend, but in relation to facts and to the present; no longer losing itself in a dream world, but mobilizing the forces of that dream world to the profit of the State. To be German, and particularly to be a modern German, took on a restricted sense, corresponding to the notion of a civilization which was to produce a fixed type. This in itself was contrary to the true Germanic temperament. The Germans were forcing themselves into organization merely by reaction against their tendency, pointed out by Nietzsche, to delight in the indeterminate, in shadows and in everything that partakes of the nature of shadows.

In so far as it was consistent, this conception of Germanity, solidified in terms of Hohenzollern civilization, was insufficient fully to contain the German spirit. It was merely a collectivity; beneath it brooded the old individualism, seeking an avenue of escape. To assign definite limitations to the activity of the individual thwarted his natural taste for the infinite. To attempt to give a national aspect to all the manifestations of the individual shocked his sense of the universal, which in spite of everything still remained an integrating factor in the German heritage.

"It hurts us to have a goal, an objective, continually set for us"—this was the growing complaint of the young writers and thinkers who conceived of the future of Germany as surpassing national limitations. They felt that they were being strait-jacketed at birth. And they represented not merely German spirituality struggling against the limitations of *Realpolitik* and *Kulturpolitik*, but also the rebirth of the eternal spiritual need to escape from the necessities of time and place, to go beyond the acquisitions of a civilization, not to let oneself be sealed within its monuments—the need which Goethe felt when he said, "Limitation is a concept unknown to Nature; on the immobile she has laid her curse."

This struggle to achieve freedom had been proceeding without a break ever since 1890; but the writers who carried it on during its early period remained isolated. It was only with the generation which began to write after 1910, and which had been roused by the revolutionary spirit of some of the elder writers, that the expressionist movement became general. Expressionism was chiefly an escape of the German spirit from the forms which Hohenzollern civilization was attempting to impose upon it, a new *Sturm und Drang* carried on by revolutionaries determined to free themselves of the restraints imposed upon them by a culture this time not of classic France but of modern Germany, and to rediscover nature—not a Germanic nature, but a universally human nature.

The term expressionism has indeed been so abused that it is in danger of coming to signify merely a literary fad. But a clear distinction should be made between the often mediocre writing to which expressionism gave birth in Germany, and the expressionist movement itself, which went far beyond the field of literature and for that matter was by no means limited to Germany. Not that it was a foreign importation. Doubtless there is in it evidence of the influence of Whitman, Verhaeren, Rimbaud, Dostoievski, Strindberg; but these were influences which were to be found widely scattered throughout Europe and America—influences opposed to the nineteenth century, tending to upset the order established by the science, the philosophy, the moral systems of that time. A bourgeois civilization had brought man down to the dimensions of utilitarian things, bound him with the bonds of a self-styled necessity of place, and he was throwing off these inherited restraints, seeking to affirm his freedom, even if only with the madman's gesture of a Kiriloff.

Opposed to the automatism of a society bent on depersonalizing the individual, and to the flabbiness of impressionist art, was an individual dynamism demanding like Nathanaël in *Nourritures Terrestres* "rather a life of tragic action than tranquillity." Nietzscheism was in the air, although Nietzsche himself was gone; he served to supply the spark which set afire the gas that filled the European atmosphere. The need to break with an inert past appeared in the Slav countries, the Scandinavian countries, in Britain and in France, as well as in Germany. Fantasy, sensibility, sensuality, instinct, burst over the dam. There poured forth a dynamic literature whose variety and lack of constraint are indicated by the names of only a few of the authors—Péguy, Gide, Proust, Giraudoux, Aragon, Joyce, Strindberg, Heinrich Mann, Wedekind, Werfel. Fervent or passively sensual, escaping into the world of dreams or passionately dealing with the world of reality—and most often all or this together—the quivering humanity which they revealed had nowhere in Europe a clearly defined outline or a clearly stated ideal; but everywhere the forms and the substance of the nineteenth century were being destroyed.

In Germany the false values which had arisen in the years following Goethe, Jean-Paul, and Hölderlin were being melted down and cast away. The German was getting rid of the waste matter of a century of political and philosophical realism, breaking the mold which had been turning out a type designed to be employed for purely German ends. The return to Goethe, to Jean-Paul, to Hölderlin, and to the revolutionary Georg Büchner by no means meant that these new writers proposed merely to return to a tradition of the past, to pick it up again where it had been broken off, to take over an already stated system of ethics and esthetics. What they sought in these neglected writers of the past was energy and inspiration to enable them to destroy already fixed and existing esthetic and moral systems. "*Das Motorische*," motive power, was more important to them than the things which the motor might produce. Whether from Nietzsche or from Goethe, from Gothic art or Negro art, the expressionists seized upon everything that could serve to inspire the "new feeling," everything that had the power to shatter the old.

No expressionistic formula was ever developed, any more than there was ever an expressionistic school. The movement was a sort of endemic revolution. It began before the War; the War served only as a stimulus. In the political revolution which followed, the expressionists saw only a chaos which would permit them the better to destroy the materialistic order against which they had been fighting, and to give free rein at last to the flood of feelings and ideas which was welling up within them.

From 1910 forward, signs announcing the tempest began to appear at various points on the horizon: Heinrich Mann's manifesto, *Geist und Tat* (1910); the founding of the reviews, *Sturm* by Walden (1910), *Aktion* by Pfemfert (1911), *Pan* by Kerr (1910), *Die Weissen Blätter* by Schickele (1913), *Das Forum* by Herzog (1914). There was a growing will not only to settle once for all with the literary accomplishment of the thirty years from 1880 to 1910—these young writers wanted to retain no one but Hauptmann, Dehmel, Wedekind, and George, and retained these only with reservations, setting up against them Rimbaud, Baudelaire, Balzac, Stendhal, Dostoievski, Whitman—but also to do away with the social accomplishment of a society which, whether bourgeois or socialist, had ground heaven into earth, and to rediscover the sky and the open spaces above.* "The Revolution is not a French thing only; it belongs to the whole world"—in May of 1914 Heinrich Mann reminded the Germans of Michelet's famous phrase, and prophesied a time when the peasant of Thuringia would light the flame of revolution for the peasant of Touraine.

* *Von dem Charakter der kommenden Literatur*, in *Die weissen Blätter*, Number 1, September, 1913.

The term expressionism was first used in 1911 by the poet Otto zur Linde, to describe the reaction of the "Charon" group against impressionist art. By the time it had been made fashionable by such manifestos as Kasimir Edschmid's *Über den Expressionismus* (1918), and Bahr's *Expressionismus* (1920), it seemed to have become a tag to express novelty in literature or in painting. In actual fact it gave a name—a poor one, perhaps, but a name—to a revolutionary movement which had been fermenting for some years.

That movement was nothing so simple as the revolt of the younger generation against their elders. Its youthfulness was a youthfulness common to men of forty and to men of twenty—to Heinrich Mann, Döblin, Däubler, and to youngsters like Franz Werfel and Kasimir Edschmid. Nevertheless it must be noted that the youngsters of the period introduced a note which had not theretofore been heard: the theme of the unsubmissive son. Until that time, although writers from Conradi to Wedekind had unsparingly criticized authoritarian education, no one had dared show the son thirsting for freedom opposed to the father drunk with authority. This was what Walter Hasenclever* did in *Der Sohn* (written in 1913, published in 1916). "We are not fools, we are *men*, and we *live; we* lead a double life, for you are trying to kill us. . . . *Give, O give me freedom!*" cries the son, revolver in hand, to the father who is threatening him with a horsewhip. The father calls the police and then, without the son pressing the trigger, falls dead, stricken with apoplexy. The success of this drama arises from something more than its unquestionable artistic excellence.

Many a twenty-year-old recognized in Hasenclever's esthetic lyricism the struggles of his own soul. This

* Walter Hasenclever (1890–   ). For bibliography see p. 298.

tragedy was the tragedy of their own families. The father was the symbol of the enemy. He incarnated a social tyranny which youth felt was frightful, and against which it saw no remedy save a symbolic parricide. The mere departure of the Prodigal Son from home was no longer sufficient to the circumstances.

From 1917 onward, André Gide's novels, translated into German by Rilke, created a stir to which the number of editions they ran bears witness; but it was only gradually that an influence whose first traces are found in Werfel's *Spiegelmensch* (1920) took effect in all its nuances without losing its intellectual quality. Before such very young writers as Süskind could feel themselves free to speak, a new gesture like Karl Moor's was required. It had been prepared by Strindberg and by Wedekind; it was outlined in Sorge's *Bettler* (1910); it became precise and ritualistic in a series of books ranging from Werfel's novel *Nicht der Mörder, der Ermordete ist schuldig* to Bronnen's *Vatermord*. The dominating theme was: "not the murderer, but the victim is guilty."

With the help of the catastrophic course which events were taking in Germany, the rebellion against the father, the mother, the teacher, and the elders became a literary theme which raised echoes everywhere and which was exploited by writers of such varied temperaments as Leonhard Frank (*Die Räuberbande*, *Die Ursache*), Fritz von Unruh (*Ein Geschlecht*), and Hermann Ungar (*Knaben und Mörder*). A Freudian influence also appeared, and in Leonhard Frank, Werfel, and Ungar, for instance, to the moral motive of rebellion was added the psychological motive of feelings repressed in childhood and bursting forth at last in the monstrous act.

This explosion of repressed feelings is the most general characteristic that can be attributed to expressionism. The movement was essentially an incoherent gushing forth of a lyricism which the consistent realists had taught must be repressed. It had reappeared from time to time, socialized in Dehmel, turned bourgeois in Hofmannsthal, stylized in George; but now it took on an explosive character for the first time since the *Moderne Dichtercharaktere* of 1885 and the forgotten writings of Conradi.

Henceforward nothing could withstand its violence. The political revolution, while it did not inspire the movement, gave it, so to speak, its civic rights. From 1918 to 1920 publishers brought out any number of books, symposia and anthologies announcing that literature was setting forth upon a new path. As early as 1916 Kurt Wolff, whose publishing house performed the same service for the expressionists that S. Fischer had performed for the naturalists, brought out *Der Jüngste Tag*, where side by side with Strindberg, Claudel, and Francis Jammes, the writings of Gottfried Benn, Johannes R. Becher, Hasenclever, Kafka, Schickele, Sternheim, Georg Trakl, and Werfel announced the coming of a new era. In 1920 Paul Cassirer, who was as much interested in new poets as he was in new painters, published *Unser Weg*, in which the new influences were proclaimed again by Hasenclever, Kasimir Edschmid, Else Lasker-Schüler, Schickele and Toller, Barlach, Kokoschka, and Georg Grosz. In 1916 Georg Müller had brought out the review *Das Ziel*, in which Heinrich Mann, Kerr, and Rudolf Kayser had appealed for a spiritual dynamism which was to fill the same rôle in German politics that it had filled in the politics of the English and especially the French; and for a literature closely tied to public life, a literature now become action, preparing the people for autonomy.

Under the name of activism there emerged a tendency to bring the political into intellectual life and the intellectual into political life. During the political revolution the organ of the activists was *Das Ziel*, which had by then passed into the hands of Kurt Wolff with the subtitle *Jahrbücher für geistige Politik*. At the same time appeared such anthologies as *Die Erhebung*, published by Fischer; *Menschheitsdämmerung* and *Die Entfaltung*, published by Rowohlt, and *Verkündigung* published by Rudolf Kayser at the Roland Verlag. *Menschheitsdämmerung* caused a sensation. In the manifesto which served as preface for this "symphony of recent lyricism," Kurt Pinthus stressed the dual character of the movement—*Dämmerung*—the twilight of one humanity and the dawn of another. "We have realized more and more clearly," he wrote, "the impossibility of a humanity completely dependent upon its concrete accomplishments, its science, its technique, its statistics, its commerce, and its industry—in short, a petrified social order. We have tried to awaken, to save, what is human in man. . . . The essence, the determining power, lies not in institutions, in inventions, in laws established on the basis of observations, but in man himself."

This literature may be termed a literature of shock, but a distinction should be made between those who administered the shock and those who merely underwent it. Among the latter some were full grown men like Unruh, in whom the course of events caused a complete upset in sensibility and imagination. Others, like Ernst Toller, J. R. Becher, Hasenclever, found themselves caught at twenty among the dead in the trenches, where the world seemed all incoherence, and destruction absurd. *Wir Sind*, the title of a collection of Werfel's lyrics, took on a moving significance: "We exist!" expressed the naïve feeling of youth resisting annihilation, appreciating what a boon it is merely to be alive. This was neither individualism nor egoism; it was essentially an instinct of conservation. The beliefs of these writers seemed revolutionary only in contrast with the demands of patriotism. Their chief demand was for life for its own sake, life for all who wish to live. Here was no such hymn to torrential forces as had been sung by Whitman or Verhaeren, and the ego which was demanding its rights had none of the ascetic heroism of Nietzsche. Indeed the favorite themes of the new lyricism were goodness, tenderness, love of man, of all men without distinction. There arose a wave of sentiment which recalled the effusions of Rousseauism, of romanticism, of naturalism. But the naturalist effusions all took place within the established limits of German society.

The newness of this lyric movement was that it was stripped of nationality and class. These writers were no longer concerned merely with the development of the Germanic nature, or with pity for the misery of a particular social class; the grandeur and the misery which they felt were those of all humanity. Like Kant and Lessing and Herder, they felt themselves part of a whole that was larger than their own people. At the same time, their humanitarianism was not the rationalist's abstract conception of humanity. Their fraternization implied no political ideology like that of the soldiers of the French Revolution. It was a purely sentimental communion between hearts which shared a sort of Rousseauistic faith in man. Leonhard Frank denounced the survival of man's ancient ferocity in *Der Mensch ist gut*, a book which had the same effect upon the public as the writings of Barbusse and Duhamel.

A current of Franciscan sweetness, of evangelic love, entered into the poems and plays of Werfel, Unruh, Toller. This desire to clasp hands was more widespread in Germany than in France, where it was felt in this form only by men like Duhamel and Vildrac, together with

Martinet and the Belgian Guilbeaux. Sensibility never reached a position of mastery in writers like Romain Rolland, Jules Romains, or Jouve. Almost without exception it did reach such a position among the younger Germans; the idea of Europe threw them into a state of ecstasy analogous to that into which the idea of Germany had thrown their fathers.

Ecstasy, however, is not a state that can last very long. Trench fighting had been followed by street fighting. Even among those ecstatic people who had begun the revolution in the middle of the War by casting away their guns, there were some, such as Toller, who underwent a reversal of feeling and after a struggle with their consciences picked up the discarded weapon in order to make use of it in the civil war. Insurrection complicated pacifistic lyricism. Souls floating undetermined between indolence and violence were suddenly galvanized into action by political considerations, either bolshevistic or republican. A stiffening, a tenseness, became evident; something more was needed than J. R. Becher's appeals to revolt, Rudolf Leonhard's exclamations, Stramm's incisive cries, Werfel's and Hasenclever's entreaties.

The newly risen will to action could finally no longer be served by poetry, and turned to the drama instead. The drama increased in importance as it became more and more clear that it offered the only effective means of propaganda. But the consequent dramatic activity of such men as Sternheim, Kaiser, Unruh, Goering, Hasenclever, Brecht, Bronnen, and Toller contributed more to the formation of a new political philosophy and a new system of ethics than it did to esthetics.

Even revolution has its traditions, and in Germany there is a particular tradition about literary revolutions. That tradition was not broken by expressionism. The movement had many aspects, but among them was one which clearly betrayed the old German mistrust of art itself. The expressionists did not admit this; they said that what they were opposed to was "art for art's sake"; but in reality there was growing up a secret hostility toward art itself, which the expressionists did not feel was a sufficient end. They were opposed to all discipline, even that which Goethe had handed on to George, and they underestimated the creative power of the word. Forgetting that nothing exists until it has been given a name, they fell into a contempt for all artistic effort; they were able to conceive of the word only as placed at the service of a cause, as useful to an idea, in a sort of mixture of pedagogy and applied art. What they were really doing, indeed, was setting up a pedagogy and an esthetic of violence and love. Some of them quoted Rimbaud. "I am not a prisoner of reason," the author of *A Season in Hell* had said. But when Rimbaud gave himself up to the demoniacal, he had in his blood a drop of classicism. The French literary revolutionaries retained a lively intellectual and esthetic curiosity. To destroy meant to them not only to find the new idea but to find the new expression which was to kill the old idea and the old expression. In the same gesture with which they crushed the old, they formed the new, and that gesture always represented reason in an exasperated search for order.

Expressionism in Germany, on the other hand, led to everything except expression. It led to nothing in painting, it resulted in no poetry save the poetry of effervescence. The German expressionist poets allowed their inspiration to turn to mere babbling; they yielded to a naïve iconoclastic fury; they reached a paroxysm without inventing the corresponding esthetic. Dadaism was merely one of the pits into which they fell, one aspect of the religion of extremes which drove them to seek the maximum of freedom in the maximum of absurdity. What they had really done was merely to exchange one automatism for another. For the mechanism of the social ego, the objective ego, they merely substituted the mechanism of the instinctive ego, the subjective ego. The individualism that was to rise again was so far only the individualism of a group, a crowd within a crowd, the statement "*Wir sind*" rather than the statement "*I am*." From some points of view it resembled the subjectivity of the romanticists seeking escape in the infinite. But the mists of expressionism were neither tepid nor languid; expressionism differed from romanticism in that it was a high-temperature phenomenon.

The natural result was a return to dispassionate order which concurred with the restoration of political order. When the mass exaltation fell, the flood of lyric effusions ceased. Illuminism was followed by a new realism. The visionaries who had believed in a magic metamorphosis awoke from their dream. They had to rid themselves of the illusion that harmony could be born spontaneously out of chaos. They no longer assigned an apocalyptic character to the convulsion through which Germany had passed. That convulsion came to seem after all merely human. The transition to the order of the future required something more than religious impetuosity; realities had to be dealt with once more.

The revolution had indeed changed the relations between things, but it had not annihilated the things themselves, nor created others in their place; it had been merely the bringing about of a condition in which resurrection could begin. Before that resurrection could actually take place, men must still their sensibilities, see the world clearly rather than fanatically, call upon their naked intelligence—and for the time being forget themselves. The ego which had exuded into a disordered universe and been buffeted again and again was now astonished at the resistance it had encountered and cut off all communication with that universe, withdrew within itself, prepared itself for knowledge.

This movement from a state of ecstasy to a state of knowledge is what was called "*die neue Sachlichkeit.*" Eyes newly opened saw the objective world again. Not that the objective world was to be returned to the high place it held before the War, with the thinking ego subordinated to it; it was merely that the thinking ego, having broken with determinism, nevertheless realized that in spite of all kinds of revolution the external world still existed. Before one can take a sovereign attitude toward it one must observe it coldly. "*Die neue Sachlichkeit,*" like expressionism, was a question of temperature. The spirit seeks to possess itself with complete sang-froid rather than merely to achieve an objectivity which, in spite of the addition of the word "new," has unfortunate connotations of reaction.

But the achievement of that sang-froid is no easy matter. The only really effective writers were those who had kept their heads even during the expressionist crisis. On the one hand they proceeded to a critical examination of false values—values which, thanks to inertia or clever camouflage, had remained current ever since Hohenzollern days, as well as those values of the revolutionary period which contained very much of the sentimental and very little of the intellectual. On the other hand they attempted to choose among the things of the objective world, to examine and weigh the realities of a Europe, an America, an Asia whose sudden development was gradually coming to seem the greatest of revolutions. Before the possible connection between various astonishing facts could be comprehended, before laws could be formulated and an Utopia and an idealism be set up, the facts themselves had to be grasped. To throw oneself into this task became a feat of intellectual gymnastics. It cost men of no more than thirty or forty the tremendous effort required, when one thinks one knows, to *umlernen*, unlearn, abandon one's point of view in order to learn all over again. The true grace entered only into the younger writers, who were born with a detachment which permitted a complete spiritual reconstruction.

It is only in Werfel's work that the contradictory tendencies of expressionism are fully represented. Werfel is the poet of the expressionist crisis; his inspiration was born of that crisis and is co-terminous with it. The writers whose names appear beside his in the manifestos of the time belong for the most part to the two preceding decades, and they moved through the expressionist revolution in an unfaltering line.

Gottfried Benn,* the most robust of the group, was never caught by the sentimentality which was reborn in revolutionary form. His hard, compact lyricism arises from a type of thinking which has not yielded to emotion; his temperament is much like that of Hebbel, whom he equals in arrogance when with plastic gesture he sets his personality against the world. Compared with the handful of poems which Benn published, the collections of Else Lasker-Schüler's verse seem devoid of humanity, jewels glittering with a chill fire in the sarcophagus of some Theban queen.

Alfred Mombert,† the only imaginative poet of expressionism, seemed to the younger writers like a distant volcano with which their own subterranean fire had no connection. Twenty years before them he had hit upon a lyricism of the incoherent through the cosmic wanderings of a strange fantasy. But he remains in the regions

---

* GOTTFRIED BENN (1886–   ). For bibliography see p. 282.
† ALFRED MOMBERT (1877–   ). For bibliography see p. 313.

of phantasmagoria; he lacks the passion which led a William Blake to attack the problems of Heaven and Hell. His images of chaos and genesis fall scattered and dead to earth like burned-out fireworks; nothing remains but an hallucination of the eye.

Jakob Haringer sang childishly of his distress with all the naïveté of a Verlaine, but it was the song of a minor Verlaine. The death at the front of Georg Trakl, August Stramm, and especially the Alsatian, Ernst Stadler, deprived the new-born lyricism of three poets who had not yet had time to give full indication of their ability. Ivan Goll, following along behind the revolution, apparently decided that French forms were the best, or at least took Rilke as an example and sought in both French and German a parallel manifestation of his talent. Alfred Wolfenstein and Paul Zech have written verse full of fine feeling; but they serve to give one more example of the fact that enthusiasm is not a state in which art can be produced, but merely the prerequisite of creation.

Franz Werfel* is not the kind of writer who sets new currents in motion. He merely had sufficiently delicate antennæ to sense fresh paths of inspiration and to see coherence in their chaos. What was radical in the expressionist movement, either of the sensibilities or of the intellect, he avoided. He conceived of the revolution as an evolution moving forward in a temperate atmosphere in which even opposing inspirations ended by following a law of alternation; order was established and creation became possible.

Werfel's relation to expressionism was very similar to Hauptmann's relation to naturalism and Hofmannsthal's

---

* FRANZ WERFEL (1890–   ). See p. 322 for bibliography.

relation to symbolism. Each was a poet of sufficiently feminine nature to absorb disparate tendencies, and each was sufficiently talented to have them polarize within him. And with Hofmannsthal, Werfel has other things in common. Like the Austrian poet, he had something of the boy prodigy about him. He was astounding the public with his virtuosity at twenty; as he approached forty it began to seem as if he was marking time. Werfel also shared with Hofmannsthal that refined sense of enjoyment which is equally possible in Vienna and in Prague; the gift of "*Einfühlung*," or the ability to throw off one's own personality and enter into the skin of the character one is creating; and a musicality of language. But Werfel uses these talents differently. His imagination, his desire, caress the world; but whereas for Hofmannsthal the world was the world of things, with which the living being tends to identify itself, Werfel seeks the world of living beings themselves. And in Werfel's view to be is not to conform, to receive the impress of the forms of civilization. He introduced a revolutionary note into Goethe's phrase: "This heritage from which you cannot escape—*kill it* in order that you may possess it." The beings to whom his tenderness goes forth recall Hauptmann's characters, suffering because they have not been fully born; but that affection is no longer on the social plane, as it was with the naturalists; it extends not to a class but to all humanity. In *Wir sind* the protesting ego is neither German nor proletarian; in *Einander* it demands not a right but a gift, a gift of the self to the self, a request which was not without eloquence in 1915 when these poems were written.

Motifs which might have been considered hackneyed seem in Werfel fresh again. The theme of pity, for example, seemed doomed to banality after Hauptmann's *Die Weber*, just as Hofmannsthal seemed to have doomed the theme of the human soul flowing like music among things and creatures, brushing lightly against the sorrows and joys of the universe. Werfel, however, restores their emotional power by praying his God for the humility that changes us into two pleading hands, into a voice which rises like a song of love, into feet moving through a thousand streets to meet souls that slip away each night "like leaves in an autumn of dreams"—to be "all slumber, tear, shelter, kiss, community, childhood, and maternity . . . wing and messenger; to know nothing of oneself, and in the morning to awake with the dew of Heaven on one's hair."

Such humble Franciscan pleas were replaced by violence in *Der Gerichtstag* (1916–1917). Between the dead heavens and the deadly earth, above the folly of carnage, Werfel evoked the image of a skylark, life contracted to a point in space, a point in which lying becomes impossible: "Thou livest only the things of thine own life—to soar, to sing, to be what thou art."

An inspiration which took its tone so easily from events was now and again capable, with its religious accent, of producing beautifully musical verse. But if Werfel had not possessed a controlling intelligence which permitted him safely to feel out all his emotions, he would have produced mere journalistic lyricism and would never have risen above the level of the sentimental writing which the War particularly encouraged. Abandonment to the emotions, however, is with Werfel a game played by an expert. The recurring theme in his work, the theme which gives it its breadth and its unity, is not sentimental but intellectual; it results in poetry, but it springs from a psychology, the psychology of the thwarted ego. Werfel conceives that ego as thwarted not merely by the things of objective reality—this would be no more than neo-romanticism—but also by another ego which muddies and soils its initial purity. "Father, I have an enemy who sits at my table and fills himself with my food. . . . Why, Father, hast Thou created me with this enemy within me, why hast Thou caused me to be born thus double and divided?"

Is this perhaps a Faustian duality of soul? Indeed Werfel has used the Goethean motif. In the magic trilogy *Der Spiegelmensch*, in which Thamal turns his dangerous double loose upon the world, Werfel has imitated and almost parodied Goethe, dissociated the personality of Faust, not by creating a new character but by simply breathing life into the self-indulgent image which grimaces at Thamal when he looks at himself in his mirror. Thamal's own ego is merely a witness, an accomplice struggling against complicity, recalling the ego of the impressionists invaded by sensation; it differs from this latter, however, in its will to defend itself against invasion, its will to self-possession. It feels itself possessed by another, and the drama lies in its struggle to possess itself again.

At first this drama seemed to Werfel the drama of his own generation. In his novel *Nicht der Mörder, der Ermordete ist schuldig*, the parricide's gesture is the gesture of youth repressed by the Hohenzollern machine. This younger generation had to rid itself of its fathers by a symbolic murder, just as its fathers had attacked the generation before 1870. Freudian influences, which have clearly had their effect upon Werfel, make the deliverance seem like an explosion of repressed feelings rather than a premeditated combat. The revolt takes place in a sort of second state of consciousness, like that of the younger son whose martinet father takes him to the fair, makes him watch a bloody combat, forces him to a trial of strength and military dexterity; whereupon the boy, without knowing why, hurls the missile in his hand at his own father's head. The unconscious bursts the bonds of custom, although youth never achieves a realization of what it is doing.

"*Wir sind*" was but a hesitant lisp, the cry of a personality which had become differentiated from its enemy, present society, but which still felt collectively. Afterward Werfel set out to extract a few great individual figures from that collectivity. He made Verdi the hero of a novel; Maximilian, Emperor of Mexico, the hero of an historical drama; the Apostle Paul, the hero of a play. The originality of these characters is in their uneasiness; the sympathy we feel for them arises from their struggle to be wholly themselves, to overcome the opposition of fate. They are porous in the extreme; they are not merely invaded by the enemy ego, they are inhabited by it, haunted by it; they feel hatred and love for it at one and the same time; it is not to be exorcised until their hatred is entirely changed to love, and the approach of death brings about a transfiguration. Verdi, obsessed by the thought of Wagner, is for some years unable to compose a line. He has never met his rival, he keeps a score of *Tristan* in a drawer unread; but that rival haunts his nights and his days, prevents him by some baleful magic from writing a note. At last Verdi comes to Venice to face his adversary. But on the very day on which he finally goes to call upon him, having at last mastered his hatred, Wagner dies. Love triumphing with the aid of death restores Verdi's inspiration, and the result is the composition of *Othello*. Maximilian, at the height of his struggle with Juarez, has learned to love his enemy, and goes to his death in an ecstasy of freedom won through sacrifice of self and assent to the triumph of the opposing force. Saul, persecuting the Christians, throws off his old personality when his ego is invaded by Christ and becomes Paul, haunted by the God whose word he spreads abroad.

In each of these works, the problem of a civilization whose intellectual, moral, and religious aspects are in process of change is superimposed upon the individual and psychological problem. Wagner blocking Verdi's career is German music overthrowing Italian music; two esthetic systems oppose each other, and beyond them are two ways of looking at the world, at life, and at man. This novel likewise gives Werfel occasion to criticize the tendency to escape from reality at the risk of compromising the artistic creation which is impossible without it, and also to point out the limitations of the Mediterranean mind, which is too deliberately closed to romanticism and sees in it only the abyss of madness. *Juarez und Maximilian* states the problem of a political revolution destroying a princely power which the prince himself feels is a delusion and whose destruction he hence welcomes. *Paulus unter den Juden* is the drama of civilization, of the Jewish religion resisting the wind of Christianity, but resisting it like a tree from which that wind strips and scatters seeds as well as leaves.

Werfel does not turn these problems into set theses. Indeed what interests us is the very mobility of the mind which states them, the ingenious change of perspective, the shift of assumptions from one chapter, one scene to the next. It is a mobility which gives us all the pleasures of the chase, but the game always escapes. Werfel never succeeds in giving a sufficiently broad development to any one character so that we are really overpowered by it; instead of a novel or a play, we are left with a series of kaleidoscopic scenes.

Werfel's art is fragmentary, like his personality. His critical lucidity is so great that he detaches himself from his subject at the very moment when he is getting closest to it. He is a Freudian, but he does not hesitate to exercise his irony upon Freudianism; he is a revolutionary, but he points out the pettiness of revolutions. He is a poet of religiosity, he wavers between pure poetry, sensualism, and the Jewish religious tradition; yet he remains without religion. He is touched with messianism, yet he is too intelligent and his intelligence is too acid to permit him to achieve true evangelic love. He is highly cultivated, but the cerebral nature of his culture prevents him from throwing himself wholly into his outbursts. He controls them, directs them, and although unlike the merely emotional expressionists, who are satisfied with a lyric wail, he finds a mode of true artistic expression for them, it is a restricted art in which the full expression of his inspiration is blocked.

That full expression is only to be had through musicality. Werfel's best work so far is in those of his poems in which inspiration and expression join in a perfect musicality. In his lyric writing the author of *Spiegelmensch* tends, like Hofmannsthal, to fall into opera. The desire for polyphonic expression felt by a brilliantly differentiated individual is stronger in Werfel than the desire for harmony between the profound elements of the being. His poetry, which is admittedly arresting, usually depends upon chiaroscuro effects, with no great strength of either light or shadow. The result is musical, but really belongs to the graphic arts; the whites are suggested in the blacks, and both blacks and whites are so delicately handled that the result gives the impression of a mind remarkable for its versatility rather than for its power. It touches upon a mass of mysterious and living things, preserves their mystery and their life, but never carries that life to a higher plane.

Werfel has one advantage over the other writers of his generation: he has genuine literary talent. Although there are shadowed places, vague effects, he nevertheless has the ability to clarify contours and actually render what others can merely suggest. His poems, his plays, his novels, are filled with successful passages, fragments of melody, well-drawn details, scenes in which electric tension gathers and is discharged. The martyred and rebellious younger son; the prodigal Thamal playing at Faust; Verdi in quest of Verdi; Juarez never appearing on the stage but hovering always over Maximilian of Austria; the Apostle Paul rising up from an overthrown Judaism; even the episodic characters, personalities barely sketched out like those in *Bocksgesang*, are really quarried out of formlessness. Werfel is not, like many revolutionaries, direct and gross; he does not limit himself to the elementary opposition between an ego seeking to magnify itself and a society which it must overthrow. He can speak of himself and his generation without abusing "I" and "we"; he creates characters in which "I" and "we" are reflected according to a carefully planned angle of incidence. But the ego which he rediscovered for his generation is dispersed in iridescent drops; the light passing through them makes a rainbow, but no view has been opened upon the sky.

Sometimes his work includes an element of Claudelian religiosity which indicates a desire to be conquered rather than to conquer. That religiosity contains only the intelligence and the sensibility of a Proteus inspired by his own metamorphoses; Prometheus is kept without the door. One cry in *Die Versuchung* reveals a distress common to many men of Werfel's age: Werfel prays for a verity that shall be his own, "a character," the power to make his way through the forest of the unconscious, to find a familiar path, by thinking out his thought to the end and nevertheless at the same time permitting a profuse sensibility to burst forth in every direction. This is an admission of powerlessness to proceed by a process of selection, to develop other than a hybrid personality—

a powerlessness which is perhaps the impotence of our age to dominate the ideas and the feelings that trouble us, to invent a psychology, a morality, an art, other than the psychology, the morality, and the art of uneasiness.

Ridding oneself of impurity through confession or death, and making death the supreme moment of life, is a lazy solution in contrast to Goethe, who counseled us to live immediately, now, with no necessity of seeking the maximum intensity of life and desire in the maximum of deprivation. "Deliver me, purify me, O my Father, drown this enemy, kill me, kill this me!"—this is the prayer that is always dear to souls who have yet to find themselves. They deny that they are subject to a materialistic fatality, but they still call upon fate, without sufficiently realizing that fate is an inner thing, something in their own power to sway. If they look within themselves at all, they see only the demons that Saul saw, the serpents that appeared to Thamal in the cave.

This happens even where there is no Freudian influence. Psychoanalysis, indeed, is only one expression of a general European curiosity. Wedekind, Strindberg, Dostoievski merely sharpened the public's appetite for searching into the obscure. And the explanation of the return to the primitive does not lie in a specifically German reaction against the hyper-organization of industrialism and militarism. The forms in which the conscious had nominally been contained had simply grown rotten, and from one end of Europe to the other the unconscious was freed. National civilizations, bourgeois in every case, had no opposition to offer to the thrust of instinct save decadent religions, decadent moral and esthetic systems. Nietzsche had an open field. But the writers who followed him, incapable of feeling his urge to reconstruct, dallied behind at the stage of mere dissociation. They tended to take the part for the whole, and the anomaly which admittedly exists in nature for nature itself and nature's law. It was easier to explore the depths and pronounce them deep than it was to attempt to raise oneself from the abyss. Even honest writers were caught in this trap, and their naïveté led them to assign an absolute value to mere pathological curiosities.

Werfel, however, was never caught. His Stanya in *Bocksgesang* is for Werfel a creature of the imagination and no more; she sees, in terms of the same sensual mysticism, the peasant to whom she betrothed herself, the revolutionary student to whom she gave her passionate devotion, and the abortive child with the goat's head which her body conceived.

But the mental disturbance, the dualism with which Werfel was struggling, finally came to seem intolerable to him. And the only solution he could find was the conversion foreshadowed in *Paulus unter den Juden*. What he renounced, however, was not so much the world, in the religious sense of the phrase, as the human intelligence which presumes to guide the world, that "damned intelligence" with which Engländer, the decadent Jew in *Barbara oder die Frömmigkeit*, expresses his disgust. In short, Werfel has yielded to the romantic weariness of those who pass the responsibility for the universe over to God—a weariness which is to be seen in his own writing. *Der Abiturientag* is valuable only as a document bearing upon adolescent pathology. *Barbara*, the long novel in which the motifs of the novels of the War and post-War period are revived, is clear evidence of a mind which has given up the struggle, a manifest renunciation of originality. The problematic aspect of life yields to the certainty of a pious mind—a mind whose piety is unfortunately so artificial that we cannot but prefer the old dramas of troubled religious emotion.

In *Knaben und Mörder* and *Die Verstümmelten*, Hermann Ungar* takes pathological curiosities seriously. His stories of adolescents seeking the dual pleasure of inflicting and undergoing humiliation, his astonishing little human dramas written with the brilliance of a gifted observer, would provide a novelist with precious documents on sadism and masochism. But Ungar is not himself that novelist; he deals with miserable creatures and leaves them just as miserable as they were created; he has not, like Dostoievski and Gide and Kafka, discovered the secret channels through which the strange communicates with the human. To reconstruct a psychology after one has explored pathology; to invent a new morality after a revolutionary amoralist movement; to develop a great art from a chaos of esthetic systems: that requires genius.

Wherever that new esthetic may appear, it seems certain that it will be applicable to all Europe. The movement which is leading up to it is in no instance local in character; it has not arisen in response to the specific and immediate needs of a particular society, nor to the temperament of any one people, whether Germanic, Celtic, Slav, or Latin. It has been called unanimism, dadaism, surréalisme, or expressionism according to the place and the moment the name has been given; but everywhere it is the same—a revolt against tradition, a passion for freedom—without one's ever being able to localize its beginnings or to speak of either the influence of one literature upon another or the supremacy of one literature over another. The revolutionaries had, of course, spiritual fathers: Nietzsche, Dostoievski. But even before these two, titanism and demonism had been reintroduced by Goethe, Blake, Stendhal. The struggle

---

* HERMANN UNGAR (1893–1929), *Knaben und Mörder*, 1920; *Die Verstümmelten*, 1922; *Die Klasse*, 1927.

between spirit and flesh, God and the devil, simply continued through Strindberg, Wedekind, the modern French writers, Wilde, and Joyce. Stendhal, Rimbaud, Baudelaire, and Gide, for instance, may have served as a stimulus to the Germans, but it is not as if they had given the initial impetus to a new movement in an inert mass. They merely assisted in the release of a dynamism which as early as Nietzsche had already escaped the bounds of Germany.

The rest was accomplished by the brutal reëstablishment of contact brought about by the War, which was followed by a rebirth of the spirit of literary cosmopolitanism that has been essential to every great period. The same themes were taken up simultaneously by writers all over Europe: the return to the human personality; the revolt against the mechanization of bourgeois societies; the explosion of primitive sensuality; the renunciation of fathers, of teachers, of fixed standards; the amoralism, escapes, adventures, and worries of adolescence; the eroticism of puberty; sexual disquiet, sign of a disquiet in every instinct, in every part of the consciousness of European man. When P. J. Jouve wrote *Vous êtes des hommes* and Jules Romains wrote *Europe*, when Romain Rolland and after him Duhamel became popular, the new literature which arose in Germany around variations of the theme *Mensch*, *Freund*, *Bruder* was in no way indebted to their work. It was simply a parallel development, or, better, a development which grew from the same swelling subterranean forces.

Those swelling forces were sufficiently spontaneous and sufficiently general so that what might have remained merely a literary theme actually gained wide public acceptance. Side by side with distinguished innovators like Werfel appeared popularizers like Leonhard

Frank* who achieved his first success with *Der Mensch ist gut*. Frank did not limit himself to the theme of humanitarian denunciation of the war spirit; in his novels he used all the current stencils: children running away from their families and organizing themselves into a band of brigands in Würzburg; a student whose repressed hatreds explode in the assassination of the teacher who ragged him in his youth; the comic adventures of a group of former brigands of Würzburg turned bourgeois and then thrust outside the bourgeois system by post-War conditions; the sensuality of first love; the sporting spirit of youth. All these he handled strikingly, appealing both to the indestructible reservoirs of sentimentality in the mass public and to that public's never-sated appetite for new objects for that sentimentality. The novel that he writes according to these formulas is clean-cut, quick, alive, but absolutely without promise for the future.

Out of expressionism, and rising above it, there appeared a double current—religious and historical—which responded to a vague desire to react against the spirit of dissociation, to return to fully composed characters—people in whose unity one could believe; heroes who, like Brod's Tycho Brahe and Rëubeni, could be set up as examples to those who were seeking to integrate their own personalities; prophets who gave hope of a resurrection of the divine. In addition to such solid works as Gundolf's *Goethe, George*, and *Caesar*, Bertram's *Nietzsche*, Vallentin's *Napoleon*, Kantorowicz's *Friedrich II*, the public was fed a great quantity of fictionalized biographies after the French manner like those of Emil Ludwig, in which Goethe, Bismarck, and William II were served up with an up-to-the-minute sauce that smelled of the cook's fingers. The exigencies of the book trade of course are not completely foreign to such

* LEONHARD FRANK (1882–   ). See p. 296 for complete bibliography.

writing; but after all it does represent a response to a desire for knowledge on the part of the public—a large part of which would perhaps be better pleased with something not so cheap.

After Kafka's *Der Prozess* and *Das Schloss*, Döblin's *Manas*, and Werfel's *Paulus*, with Thomas Mann's new novel *Joseph und seine Brüder* a sincere and semi-mystic yearning for the past begins to appear. Ernst Weiss[*] in 1924 had sketched an adolescent *Daniel* who did not weep for a lost Jerusalem, who broke away from his mother and his people, who prepared himself, not to confess the faith that was gone, but to live, to carry the message of the faith that was to come. Weiss is a versatile and gifted writer; with bold fantasy and a disconcerting taste for the hybrid, he wrote first, in *Tiere in Ketten*, a novel about a woman that was a hymn to animality, then, in *Nahar*, a novel about a tigress that was a hymn to femininity. He returned to more normal subjects when, taking Balzac as his central figure, he wrote *Männer in der Nacht*. The episodes are lively, but they are too close to newspaper scandal-sheet style; and Weiss's talent as a portraitist does not match his admiration for the great author of the *Comédie Humaine*, in whom other Germans have pointed out elements of metaphysical grandeur which, in spite of their importance, even the French have tended to overlook. Wassermann, who was also an admirer of Balzac, escaped the perils of fictionalized biography in *Der Aufruhr um den Junker Ernst*, just as he had in *Caspar Hauser*, by writing always in an atmosphere of legend.

Alfred Neumann,[†] who, without approaching the stylization of C. F. Meyer's *Der Heilige*, revived in *Der Teufel* the character of Oliver le Daim, won his success

[*] Ernst Weiss (1884–   ). See p. 322 for bibliography.
[†] Alfred Neumann (1895–   ). For bibliography see p. 314.

synthesize is no longer a national being, a function of geography and local history; it is man, man of all times and all places, man with divergent aspirations whose unity must be rediscovered. It is therefore not surprising that their search takes them as far back as Jesus and Confucius, as far afield as Asia and Palestine. They are moved by the feeling that there has always been a secret unity in divided humanity, and that though there is division into sects, there is unity in religiosity of desire.

Examples like that of Fritz von Unruh* indicate the speed with which complete changes of point of view, if not changes of mental make-up, can take place. Just before the War the author of *Offiziere* and *Prinz Louis Ferdinand* was body and soul a guardsman. He had achieved certainty through a military and Frederician philosophy, tinctured with mysticism. The battle of Verdun transformed that certainty into a certainty of a very different nature, in which humanity took the place of Prussianism and Goethe was the directing force. Fritz von Unruh changed from one emotional inspiration to another. Where Werfel had too much intellect and too little naïveté, Unruh had the reverse; his naïveté is absolutely complete. When he wrote three hundred pages of *Flügel der Nike* on the basis of an abandonment to the sensations of a week in Paris, he had not the slightest idea that what he wrote might shock the public. He is an enthusiast who holds the delirium of his fantasy sacred and listens only to the divinity which has chosen to dwell within him. He is neither intellectual nor artist nor, in spite of this, a man of action—at least he conceives of action only through eloquence. *Opfergang*, indeed, had its own special eloquence, despite its borrowings from Shakespearian rhetoric—the eloquence of the conversion of a Prussian officer and professional soldier

* FRITZ VON UNRUH (1885–   ). See p. 321 for bibliography.

who in the midst of the battle of Verdun sees destroyed
in his mind the logic of the battle and with it the whole
Prussian system. In that book phantom characters
served to emphasize the tragedy of a situation in which
the living are merely shadows of the living.

Unfortunately in succeeding plays this depersonaliza-
tion is carried even further. Unruh feeds entirely upon
himself. His mouthpieces are pure abstractions. It is
true that Goethe used symbolic figures at the end of the
second *Faust;* but "*Sorge*" and "*Schuld*" and "*Not*"
had drunk of Goethe's blood for half a century and been
given life; whereas in Unruh's *Ein Geschlecht* "Mother"
and "Daughter" and "Son" represent merely a sudden
conflict of ill-organized ideas and feelings common to
the opposition elements of the younger generation. Unruh
contributes nothing in the way of personality to revolution and fraternization save a touch of feminine receptivity. The pathos of his plays might have been like
Kleist's but it remained merely that of an impulsive age.
A different age might have produced a different Unruh.

Was this because the demands of the theatre tend to
attenuate the emotions? German writers were slow to
publish recollections of the War. The journal of Bernhard
von der Marwitz did not appear until 1924, the recollections of Rudolf G. Binding* (*Aus dem Kriege*) not until
1925. In the latter, as in *Erlebtes Leben* and *Rufe und
Reden*, a well-connected soldier, as closely bound to the
old régime as he was to his squadron, writing with a
critical detachment in strong contrast to Unruh's excited
manner, enters frankly into an examination of the forces
working upon his milieu and expresses the aristocratic
regret that he let himself be out-distanced by a revolution
which he should have helped to make rather than merely
have submitted to.

* RUDOLF G. BINDING (1867–   ). See p. 286 for bibliography.

Hans Carossa* in his *Rumänisches Tagebuch* gave a too little known example of how a well-born soul can accept a war into which the body is drawn willy-nilly, and in spite of everything draw from it a serenity reminiscent of Goethe in the campaign against the French. Later Arnold Zweig with *Der Streit um den Sergeanten Grischa* (1927) and Georg von der Vring with *Soldat Suhren* (1927) presented in fictional form documents bearing upon the psychology of the German soldier, which was a great deal more complex and was evolving much more rapidly than news from the enemy camp led one to infer at the time.

When Siegfried Kracauer, with the talent of a Jules Renard, wrote *Ginster* in 1928, maintaining his anonymity because of the boldness of his conception, it was the first time an ex-combatant dared to take a jeering attitude toward the whole military system, which until then had been attacked only with high seriousness. This humorous approach to such a subject is a clearer indication of the change of viewpoint which had taken place since Beyerlein's *Jena oder Sedan* than almost anything else could be.

It was *Im Westen nichts Neues* that let loose in 1928 the flood of war novels. Its sudden and world-wide success had little to do with the author's literary ability; indeed it was perhaps precisely because Erich Maria Remarque presented only a normal, average picture of the War that he appealed to the great average of the men who had fought in it. No matter what their nationality, they found stated in that novel their common wretchedness, and, so to speak, a common measure of the heart of man faced by events which he cannot understand.

* For bibliographies of CAROSSA, ARNOLD ZWEIG, VRING, and REMARQUE, see pp. 291, 324, 322, and 316 respectively.

Usually the novels* fall into two categories. Those in the first category (Renn's *Krieg*, Johannsen's *Vier von der Infanterie*, Plivier's *Des Kaisers Kulis*) express a persistent hatred for the horrible things into which the troops were forced. Those in the second category (of which the best example is perhaps Ernst Jünger's *In Stahlgewittern*) are dominated by the desire to redeem war as an opportunity for the individual to surpass himself and as a school for nobility through sacrifice.

At the same time still younger writers, the non-combatants, those born around 1900, were painting their own picture of the War. Most of them, like the characters in Glaeser's *Jahrgang 1902*, looked upon what they had seen and remembered as monstrous. At an age when one ordinarily takes a trusting view of life, they were drawn into the maelstrom; they came out shocked and without illusions about their parents. Ernst Glaeser has cleverly chosen his young spokesmen from among various classes of society, and has distributed sets of feelings among them in such a way that their sum is a very fair statement of the emotional reactions of his generation. He is a splendid observer, lively of mind, humorous with a touch of irony; he not only painted a picture which clearly recalled the past, but he also gave his own generation an opportunity to forswear through him the beliefs of the generation preceding. In this they have succeeded little better than their elders; and whether we watch Renn writing *Nachkrieg* or Glaeser writing *Frieden*, we cannot avoid the conclusion that no matter how hard their authors try, these post-War novels give clear evidence of an inability to recreate order out of chaos.

The literature born of the shock of the War might well be called a literature of conversion. It has its

* For bibliographies of RENN, JOHANNSEN, GLAESER, and JÜNGER, see pp. 316, 303, 297, and 303 respectively.

romanticism, which is reminiscent of the romanticism of a Schlegel, a Wackenroder, a Stolberg, in so far as the nature of its effusions is concerned; but it differs in the object which provokes them. Political faith has now taken precedence over religious faith. In France the shock of the War tended to drive the intellectuals toward the Right in search of security; in Germany, on the contrary, a large number of the converted were drawn to the Left. They felt no animosity toward the Church; they simply ignored the Church. Their religiosity was sufficiently fed by the idea of peace and evangelic love reigning among the peoples, and particularly between France and Germany; and this served them as sufficient prop.

Their conversion is important chiefly because it is a partial conversion of the German will. The elder romanticists wanted to be German before anything else, and felt themselves the more so as the opposition between France and Germany became more clearly defined; this newer generation, on the contrary, had in common with French writers of their own age not only a will to rapprochement but now a democratic mysticism *à la* Duhamel and Jules Romains, now a bourgeois mysticism *à la* Drieu la Rochelle and Alfred Fabre-Luce, now a European mysticism containing various elements. The novelty of this political religiosity is its European character; its weakness derives from the confusion of its aims and its intellectual insufficiencies. Europe must be reborn from something more than ecstasies and ingenuity. It is intelligence that brings about revolutions; sensibility alone is capable only of reactions whose direction it cannot control.

Unruh's case is typical of that of a number of representatives of the old order for whom the revolution consisted merely of rotation around an axis that remained fixed. Others, like Ernst Toller,* went further, denying the importance of national feeling and even the idea of nationality. But their change of perspective is limited to this plane; elsewhere their conceptions are pre-War conceptions. Their inspiration is social, and differs from Dehmel's or the early Hauptmann's only by a sort of bolshevism, a shudder resulting from cruel experiences undergone. Toller's works were partly written in prison, where he was placed first as a conscientious objector, then for having taken part with Kurt Eisner in the Bavarian revolution. A play like *Die Wandlung* is no more than a succession of complaints, though it admittedly has the ring of authentic experience. In the Toller plays which followed—*Masse Mensch* and *Hinkemann*—the characters, like those of Unruh and Bronnen, never rise above the schematic; their importance lies not in what they are or what they do, but in what they say; their speech itself is far from realistic or natural; but they are interesting because without ever achieving a higher realism they are nevertheless above realism. Toller's art—and in this he adapts himself to the demands of the theatre, which gains its effects from magnification—lies not in rendering moral nuances, but rather in a choice of dramatic situations which catch the interest of the public either because they reproduce recognizable experience, like that of the soldier fighting for a nationalism that he has renounced, or because they are unusual, like that of the disabled hero coming back to his wife without his virility.

Toller differs from Unruh in that he has a strong sense of theatre, a vein of lyricism which comes out like a song in *Schwalben*, and a sense of humor. The peasant Pickel, who in *Hoppla, wir leben* finds himself changed overnight from subject into citizen, is not merely droll in his

* ERNST TOLLER (1893–   ). See p. 320 for bibliography.

exercise of unexpected prerogatives. He represents the embryo of a new psychology and a new sociology, as does the revolutionary Karl Thomas in *Hinkemann*. Thomas might have been merely the tribune of the people declaiming against a society in which revolutions are turned to the advantage of profiteers; but because of the conflict in his own mind between the group he is attacking and the group he is fighting for, he becomes a truly dramatic figure. He does not believe in the latter; he realizes that neither the group nor the individuals in it are worthy of his ideology; and Toller does not hesitate to ridicule that ideology itself.

The result of all this is that these thesis plays escape the banality of their type because the thesis is divided, and sometimes even divided against itself. In Toller's work there is more than passive feeling. The intelligence makes a choice, and the personality of the leader begins to distinguish itself from that of the group. Toller, like Heinrich Mann in *Geist und Tat*, believes in mind in action, the individual placed at the service of the social structure. There is a certain heroism in this alliance of voluntary servitude with a great demand for liberty. It is doubtful whether German art benefited from it as much as did the German Republic, but it is interesting to see political questions consciously taken up on the stage. Toller's plays, Büchner's *Danton*, Heinrich Mann's *Madame Legros* and *Der Weg zur Macht*, Jean-Richard Bloch's *Le dernier Empereur*, the dramatization for Piscator of *Rasputin* and the adventures of the good Czech soldier Schweik, the drama of German conscripts sold like cattle by a prince in the time of Frederick II (Bruno Frank's *Zwölftausend*), the tragedy of the people become rulers and driving out their king (A. E. Rutra's *Der Kronprinz*)—all these supplied material to stimulate the thoughts of a public still serving its apprenticeship at government and ready to accept the political education, which it lacks, from whatever source it can.

Toller has allowed his plays to be put on with a cinematic technique, with Piscator settings. The text is no more than a scenario; it becomes merely a pretext for invention on the part of the director, who no longer conceives of the screen as merely a projection of the stage in which more background is possible, but as a means of developing the author's creative idea with the assistance of cinema technique and without the author's text. This represents no revolution in the esthetics of the drama. It is rather the sudden evolution of an esthetic which already existed and is now being developed within the limits of strictly German tradition.

Served by a new technique, there appears anew the old German tendency to overflow the classical unities, to refuse to be bound by time or place, to reunite the action of the play with the space and the time from which the author had arbitrarily cut it, to suggest and to depict, through the new cinematographic means, the thousand images which mere words cannot suggest, to create around the play an atmosphere that gives the illusion of all life. Max Reinhardt, by the multiplication of material means, by the use of the revolving stage and elaborate lighting effects, has given the stage setting a disproportionate importance which leads to the conclusion that the director's art is at its apogee when the importance of the author's art is least. Directors in the time of the Duke of Meiningen concentrated on faithfulness to the text. They attempted to give a play its proper atmosphere; they provided local color; but the setting was always restrained to the service of the text. With Reinhardt, whose conceptions are the opposite of those of Jacques Copeau, it is less a question of serving the text than of making one's own use of the text.

Piscator goes one step further. He does not merely attempt vast syntheses—evoking behind the revolutionary Karl Thomas the revolution in the streets, behind the German revolution the Russian revolution, behind the revolutions of the present the revolutions of the past, behind all revolution war, motion pictures of the trenches, and on the same level with them the profiteers at work, the playboys in the night clubs. Influenced by Meyerhold, the Russian, he renounces the theatre for its own sake, converts the theatre into a powerful weapon of propaganda, turns upon the audience a machine-gun fire of impressions piled one on the other, leaves the spectator defenseless against his arguments. Teachers have more to learn from these new techniques than artists; from the artistic viewpoint the synthesis achieved is superficial, and results merely in a multiplication of sensations. They will not have artistic value until intellectual restraints are restored and the craftsman again becomes master of his tools.

Reinhard Goering in his *Seeschlacht* (1917) gave promise of supplying what this new theatre lacked: profundity of conflict rather than effusion; internal drama rather than tableaux; return to and concentration upon the ego rather than escape and dispersion of the ego; precision and poetry of expression rather than rantings and stammerings. The whole action of the play takes place in a single hour during the battle of the Skagerrack. Seven sailors in the turret of a cruiser are discussing the strange fate that has left them hanging between life and death; and the whole problem of the individual caught in the disintegration of society is stated for us with a breadth that recalls Hebbel. Intoxicated at once with life and with death, man is caught between two destinies: an impersonal destiny hanging over everything like the fate of ancient times; and a moral, individual destiny which is directly opposed to the first but is just as mysterious.

Here is no simple pressure of desire, but two souls within a single individual, one of them saying no to the other and refusing to obey because it is possessed with nameless, indefinable things that are contrary to the order received. The tragedy lies in the presentiment that these nameless opposing things exist, and in the question "Between man and man is the die cast; is no new relationship possible?" The great naval battle continues, the sailors are in revolt in spite of the fact that they obey, obey in spite of the fact that they are in revolt. "I obeyed, didn't I? I fired, didn't I? But I could just as well have refused, couldn't I? We were just better prepared to obey—weren't we just better prepared to obey?" This theme of the soul become the simultaneous prey of abstract fate and its own personal demon, twice victimized and doubly guilty because it can overcome neither the one nor the other influence, is taken up again in *Der Erste, Der Zweite, Scapa Flow,* and *Der Retter* (1918–1919), short dramas of a period thrown into confusion by a strange power.

Arnolt Bronnen,* in his plays as well as in his novel of the films, treats of the petty passions of petty souls exploding in every direction. Action and motivation are commonplace, whether the original impulse which frees the instincts comes from a battle of tanks at Château-Thierry, from the scuffles of the Rhineland rebellion, or from a spree at a seaside resort or in Hollywood. The presentation is invariably such that an atmosphere of storm is created about the characters, but it is always the same storm, finally breaking in a torrent of desires that are never more than bursts of hunger—sudden excitations of the libido of the male who is driven mad at

* ARNOLT BRONNEN (1895–   ). See p. 290 for bibliography.

the sight of a woman, any woman, or of the libido of the woman, whom the presence of a male throws into hysteria.

All this is presented with a juvenility, an ardor, a detachment, and an adroitness which, far from being new, is merely the old light literature of Vienna and Paris with a few touches of the then fashionable sex-hunger motif. The plays wear a jaunty parti-colored dress: sensualism, clever remarks, naturalism, *je m'en fichisme*, political motifs, pathological motifs, motifs borrowed from high tragedy, sketch, vaudeville, and operetta. Bronnen's style is alert, full of clever repartee, using nothing but dialogue. An author with more to say could have made good use of it.

Bertolt Brecht,* who with Bronnen is considered one of the playwrights best representing the newer generation, is much more persuasive and natural. His *Baal* is Wedekind in a new style; but whereas the author of *Lulu* depicted the human animal as naked and free, beautiful in its nakedness and wild liberty, Brecht depicts it as wallowing in the mire of a sorry voluptuousness. Did they not recall the nihilism of the inflation years, his pessimism and his cynicism would be no more effective than night club scenes themselves. Baal and the characters in *Trommeln in der Nacht* are inhumanly human, like Georg Grosz's caricatures; they have the accent of a period of utter demoralization, when nothing mattered save the desperate desire to go on living in spite of everything and the pleasure of getting one more thrill out of one's body before plunging to destruction in a lawless world. But they are nevertheless arresting, because of a sort of pan-animalism which is less literary than that of Ernst Weiss, an elementary and authentic sensual power.

* BERTOLT BRECHT (1898–   ). See p. 289 for bibliography.

When he subsequently dramatized the life of Edward II of England, which ended in the Tower, Brecht was trying to fit history to the current fashion. Such combinations cannot serve as a formula for a new drama, any more than could Alexander Lernet-Holenia's* *Österreichische Komödie* or his tragedy *Demetrius*. The cleverness, the grace, the brilliancy of Lernet-Holenia's comedy represent a prolongation of the Austrian tradition, but no more than that; and in the tragedy *Demetrius*, in spite of a seeking after Shakespearian effects and a use of motifs borrowed from psychiatry that recalls Hofmannsthal, Lernet-Holenia's hero, suffering from a malady of the personality, reminds one more of the Russia of the ballets and Rasputin than of the Russia of Dostoievski.

In examining the literary output of the expressionist period as a whole, one regrets that so few books had real literary value. But it would be a mistake to judge them only from that point of view. The importance of the period lies neither in single books nor in their artistic value; it lies in the movement in general, the new movement of the spirit which was awkwardly cropping out in literature. In some respects expressionism seemed to be a process of reviving naturalism, a process of whipping up the naturalist vision of the world until it became, in the words of Kasimir Edschmid,† "a fanatical vision."

But this is only one aspect of impressionism, an aspect to which Edschmid would have been the last to restrict himself. The new intensity was not so much that of a new vision as of a thinking and feeling obviously more revolutionary than that of the first *Sturm und Drang*. The crystallization that had followed the effervescence of

---

* ALEXANDER LERNET-HOLENIA (1897–   ). See p. 308 for bibliography.
† KASIMIR EDSCHMID (1890–   ). For bibliography see p. 292.

the eighteenth century had to be destroyed. Whether that crystallization was called romanticism, bourgeois spirit, nationalism, militarism, capitalism, or Marxism, the new writers attacked it all, attacked the type of humanity which the nineteenth century had produced and the psychology which conceived of that humanity as a final, unchangeable type. They felt themselves carried along on a wave which laughed at national boundaries, which was carrying with it, as Edschmid said as early as 1917, "a whole generation, an entire generation of Europeans," all of whom shared a feeling of complete liberation from preceding generations. Intelligence and sensibility fell in a torrent upon the surface slime of Western civilization and bared the substratum below.

The more gifted of the younger writers early realized that this descent in a torrent would not alone suffice. Edschmid, in the most striking manifestos which expressionism produced (*Über den dichterischen Expressionismus*, 1917, and *Über die dichterische deutsche Jugend*, 1918) stated the need for a *Bindung*, the restraining force which Thomas Mann sought in reason after he had found Frederician discipline wanting, and which alone could make the dynamism of the younger generation effective. Edschmid also stated his faith in the individual genius, but he failed to make clear what was most needed—an explanation of how to undertake a systematic conquest of the personality. Since then, in none of the younger writers has this new personality taken final form, and it might seem that after the movement's period of strength has come its period of weakness. But this is not the case. What has happened is merely that a period of liberating awareness is being followed by a period of creative awareness; and creation presupposes a withdrawal into oneself.

The younger generation never underestimated the need for adding a proportion of intellectualism to serve as an antidote for expressionist "fanaticism." Edschmid, who had one of the most brilliant minds of his literary generation, pointed out the sources from which this intellectual inspiration might come. In France and in Russia, as well as in Germany, he discovered links between the Europe of the present and the Europe of the past, made clear the possibility of an intellectual tradition that could include, in addition to Luther, Goethe, Jean-Paul, Kleist, Hölderlin, and Georg Büchner, such non-Germans as Rabelais, Montaigne, Pascal, Voltaire, Rousseau, Stendhal, Balzac, Tolstoy, Gogol, Pushkin, and Dostoievski. Every element of man is appealed to, since all of man must be changed. The revision of values demanded by Nietzsche was carried on with fine critical vivacity in Edschmid's *Die doppelköpfige Nymphe* and *Das Bücherdekameron*.

Edschmid has been called a journalist, but at least he raised journalism to a level that Heine would have approved. His essays, his newspaper articles, his travel sketches contain a great deal more than brilliant sallies; there is much wisdom in his sane opinions on men and things in the Germany and the Europe of the present day. The very nature of Edschmid's gifts tended to turn him aside from a novelist's career, although the success of *Die sechs Mündungen*, *Das rasende Leben*, and *Timur* was well merited. In their extreme intensity of plot, in their concentration with what would in former days have been a whole novel crowded into a chapter, a chapter into a page, a page into a sentence, and the sentence itself disencumbered of all the hesitant, descriptive, and qualifying elements of the past, these stories represent a type of writing which has seldom been done in Germany, and whose only precedent is in the work of

Heinrich Mann. Like Klabund's stories, they responded to the new rhythm of existence, *"das rasende Leben,"* life lived passionately, frantically.

In the slowly reconstituted German organism this passion, while it had not lessened, had certainly become tempered. And as it had become a more restrained fire, the mind was no longer prisoner, and it was now possible to introduce once more into literary creation the "dispassionate order" which Rudolf Kayser in 1924 called *"die neue Gegenständlichkeit," "die Sehnsucht zu neuer und geformter Objektivität,"* and which Sternheim made fashionable in 1926 with *Die Schule von Uznach* under the name of *"neue Sachlichkeit."* The "cold compresses" of Nietzsche's rationalistic period reappear. The demand is for an art in which the maximum of fervor shall be allied with the maximum of lucidity; an art which shall avoid effusion and dissolution by concentrating temporarily upon its object, and, instead of subordinating itself to that object as the determinists did, shall recreate it from within. Man, the artist, should impose form, his own form, upon the objective world of brute matter. To humanize by fashioning—this is the task of a neo-idealism based upon observation and reflection.

This return to "dispassionate order" has borne fruit in a number of novels and essays in which tone is clarified and penetration of thought and mastery of form are on the increase. But Joseph Roth* is the only writer in whom it has yet resulted in true art. La Rochefoucauld would have liked Roth's novels, for they are the work of a moralist; and this alone assures them of a place apart among the works of the younger writers, who are in general so closely bound up with the objects with which they deal that not enough creative personality emerges,

* JOSEPH ROTH (1894–   ). See p. 316 for bibliography.

and the document remains a collective document. *Die Rebellion* is the story of a Crainquebille, a crippled soldier who slips all the way down the scale from the highest military honors to a prison cell, without ever understanding why. *Flucht ohne Ende* tells the story of an Austrian ex-officer, held prisoner in Siberia, who makes his way back across Russia and Germany to Paris—a device which enables the author to pass all of post-War Europe in review.

Joseph Roth himself has been back and forth across that post-War Europe disguised as a reporter. His comments on the Eastern Jews, like Döblin's observations on Poland, are of a piece with the excellent books of Jean and Jérôme Tharaud. Without losing any of the richness of the sensible world, he carries out a psychological analysis in which one never knows which to admire most, the art of observation or the art of expressing those observations. He attacks with the cruelty of a lucid tenderness the war-time and revolutionary wave of sentimentalism. He has put himself into the very skin of the living dead who came back from the trenches and whose experiences in the beyond made them pitiless in their judgments of the forms of life which they encountered upon their return. His sensuous intelligence enables him to prick the bubble that is Moscow, Berlin, Paris. In ten lines he teaches us more about bolshevism than we can learn from ten volumes of ordinary investigations. He is an Austrian citizen, but he was born in Volhynia and is therefore familiar with post-War Russia, having seen it from within.

His art lies in his ability to seize upon the underlying explanation everywhere, but he never presumes to set himself up as a judge. He characterizes his subject abruptly, in short words, in short sentences, and the illusion disappears. He has taught us that the Slavs, the

Teutonic peoples, the Latins, have few of the characteristics which fine phrases have led us to believe. In
them is merely life like all life—to be taken as it is. But
although he strips them naked with stinging words that
give us almost sensual pleasure, he leaves something in
the background which, however sharp and denunciatory
he may become, he does not pretend to explain. At the
same time that he gives us the exact sensation of reality,
he suggests the idea of something back of it, something
great, something which remains unrealized. This feeling
is all the more poignant because the artist's sobriety
prevents him from ever making even an indirect appeal
to the emotions. His bitterness is too deep to permit him
to use adjectives. He maintains an equilibrium between
that which is said, and said with rare perfection of
expression, and that which, with equal artistry, is left
unsaid, that bespeaks the great tradition. Roth has been
praised as a French writer using the German language.
He is more than that: a writer of the great line of writers
of all nations and all times.

The atmosphere which Roth breathes is the same as
that breathed by Aragon, Montherlant, Soupault,
Drieu la Rochelle; but through it there blows a wind
that is sharper than in Paris, the raw wind of the steppes
blowing unexpectedly westward across Europe and
carrying the dead leaves away with it. Roth's endless
flight is, like theirs, an escape from the gardens of
Barrès, a new *mal de siècle* felt by those Europeans who
have been born under the sign of change. But change
toward what? They are barely willing to ask themselves
the question. So long as the wounded organism asked
only to forget its hurt—a state of soul characteristic
of soldiers suddenly demobilized, whose combativity
finds no outlet in time of peace—there was something
bitter and delicious in mere movement for movement's

sake, mere self-evasion. They must be given time to re-adapt themselves—either to resign themselves to things whose measure fits them ill, or to impose their own will, change the measure of things, introduce into a cowering world a scale of values worthy of both their fundamental robustness and their nostalgia. Their sickness is that they cherish that nostalgia too much; that they look upon the two extremes as a dilemma rather than as the end-points of a rhythm which will permit an effective application of the forces swelling within them.

No one has made the secret sadness of his generation so clear, no one has so well expressed the moving pessimism common to Frenchmen, Germans, Russians, of the generation between thirty and forty, as Roth in *Flucht ohne Ende* and *Zipper und sein Sohn*. He is the witness that they needed and we needed, standing midway between destruction and creation, a destruction and a creation from which they feel dissociated and which they watch from apart while the actual participants carry it unconstrainedly forward. His evidence represents Europe's judgment of herself, and it is purifying in its harshness. There can be no sound optimism without a previous pessimism, no effective literature without this preliminary stripping away of illusions.

Joseph Roth has carried intellectual and artistic asceticism to the point where he refuses to carry his themes out to their conclusion, where he wilfully cuts short his effects at the very moment when the reader is in suspense and wonders what is going to happen to the characters. *Rechts und links* does not end; perhaps the reason is that in life itself nothing does end, and only a mediocre art tries to work out artificial dénouements. Roth hates the mediocrity of his time, and sees a refuge for grandeur only in unhappiness and detachment. His

Job is marked with the stamp of that grandeur. A Jew without money, without fatherland, he does not merely sit upon his dung-heap lamenting, like a biblical Job. He wears the poetic halo of the Wandering Jew, condemned eternally never to halt, never to possess. This poor Jewish school-teacher on the Russian frontier possesses nothing but his wife, his sons, his daughter, and his prayer cord. The Cossacks take first his daughter, then one of his sons. Then America takes away two of the other sons, who grow rich in New York. The War comes, and Mendel Singer, who has no fatherland, no possessions to defend, who lives in the untemporal, is seized by the temporal after all, swept up in the cyclone of events, turned adrift in the United States, which have themselves entered the War. Having lost his wife, lost his children, this man who has only his God left despairs of God Himself and burns his greatest treasure, the prayer cord. Yet in the darkest of worlds there is some strange power that maintains the vital spark of optimism. Mendel's last son, Menuchim, a tongue-tied invalid, comes to his father's deathbed. An abnormal and precocious child, he has become a famous musician. All the wretchedness of the Singer family thus served as a sacrifice to bring new beauty into the world.

Such is the beauty that results from Roth being harnessed to a work whose creative power swells in remarkable musical rhythm. Roth the intellectual is at the same time a poet. The spirit of his *Job* is the spirit of the verses of the Bible; the harmony of composition which makes this book a great work of art is of a more subtle sort than that of logicians and analysts. It is a song in alternating rhythms, not merely a well-constructed novel; and it awakens profound echoes in the reader. This same musicality, now softened, lends to Roth's *Radetzky-marsch* the charm of Old Austria singing her swan song.

Hermann Kesten,* who bears some affinity to Roth, learned much from André Gide—a choice of influence which alone is to his credit. Kesten has set out on the path of the moralists, and promises to be one of those who will give greater depth to the German novel, let air into the thick-growing forest, illuminate the opaque masses of vegetation with a brilliant intelligence, and give birth to a new sensibility, less naïve than in the past, aware of its own movements, conscious of its weaknesses, demanding a subtler and a franker order. This cannot fail to benefit psychology and, in the long run, morality. Kesten at once set out to attack big themes—liberty, love, happiness. He takes the attitude that none of the great motivating forces that drive humanity forward is as simple as the men who feel it believe. Lenin called liberty "a bourgeois prejudice." Kesten's young Joseph,† seeking liberty through escape from family and fatherland, finally feels cheated by his dream, but at least succeeds in discovering himself. If in this case illusion was a driving force, then disillusion, the sense of what makes reality, is another. Everyone says "the revolution" but in his heart of hearts means "my revolution." In the long run one can possess only oneself—but before one can accomplish this, one must first discover that self.

Love is an illusion like liberty; if the veil of illusion falls, there is despair—but there is also irony. Happiness —what do those who seek it know of happiness? Those who are happy, those who become happy, do so without knowing it, without willing it, without earning it. Part of life depends upon destiny, part upon one's own being. That being must be taught to laugh when it feels like crying, to restrain itself when passion threatens to carry

* HERMANN KESTEN (1898–   ). For bibliography see p. 305.
† *Josef sucht die Freiheit* (1928).

it away. This is only possible through intellectual virility, the individual feeling himself superior to his fate, his alert intelligence immediately discerning that which is relative in events, and, in spite of appearances, refusing to lend it absolute value. This is not so much scepticism as it is a sharp sense of values which are constantly changing in a world that is itself changing according to an accelerated rhythm. The mind must be continually alert if one is not to lose one's footing and fall into the abyss. The intelligence manifested in Kesten's novels is not content with mere *bon mots* and piquant formulas, of which there are nevertheless an abundance; it has a mobility which promises to be creative, and the acts of destruction which it carries out are tempered with humor. The jury which gave Hermann Kesten the Kleist Prize was honoring a brilliant and robust talent whose virility is steadily increasing.

Arnold Ulitz is a witness to the difficulty experienced by the man in the street in leaving the plane of emotivity without falling back upon the plane of organization. The Silesia of his novels opens upon plains that sweep eastward to the Ural Mountains. Across those plains, as well as through Bohemia and Austria, the Germanic world is laid open to Slavic infiltrations. In the North, those infiltrations fall upon natures less naturally artistic than the Czechs'; the result is a literature more turbid than the work of Rilke, Kafka, Brod, or Werfel, filled with mysticism and nebulous dreams.

The bolshevist revolution accentuated the elementary character of the Slavic influence; in simplifying social problems it complicated the political and psychological problems of a Germany whose antennæ were reaching at once toward Western and toward Eastern Europe, the two great cultural regions between which she is the

potential mediator. Silesia is also Hauptmann's home-
land, and in rudimentary form Arnold Ulitz* has many
of Hauptmann's traits. He might be the ideal child of
the cartman Henschel and of Rose Bernd—a being who
has realized Wedekind's desire to escape from the influence of books in order to be able to write them, and whose
books express only what he has learned from his dealings
with creatures plunged deep in the life of instinct.
He himself might be one of those creatures, but with
the gift of substituting close-packed chapters for the
awkward silences which occurred between the exclamations of Hauptmann's peasants. His novels are not
written, in the ordinary sense of the word; they are the
gushing verbal expression of a naïve sensibility, a sensibility whose manifestations have been suppressed in
France by the traditions of poetry, but which in Germany finds free expression backed by a tradition running
from the *Volkslied* and Simplicissimus to Jean-Paul's
Siebenkas and Brentano's naïve Kasperl. The effect of
the War and the revolution which followed was to stimulate in such natures an instinctive distrust of civilization, which they considered a refinement of barbarism,
and to confirm them in their optimistic faith in the virtue
of the primitive soul.

Such a movement is far from the religion of Lenz or the
youthful Goethe. The values which had been preached
by the Reich had dissolved, simply because the Reich
which had preached them fell, and not because of any
theory held in advance of the fact. Ulitz was thirty in
1918. As he watched the inflation, saw the American with
his dollars raising monuments upon the ruins of Germany,
he learned to scorn American methods, just as did his
poet turned head-waiter. Overwhelmed by apocalyptic
visions of approaching bolshevism, touched with a
breath of nihilism, Ulitz, when he wrote *Marat*, was not

* ARNOLD ULITZ (1888–   ). See p. 321 for bibliography.

far from believing that the complete destruction of the decaying world of the West was just and necessary. But he retained the traditional hope of redemption through a return to original simplicity. He sees the problem as a simple one: to begin again the work of culture at its beginnings. The essential values lie in the forests, the streams, and the fields; we must make contact with them again without any romantic masquerade, without the guitars of the *Wandervögel*, through the solitary labor of a Robinson Crusoe clearing his acre of land, through an unpretending love—the love of a man and a woman giving life to the child in whom the world begins again.

The most effective of Ulitz's heroines, *Die Bärin*, brings into the chaos of civilization a freshness and ingenuousness which Voltaire would have been unable to imagine. This girl, whom the "impulse of youth" drives across the Thuringian countryside with a group of vacationing students, is as close to elementary nature as La Motte-Fouqué's water sprite. She is the northern Bacchante imprisoned in the body of a she-bear, listening without any Mallarméan sophistication to "the eternal swarming of desire." In the end she succumbs to desire— or to her youthfulness. She bares her body to all the boys who accompany her, she seeks a revelation of sex in nature, which knows neither good nor evil; and she is driven to a tragic end precisely because she confused herself too completely with nature and could see evil nowhere. This novel states a problem of morals and of civilization which has always preoccupied the German: Can we trust to instinct, to the "*dunkler Drang*," and through discernment avoid some of the costly errors of experience? On the one hand are intuition, inspiration, the dionysiac forces of the unconscious; on the other are knowledge, the ordering forces of intellectualism. What is the proper proportion between them? This is a question as important to other nations as to Germany.

Frank Thiess* also represents an aspect of that return to nature which since the time of Rousseau has been almost constantly fashionable in Germany. Each generation discovers its own form of the *Sturm und Drang* of younger days, and the forces of obscurity and explosiveness rise in conflict with established civilization. The "*Jugendbewegung*," the impulse of youth, leads each generation to attack the artifices of education, to attack the excessive authority exercised by family, society, or the State, to destroy the machine into which they are forced like spare parts, to create spontaneously their own order, to live a life whose orientation is of their own making.

Since the War this movement has been complicated by Freudian influences, by a curiosity about the problems of sex. Frank Thiess, by playing up to these various tendencies, has achieved popularity with the undergraduate generation and with the men of all ages who have continued to think as undergraduates think. On the one hand stands civilization, which has grown increasingly corrupt ever since Rousseau denounced it, and the poison of great cities threatening to kill the soul. On the other hand is nature—the Harz mountains, Livonia, Canada, the primitive solitude of the forests, the life of the animals, with whom, thanks to a little faith in transmigration, we can feel one, and the healthy animality which is a part of us and which makes us want to live naked, lying flat and close to the earth, listening with religious feeling to the pulsing of the universe. These are the two ways of life which Thiess asks his disciples to choose between, the two poles whose alternate attraction he himself feels, with a certain complacency toward his own naïveté. His is the imperfect virility of an adult who has not progressed beyond puerility.

* FRANK THIESS (1890–   ). For bibliography see p. 320.

Conclusion—1931

WE MUST guard against drawing too many conclusions where there is not yet a goal reached but merely a revival begun. The present movement in German letters is linked with the broader movement which is changing the conception of the German being, and this latter movement itself depends upon still broader changes that are taking place in the Old and the New Worlds. One thing only is certain: what passed for *Welt- und Lebensanschauung* in the Hohenzollern period is now, if not completely destroyed (there was not a complete break with the past in 1918 any more than there was in 1870), at least on all sides questioned. There has been born in the people a spirit different from the pre-War spirit. This is the outstanding phenomenon.

The writers and thinkers, who from 1870 to 1918 opposed the things that were, did not remain entirely isolated. Their movement grew into an opposition of the élite to the masses. But this differentiation, though masked under cover of democracy, was really an aristocratic phenomenon. Only a few strong personalities had recovered their sense of autonomy, and that autonomy was effective only on the intellectual plane. Since 1918, however, this sense of autonomy has spread to the people at large, who are now experimenting with a new régime in all modes of activity. This is something more and at the same time something less than a return to independence of mind; it is a conversion of the masses.

The will to change the existing state of things and the existing state of mind has been sufficiently widespread in Germany so that, in spite of the dissimilar ends that have been proposed for it, the idea of change is the subject of all German literature, and whether one likes it or not the inspiration of all writing. That will to change has undergone rapid modifications. The movement which in public affairs was called revolution and in literature was called expressionism has not lost its violence. Critical vehemence and sentimental effervescence have been followed by a few measured steps; after the bursting forth of the ego has come an attempt at self-mastery. Intelligence has often been ignored in controlling passions. Men observe new facts and ill-understood realities expectantly, in order to intervene with reason.

What was momentarily a wave of humanitarianism, a solidarity of despair in the midst of the chaos of Europe, had become reflection upon the need for a responsible order, and the hope in concrete humanity forecast by Kant, Lessing, and Herder. The basic cosmopolitanism of Germany had reappeared; the "*Weltblick*," the world point of view, which for a time had been placed at the service of the will to power, had begun once more to serve the life of the spirit.

A new will to understand was appearing, aided by the recent extension of the literary horizon. Until 1925 German readers who looked abroad were interested only in the Latins, the Scandinavians, the Slavs, and the Asiatics; since that time they have been absorbing a flood of translations of English and American authors. Writers, too, while maintaining close contact with contemporary French* and Russian literature, have devel-

---

* There was scarcely any significant contemporary French work, from Romain Rolland to Jules Romains, Duhamel and J. R. Bloch, from Gide and Valéry to Proust, Roger Martin du Gard, Soupault and Crevel, which had not been or was not in process of being translated into German, frequently by writers for whom Rilke was the example. Sometimes too large a place was given to competent, amusing novels or to the originators of new styles, but

oped a new interest in a literature which, with the single exception of Whitman, had had scarcely any influence upon their elders. England, Ireland, and the United States have completed the cycle of their investigation of ideas and realities.

This metamorphosis in literature is the sign of a social metamorphosis which has gone much deeper in Germany than in France. In 1930, German literature unconsciously reflects the evolution of German society, indeed draws all its elements from contemporary public life. Scarcely anything is changed in the process; writers yield to outside stimulus rather than attempt to impose their own inspiration upon the world they see about them; and their work therefore has a documentary authenticity. Through that work we can watch the illusions in which the generation of yesterday delighted, falling one by one away. Kasimir Edschmid's *Hofrat Brüstlein*, who, like Werfel's *Spiegelmensch*, casts off illusion after illusion and progresses steadily toward an unpretending wisdom, symbolizes all that is most interesting in the internal evolution of Germany. And the younger writers are listening to older men like Heinrich Mann, who in his recent trilogy which opens with *Mutter Marie* has taught them that they must accept their responsibilities, learn how to suffer, learn how to enjoy themselves.

What was this more recent generation, and what promise did it hold? Some notion can be had from immediate evidence, some from elder writers who have been observing the way of life of the adolescents who are or might have been their sons,* some from the intermediate gen-

---

nonetheless a certain selectivity was exercised. Stendhal, whose influence on the younger writers keeps increasing, was particularly admired.

* Wassermann in *Oberlins drei Stufen;* Thomas Mann in *Unordnung und frühes Leid;* Heinrich Mann in *Liliane und Paul* and *Mutter Marie;* Arnold Ulitz in *Die Bärin;* Leonhard Frank in *Das Ochsenfurter Männerquartett.*

eration of forty whom circumstances have placed in the position of liaison agents between two ages.* The most trustworthy evidence, however, is to be found in the first books of the writers of the newer generation themselves.† That evidence is interesting; but it does not yet indicate a generation that has found itself, a generation whose forces are sufficiently organized so that any dominating force becomes visible. So far we have had only a prelude, a musical attack—"*Auftakt*," which is the fashionable term, best expresses this attitude of 1930.

Here, then, was a beginning. Toward what does it point? The young generation itself cannot agree. Some have changed their point of view only in the hope of a restoration of the old type of order, and have sought alliance with forces outside Germany; we need not look to them for the spirit of the future. Others, though determined upon radical changes, are still too dependent upon group support to do more than furnish man power; in their case our interest is in the direction in which that man power will be used. The only suggestion comes from the intellectual élite of the younger generation.

That élite, distrusting hyper-organization, tends toward individualism. Each makes his own choice as he

---

* Willy Haas with his *Literarische Welt* and Rudolf Kayser with his *Neue Rundschau* were in an excellent position to observe what was happening. Haas in *Das Spiel mit dem Feuer*, 1923, and Kayser in *Die Zeit ohne Mythos*, 1923, have both stated perspicaciously some of the principal problems which confront the new generation—problems which have since been taken up again by Döblin in *Wissen und Verändern*, 1931. Walter Benjamin in *Einbahnstrasse*, 1928, has both stated what was lacking then and suggested some of the means by which the German intellectual can overcome that lack.

† Notably *Anthologie jüngster Lyrik*, which contains only the works of poets under thirty, and *Anthologie jüngster Prosa*, in which the standard of selection is somewhat more elastic. Both are edited by Klaus Mann. They include the writings of Klaus Mann, W. E. Süskind, Herbert Schlüter, Hans Aufricht-Ruda, Hans Meisel, Willi R. Fehse, Wolfgang Hellmert, H. J. Wille, Zollikofer, Max Sidow, Bert Schiff, Beheim-Schwarzbach, Manfred Hausmann. For the German titles and English translations of works by these more recent writers, see bibliographies at end of this volume.

combats the order which has been broken.* The " *Wander-vögel*" even before the War were in their own way revolutionists without realizing it. Then, as new ranks of the younger generation came forward and as events gave them a clearer realization of why they were opposed to the elder régime, more and more schisms began to appear, until finally they had not a program but only a tendency in common.

The most interesting group is that which underwent the orienting influence of that astonishing revolutionary teacher Gustav Wyneken. Youth, persuaded to live outside official society, dreams that the communities which it sets up will remake civilization in a nobler form. Respect for Germanic customs, the romanticism of folk poetry and songs and vagabondage, are allied with a modernism which includes scientific hygiene and a naïve and bold attitude toward sex that leaves little possibility of danger from over-repression.

A sentimental and protestant ethic, which tends by reaction to manifest itself in sensuality and paganism, keeps troubling these young people, who take a sensual pleasure in experimenting with their consciences. A neo-idealism and a neo-paganism set up man himself as the supreme possession of mankind and look toward a humanism which has nothing to do with either humanitarianism or the academic humanities. We must will a humanity beautiful in the immediate present, accept it with what there is in it both of nature and of internal culture. The body has its holiness, and it should be exposed in its nakedness; its beauty is joy and virtue; its freedom is linked with the freedom of the spirit;

* "I stand as all my generation stands—alone in a chaos of crumbling values. The direction and the end of my existence is a new order, by which I mean an eternal rebellion. By what road are we to go? Each chooses his own road. Secret companions are waiting for us . . . at its end." (A. Weber in *Anthologie jüngster Lyrik*.)

freedom, joy, and the new spirituality assume that youth shall cut itself loose from a society which produces automatons, from families and from schools in which nothing is taught but how to grow old, how to lose youth. Youth is not the preliminary step to doing over again what our fathers did; it is a moment in life which must be lived with an unique fervor. Each new generation has a right to its own personality and its own prerogatives in order that it may prescribe its own duties.

In all this there is still no more than what we may call a group individualism. Any promise of profound revival must be sought among those who have developed a truly individual personality. Such young writers are somewhat sceptical concerning the "Decline of the West"; they are indifferent to the crises undergone by a society whose metamorphoses seem to them more interesting than its maintenance.* Chaos has not seized them for its own, but has merely inspired them to examine all its elements.

Their first act is an inner negation, their first gesture a turning of the back upon the "ideals" they found in death agony and whose remains obstruct their path. Their generation is moving toward the future with a maximum of independence from the past. They will have their own problems and their own way of stating them. The generation of yesterday had to liquidate the heritage of the century of facts; its writers, in all schools, had to take up a position either for or against these facts, for or against the philosophy which tended to sanction their authority. Meanwhile events, working to the benefit of the liberators, have overthrown the facts themselves.

---

* "The War: foul, wretched years. The Revolution: a rousing of the spirit, a pricking up of the ears, but without result. The inflation: a breeding-time for thieves, a *jeunesse dorée*, a period of deceitfulness—but so alive! The University: phantoms, quicksands. Traveling in Germany and in foreign countries: a flood of light upon one's senses, the discovery of Germany by seeing Germany from the other side of the German frontier." (W. E. Süskind.)

The factual order was no longer a constraint; a place had been made for other facts and another order.

The bourgeois ideal, in other words, then had a definite prestige; but that prestige rested upon a stability in which the present generation no longer has faith. The wisdom of experience now seems bankrupt, and no longer prevents them from imagining a life of their own in a society of their own. The house of their childhood is in ruins; they never had much affection for it, much less were they imprisoned by it. They were spared the authoritarian education of their elders. They were turned loose in the world, and in that world they find a greater hope than they can find in the disappointments around them, for which they feel no responsibility.

They love the feeling of leaving things behind. They conceive of themselves as prodigal children called upon to dissipate the last that remains of the old heritage weighing upon liberty and opposing their desire for autonomy.* Süskind's Vera Martin turning on all the electric lights, wasting light "so that something will happen in the world without bringing anyone a profit," is as significant as Hansjürgen Wille exclaiming: "Ceaselessly thou must destroy the universe which thy dreams have built— thou must break it with thy hands and exult in its fall— Take thou, radiant, the roads that climb—Thou canst not die—Be thou prodigal with thy riches, prodigal with thyself."

Twenty years ago a utilitarian generation was bringing up its children to serve specific ends. To the younger generation in 1931, utility is far less important than the act of dissipation, "the things that happen without one's

---

* It is difficult to estimate the importance of the influence of André Gide upon German writers under thirty. But, to judge both by the number of printings of the German translations of his work, and by the testimony of the young writers who refer to him, it must indeed be great.

thinking of oneself," a sort of "singing certainty" that beyond the rational and practical ends of declining bourgeois society are higher and mysterious ends. These young people are still inspired by the spirit of music, but it is not the spirit of Wagner; they have hardly heard of the Tetralogy, and the incantations of Bayreuth leave them cold. Their musical sense is a sense of life, of their own life. From the adventures of which their lives are woven they hope there will spring the melody of their times. It is a melody they hope for, not a theory.

The reasons for living and dying that yesterday held sway no longer seem convincing to them. They are suspicious of a rational structure which showed that it could not withstand the pressure of events. They came into the world to find all systems staggering, and they have lost hope in systems; they seek their center of equilibrium in themselves. In contradistinction to those who gave themselves up to determinism as to some kindly destiny, they have reintroduced into determinism the idea of will, and they acknowledge dependence only upon their own courage in the face of life.

So many beliefs are being questioned today that they are doubtless embarrassed by the "deceiving and total liberty" at which Péguy jeered, and at the same time naïvely flattered by the uncertainty of their future. On the other hand, the daily exigencies of that future compel them to deal only with absolutely essential problems. "We are probably the least problem-ridden younger generation that the world has ever seen," wrote Klaus Mann. "We talk a lot about problems, but we don't really take much stock in them. At bottom we believe in two things only: life and death." Here is an assurance which might equally well be that of a Prince Charming or that of the hard-working and passionate people who applauded *Hoppla, wir leben*, in which Toller lashed savagely at those for whom to live is to take life easily.

Nevertheless, the excess of pessimism in the atmosphere has brought about a will to optimism, and these men who are beginning their lives have a religious faith in the indistinct future. Possibilities in which their elders saw only annihilation speak to them of miracles. The Spenglerians, to mask their bitterness, called the defeat of Germany "*Untergang des Abendlandes.*" But in this (relative) defeat broader, keener minds see a virtue; they give it its true meaning—that there are things which must be undone because they have been badly done, and they must be courageously made over again with no implication either of revenge or of restoration. Everything has become possible to a generation which was present at the impossible and feels none of the shock that its elders felt at the overthrow of fixed categories.

Circumstances have forced these young men to "live dangerously." But they are not, like Nietzsche, ascetically and heroically reaching toward sanctity. They saw the fall of the great exaltation of the Reich; they have passed through the species of spiritual vacation-period brought about by a break-up of values. And they proceed toward the perils that confront them with the freshness of forgetfulness, or at least unhampered by the now obliterated memories that their fathers had. They have brought a new confidence to life; it seems to them in 1931 more demanding and more attractive, since a thousand idols and a thousand fears have been swept away in the cyclone. Their optimism does not arise merely from juvenility; the path is actually more open before them. It is full of uncatalogued joys and suffering; the element of unpredictableness inspires the personality to conquer itself, whereas the old organized system merely left it the choice between yielding or rebelling.

The new German generation of yesterday felt that it had started with its ego completely free amid a mass of ruins, and the contrast was so great that merely to live seemed beautiful. For them the word life took on its full significance. It does not mean abandonment to the mobility of a desire which changes constantly as its object changes. The block-like unity of things, or what had been presented as such, had fallen to pieces; but it is not enough that we should merely thrust aside those things which are inert and which compromise the development of life, and then let ourselves be simply carried along with those things which have the power of growth.

Movement must be introduced not only into things themselves but into the idea of things, the "*Weltanschauung.*" The members of the young generation have their reverence for the existent, but it is a different reverence from that of sub-Hegelians standing in admiration before a political State and a state of things which for a time seemed to represent well-being. They come close to Goethe's conception of the being taken in its organic totality, implying a growth in profundity, a qualitative becoming. They think of the German being as breaking the temporary shell which it had formed for itself, retaining only that which can be reabsorbed into the organism, and beginning to join itself to the universal being.

It is because he proclaims the necessity of a new "spirit of Utopia" that Ernst Bloch* has succeeded in capturing the imagination of some of these younger Germans. It is because of its Utopian qualities rather than because of its accomplishments that bolshevism has attracted others. For those who are interested in it,

---

* ERNST BLOCH (1885–   ). For bibliography see p. 287.

Communism is primarily a symbol. The term *"Edel-kommunismus"* includes more than the idea of anarchy in white gloves. It suggests the idea of a community that shall not be dependent upon class distinctions, which indeed are already partially broken down, but shall find its own distinctions on another plane. Technology, ceasing to be an end in itself, is to assist the process of ennoblement. This is a long way from Americanism. Indeed the young engineer in *Tordis*, in spite of the fact that he bows to the rhythm of business when he is in America, brings back with him to Germany a disdain for the impersonality of material civilizations.

The members of the younger generation are evolutionists rather than revolutionists; they do not cast away the acquisitions of the past without careful examination. Allied with their faith in themselves is a certain disquiet. They are precocious; they early yielded to a torrent of inspirations, and they are now looking back over their shoulders, wondering if anyone is crying after them a warning of dangers ahead of their feet. And they also welcome advice from some of the "young men" between forty and sixty. As an epigraph for *Heute und Morgen* Klaus Mann uses a quotation from his uncle, Heinrich Mann, concerning the necessity of reconciling reason and the mysterious urgings of the heart in an idealist faith. Stefan George, Heinrich Mann, Thomas Mann, Wassermann, Döblin, and Däubler all have their disciples. Süskind's Raymond returns from his adventure by the path where treads the common man and which is soft from the pressure of many feet.

Basically this younger generation's chief characteristic is its will to keep itself unattached and at the same time not to miss an opportunity for effective action. There has rarely been such a combination of the faculty of marveling at the aspects of life in a way that recalls

Rilke, and a strong sense of restraint, as in the youths depicted by Herbert Schlüter.* The realization that "the preceding generation, when it began, had a great future before it, whereas we have only a great past," arrests their desire to participate in action and gives them from time to time a "melancholy smile."

No one can predict the kind of Europe toward which this state of mind points; but we can safely expect in German letters a revival springing from a broader base than literature itself. The style of German writing in 1931 is better evidence of a psychological change than any amount of new doctrine would be. It has cast out verbal pathos, it contains and nourishes a severely self-restrained intellectuality and sensibility. The simplicity that we find in Joseph Roth, Edschmid, Bruno Frank, or Süskind is no affectation, no mere banal return to nature. It is an approach to the natural which comes as the fruit of the artistic evolution of preceding generations; and what finally stands revealed is a pure and certain sense of values.

The new-born German style will be neither a romantic escape into the indeterminate, nor a return to the standards of the dead who are yet unburied by history, nor the result of a modern and inhuman technique. Catchwords are still to some extent effective upon the man in the street, but the very diversity of the present catchwords, the multiplication of groups and the growing opposition among them, indicate an increasing differentiation within the masses. A sense of discrimination is

* A restraint composed partly of regret for a ruined greatness and of disdain for the attitude of the elders: "There they are, the fathers of our time: incapable of all human grandeur, cowardly to the depths, they allowed great things to happen, looked at them in astonishment and—whether for success or defeat—they shifted their ground. That was their great source of strength: they shifted their ground. They escaped from fate, they fled destiny, they shifted their ground. . . . " (*Das späte Fest.*)

overcoming the taste for ecstasy. The *neue Sachlichkeit* represents a more intellectual sensibility than that of the past, a sensibility governed by a clearer mind. Even should the overthrown forms reappear, they would no longer respond to the changed inspiration. There is a growing desire to change humanity from within rather than attempt to superimpose civilization upon it like an ornament or set up a universe beside it like a symbol. The style that is being born with it is being born from within, and reconciles the soul with the sensible world.

This conception of an élite sometimes takes on a political color, and not in Germany alone. Aristocrats like Steinböhmer,* party men like Ernst Jünger,† while realizing that the world must change, make every effort to preserve the values which they feel are being compromised through democratic revolutions, by fighting for them with what Hofmannsthal called the "conservative revolution." The year 1930, as the world vividly recalls, marked a turning point in Germany's road to destiny. The sudden expansion of *Nationalsozialismus* made manifest the serious confusion into which a disoriented, demoralized people had fallen, showed their dangerous uncertainty, their willingness to let their more violent members take the responsibility of getting the wagon out of the ditch. The National Socialists had no program worthy of the name. Their catchword, action, gives no indication of the final direction in which that action is to take place, but seems to be alternating between the extremes of reaction and revolution.

Here is a state of endemic war, of civil war everywhere, reminiscent of the days of Luther. Its essence is to strike, letting each day provide the enemies to be stricken. The feelings inspired by Hitlerism and Communism are

* *Abtrünnige Bildung,* 1930.
† *Krieg und Krieger,* 1931.

in part feelings of desperation, the feeling that there is nothing to be lost and everything to be gained in changing a state of affairs which is admittedly intolerable. But more marked than this despair is the indifference that can also be seen, a gloomy and dejected indifference toward anything that may happen, a passive attitude toward what events may bring that arises from the conviction that no matter what happens it will be catastrophic. With such an attitude, why should the masses worry about the particular form the catastrophe will take? They simply abandon themselves to the stimuli offered by a literature which is turned almost entirely to political ends.

Arnolt Bronnen is a specialist in nationalist agitation who in *O.S.* and *Rossbach* has magnified the exploits of the *Freikorps*, secretly armed bands carrying out, with a certain heroism, acts of violence such as those attempted in Upper Silesia. To be outside the law has become a matter of pride to the young men whose true story Ernst von Salomon* tells in *Die Geächteten*. They are misled adolescents whose ringleaders have whipped them into a fanatical frenzy that leads to political crime; they carry their resolve through to the end, assassinating Rathenau, tomorrow assassinating whoever shall be pointed out to them by a blood tribunal arisen from the Middle Ages, simply because they have become convinced that "intellectual conquests require bloodshed, and the spirit is born only thereafter."

Those intellectuals worthy of the name have attempted, by means of "*ratio*," to check the glorification of elementary forces loosed by a mass hysteria in which there is a strong religious element and which is compounded of a barbarous mysticism and an ultra-modern sadism. Heinrich and Thomas Mann, preachers of

* ERNST VON SALOMON (1902–   ). For bibliography see p. 317.

reason, were seconded in this effort by a group of young writers all of whom were trying to make the German Republic a reality in the German mind. Prussia with her tradition of lucidity, Berlin with her strong position as capital, were looked to as enlighteners in a country in which the *Aufklärung* of the eighteenth century had been cut short by a romanticist invasion.

The theatre was fast becoming a forum in which to debate political questions. Wilhelm Herzog,* who wrote the best biography of Kleist, gave in *Rund um den Staatsanwalt* a striking picture of the fall of the Imperial régime in 1918—a fall that was followed by chaos. There remained the necessity of clarifying the opinions of a people who had had no political education, who lacked training in self-government. As opposing parties faced each other, those in power did not know which way to look; a return to first principles was necessary, a definition of the idea which the republicans were uphold-ing. The success of *Die Affäre Dreyfus* proved how urgent it was that questions which were exercising a people suddenly given autonomy should be treated publicly; how pressing was the need to learn whether continued support should be given the authority of the existing State, the system already developed, or whether the existing State should be modified in an effort to achieve greater human justice. Judicial crimes were attacked by Herzog and by Wassermann. Dreyfus Case or Maurizius Case, there was growing in Germany a feeling that con-science should be placed above reasons of State. It is therefore not surprising that into the argument were pitched all the relevant similar trials in France, with Herzog reviving the Panama scandals after the Dreyfus

* WILHELM HERZOG (1884–   ). *Kleist*, 1911; *Rund um den Staatsanwalt* (*Die letzten Tage des kaiserlichen Deutschlands*), 1927; *Die Affäre Dreyfus*, 1929; *Panama*, 1931. For completer bibliography see p. 301.

Case. Every crisis through which the French Republic had passed, and particularly the crisis of Boulangerism, was being reproduced with striking parallelism in the young German Republic, and the lessons of history were not to be lost.

Writing under the name of Bruckner*, Theodor Tagger in *Krankheit der Jugend* and *Die Verbrecher* has brought social problems to the German stage. His excellent craftsmanship, his cleverness in using a vertical section of a house so that the various floors serve as so many slices of life superimposed one on the other, and a style that is sober, sinewy, and hard as the lives of his characters, won him a success with these two plays which he could not repeat with *Kreatur* and *Elisabeth von England*.

Döblin in *Die Ehe* (1931), with his usual ardor and generosity, draws up a powerful indictment of the kind of birth control law which condemns a poor family either to have more and more children or to turn to an illegal and uncontrolled abortion. Abortion in Germany had become so widespread that it was to the interest of the community as well as of the individual to make it legally possible for doctors to perform the operation, which is otherwise left in the hands of criminals.

Peter Lampel* treats of both social and educational problems in his *Verratene Jungen* (1929) and particularly in the sensational drama *Revolte im Erziehungshaus* (1928), in which the abuse of authority in a "reformatory" drives the inmates to rebellion.

This same theme of revolt is taken up also in Toller's *Feuer aus den Kesseln* (1930), whose characters are the same sailors of the battle fleet, the same "coolies of the Kaiser" whose revolt against the machine which they were condemned to serve had already been depicted in Plivier's plays.

* For bibliographies of Bruckner and Lampel see pp. 291 and 307.

Of the plays produced in Berlin during the season 1929–1930, four were indictments of justice and the legal system, three were indictments of the educational system, two attacked the intolerance of man for man, seven depicted war as a calamity, only one was nationalistic. In addition to the legitimate theatre, soon transformed into a forum, there were satires expressed in the form of songs such as those in Brecht's *Dreigroschenoper* (1928) and in Walter Mehring's* jazz songs, with their caustic verve, their verbal fantasy, and their poetry. This "poetry for every day and every use" is a new literary genre in Germany, at which both Erich Kästner† and Kurt Tucholsky ‡ were also eminently successful.

This turning of the theatre to the service of political agitation and political ideas left little room for drama for its own sake. Ernst Barlach§ has genius as a sculptor, but when he writes for the theatre he is inclined to stray into metaphysics. Yet he has treated Faustian problems on the stage, as in *Der Blaue Boll*—an effective mixture of mysticism, realism, and humor. Here is the tradition of Hoffmann and Arnim cropping out again against a Mecklenburg background, together with a reminiscence of the strange visions of William Blake.

Volpone, which Stefan Zweig borrowed from the classic English drama and put into modern form, brought back to the stage a theme as eternal as the power of money. Mary Baker Eddy, the founder of Christian Science, is the heroine of a play called *Wunder in Amerika* (1931) in which Toller and Kesten are concerned with teaching their compatriots an indirect lesson of the dangers of yielding to the healers who have sprung up in Germany.

* Walter Mehring (1896–   ). For bibliography see p. 311.
† Erich Kästner (1899–   ). For bibliography see p. 304.
‡ Kurt Tucholsky (1890–   ). For bibliography see p. 321.
§ Ernst Barlach (1870–   ). For bibliography see p. 285.

There are few merely pleasant plays like Hasenclever's *Ehen werden im Himmel geschlossen* (1928). But the desire to laugh, to yield to innocent gaiety in the theatre was not entirely dead. Zuckmayer,* who received the Kleist Prize, has charmed the public with his plays about the life of the humble people in villages and small cities, drenched in provincial atmosphere, experiencing their little pleasures and their little vexations, loving life in the Rhineland manner, forgetting, and making us forget for a moment, the larger problems. Here is a realism which the Germans once before enjoyed in the time of Kotzebue.

In spite of the prevailing indifference toward pure lyricism, some of the work of the younger poets has appeared, at least in anthologies.† They mark the end of the expressionist paroxysm, a desire to rediscover the harmony and the perfection of form which are ultimately to express perfection of soul.

But this approach to classic equilibrium is manifested only among the privileged few. The novel is still a popular form—everyone can write a novel, everyone has a chance of selling the American translation or the film rights, everyone has something to say about the problems of the day—and facile novels have poured from the presses without resulting in any advance in the novelist's art. A man like Robert Neumann,‡ for instance, writes amusing parodies, but his is mainly a paroxysmic art representing the chaotic post-War world with its dubious speculators, its hangers-on and adventurers like those in *Sintflut*. Though the details are authentic enough, they make us regret real painters of the stature of Balzac, Zola, and Heinrich Mann, the authenticity of whose pictures is a result of choice and synthesis.

* CARL ZUCKMAYER (1896–   ). See p. 324 for bibliography.

† *Anthologie jüngster Lyrik* (Enoch Verlag, 2 volumes, 1927–1929); *Junge deutsche Lyrik* (Reklam Verlag).

‡ ROBERT NEUMANN (1899–   ). See p. 314 for bibliography.

This choice and this synthesis are carried out with a rigor that approaches dryness in Anna Seghers' novels, but their atmosphere is nevertheless passionate. Both author and characters are carried along on a great social faith. Crowds in the heat of a strike or of a demonstration in front of the American Embassy are for a moment endowed with a unanimous power, carried away by a collective obsession. In spite of the internal resistance of the individual, they all rush to their goal, live to the full their moment of enthusiasm or madness. This is all the more effective because it takes place in an atmosphere that is almost indifferent, among people who are niggardly with words and with gestures. The result is a dry-point, a black-and-white effect which places Anna Seghers* among our really distinguished engravers.

Joseph Breitbach's characters are bathed in a softer light. In *Rot gegen Rot* (1929), his little working people are forced to choose between the red of love which life denies them and the red of revolution toward which life drives them; the tragedy of their fate is tempered by the author's common sense and subtlety, and by a touch of humor between the lines. These same qualities, with more refinement and more fantasy, are to be found also in Heinrich Eduard Jacob's *Jacqueline und die Japaner* (1928), and again, but used with more concentration, in Marieluise Fleisser's *Ein Pfund Orangen* and *Mehlreisender Frieda Geier* (1931).

The attraction exerted by the United States upon the younger generation, and the need for wide open spaces after living among a people who complain of being cramped (*Volk ohne Raum*), have given inspiration to a whole literature of travel books and novels. Erika and Klaus Mann in *Rundherum, ein heiteres Reisebuch*

* For bibliographies of SEGHERS, JACOB, FLEISSER, HAUSER see pp. 319, 303, 296, 301, respectively.

(1929) have gaily told the story of their youthful trip around the world. Heinrich Hauser, after writing a novel about a sailor (*Brackwasser*) and descriptions of life at sea (*Donner überm Meer*, 1929), of the Ruhr (*Schwarzes Revier*, 1930), and of the last sailing ships (*Die letzten Segelschiffe*, 1930), set out to explore the valley of the Mississippi in a Ford (*Feldwege nach Chicago*, 1931). Manfred Hausmann*, who made an early name for himself with a novel of a tramp, full of the poetry of vagabondage and the freshness and perfume of the roads that lead to nowhere, has discovered in *Kleine Liebe zu Amerika* not the America of trusts and vast problems, but an America where one can idle and enjoy the little incidents of an unplanned itinerary. Kurt Heuser was a planter in his early youth, and the spirit of adventure nourished within him the sensibility of the true artist. He has something in common with Joseph Conrad in his divination of the mystery surrounding Africa. His *Elfenbein für Felizitas* (1928) and his *Die Reise ins Innere* (1931) are more than the exercises of a gifted littérateur: they are the work of a writer of the true breed attempting to unite great themes of individual life with those of the life of the universe.

In short, between the sharp harsh realism of those who wish to have no illusions about themselves and the world, and the romanticism of those who, fleeing from themselves, yield to the appeal of the far-away, melt into a whole which is larger than themselves—nature, foreign lands, their own nation, a political party—there is room for a new realism, a realism for those vigorous minds that are seeking to give reality significance.

Especially striking is the contrast between Matzke's *Jugend bekennt* (1930), the work of a young man who is strongly sceptical about everything that does not

---

* For bibliographies of HAUSMANN, HEUSER, TRITSCH see pp. 301, 303, 321.

fall within sharply defined lines, and Tritsch's *Europa im Zwielicht* (1930), written by a man who, although he is ten years older, has reflected upon the disappointment which would follow if the *neue Sachlichkeit* did not result in creative activity. "The most civilized man," he writes, "the man who is most closely in touch with the technical and economic complexities of the modern world, is today the poorest of all in spirit, the most primitive, the most impersonal . . . a super-monkey." We must give ear to the demands of men such as Tritsch, who no longer wish to "skip over everything that is essential in humanity," nor disdain "the deeps of the soul."

It is this same demand which lends significance to some of the younger writers represented in *Vierundzwanzig neue deutsche Erzähler* (1929), and *Vorstoss, Prosa der Ungedruckten* (1930).

The crisis which is affecting Germany, and other countries as well, is primarily a crisis of the spirit: a consciousness of the contrast between the things of the past and the things of the future, between Europe and the rest of the world, between the nation and higher unities, between collectivism and individualism, action and thought. To literature, itself divided between action without thought and thought without action, has been assigned the great rôle of helping to bring about a synthesis.

BIBLIOGRAPHIES

NOTE

The following bibliographies include only those German authors mentioned in Professor Bertaux's text and still living at the end of 1934. The bibliographies, which are limited throughout to works published in book form, have been carried down to this date, though Professor Bertaux closes his history with 1931. Dates for publication in German are, wherever possible, based upon the earliest edition. In listing translations into English, the year of British as well as American publication is given.

I wish to acknowledge the many courtesies accorded me by the staffs of the British Museum Reading Room and the Library of Congress. For information and assistance given by Dr. Andor Braun, formerly of Vienna, Dr. Heinz Placzek, formerly of Berlin, and by Mr. B. W. Huebsch, Dr. Harry Slochower, and Mr. Albert Daub of New York, I am also grateful. I especially wish to thank Mrs. Stefi Kiesler of the New York Public Library for invaluable aid throughout the preparation of the text and the bibliographies.

J. J. T.

BIBLIOGRAPHIES

AUFRICHT-RUDA, Hans, b. 1899, novelist

Die Verhandlungen gegen La Roncière, novel, '27 (The Case for the Defendant, Boston '29, Lon. '29)

Der Jahrhundertbogen, novel, '27

BARLACH, Ernst, b. 1870, dramatist

Figuren-Zeichnen, '09

Der tote Tag, drama, '12

Der arme Vetter, drama, '18

Die echten Sedemunds, drama, '20

Der Findling, drama, '22

Die Sündflut, drama, '24

Der blaue Boll, drama, '26

Ein selbsterzähltes Leben, autobiog., '28

Die gute Zeit, play, '30

BECHER, Johannes Robert, b. 1891, poet

Der Ringende, Kleist Hymne, '11

Erde, novel, '12

Die Gnade eines Frühlings, poems, '12

De Profundis Domine, '13

Verfall und Triumph, '14

An Europa, poems, '16

Verbrüderung, poems, '16

Das neue Gedicht, '18

Die Heilige Schar, poems, '18

Päan gegen die Zeit, poems, '18

Gedicht für ein Volk, '19

Gedichte um Lotte, '19

An Alle, '19

Zion, poems, '20

Ewig im Aufruhr, '20

Um Gott, '21

Der Gestorbene, poems, '21

Verklärung, hymn, '22

Vernichtung, An den Deutschen, Mord, 3 Hymnen, '22

Hymnen, '24

Am Grabe Lenins, poem, '24

Arbeiter, Bauern, Soldaten, drama, '24

Vorwärts, du rote Front, prose, '24

Roter Marsch—Der Leichnam auf dem Thron—Die Bombenflieger, '25

Der Bankier reitet über das Schlachtfeld, novelette, '26

Maschinen-Rhythmen, poems, '26

3 As oder Der einzig gerechte Krieg, novel, '26

Die hungrige Stadt, poem, '28

Im Schatten der Berge, poems, '28

Graue Kolonnen, 24 neue Gedichte, '30

Ein Mensch unserer Zeit, poems and prose, '30

Der grosse Plan, Epos des sozialistischen Aufbaus, '31

BEER-HOFFMANN, Richard, b. 1866, dramatist, poet

Novellen, '94

Der Tod Georgs, novelette, '00; new ed. '28

Der Graf v. Charolais, tragedy, '06

Gedenkrede auf W. A. Mozart, '06

Jaakobs Traum, ein Vorspiel, '18; new ed., as Die Historie von König David, ein Zyklus, '20

Schlaflied für Mirjam, poem, '20

Der junge David, dramatic poem, '33

BEHEIM-SCHWARZBACH, Martin, b. 1900, novelist

Antwort eines Deutschen an die Welt, '33

Sechs Bekenntnisse zum neuen Deutschland (with others), '33

Deutsche Jugend vor den Toten des Krieges, '33

Vom Leben der Plastik, Georg Kolbe, '33

Dichtungen, Auswahl, '33

Wir fordern Reims zur Übergabe auf, *novelette*, '34

BLEI, FRANZ, b. 1871, *essayist, biographer*

Die rechtschaffene Frau, *drama*, '93

Der dunkel Weg, *farce*, '06

Das Lustwäldchen, *poems*, '07

Das Lesebuch der Marquise, '08

Felicien Rops, '08

Die Puderquaste, '09 (The Powderpuff, Lon. '09, N. Y. '10)

Erdachte Geschehnisse, '11

Gott und die Frauen, '11

Das Rokoko, '11

Das schwere Herz, '11

Der Dichter und das Leben, '12

Vermischte Schriften, 6 vols., '11–'12

Landfahrten und Abenteuer, '13

Über Wedekind, Sternheim und das Theater, '15

Menschliche Betrachtungen zur Politik, '16

Logik des Herzens, *comedy*, '16

Das Evangelium des Apollonios, '19

Die verliebte Weisheit der Ninon, '20

Die Abenteurer, *short stories*, '20

Die Sitten des Rokoko, '21

Der bestrafte Wollüstling, '21

Leben und Traum der Frauen, '21

Lehrbücher der Liebe, 4 vols., '22

Das grosse Bestiarium der modernen Literatur, '22

Der Geist des Rokoko, '23

Der Knabe Ganymed, *novelettes*, '23

Das Kuriositätenkabinett der Literatur, '24

Die Frivolitäten des Herrn von Diesemberg, '25

Der persische Dekameron, '26

Glanz und Elend berühmter Frauen, '27 (Fascinating Women, Sacred and Profane, N. Y. '28)

Wiedergeburt der Venus, '27

Frauen und Männer der Renaissance, '27

Frauen und Abenteuer, '27

Himmlische und irdische Liebe in Frauenschicksalen, '28

Ungewöhnliche Menschen und Schicksale, '29

Formen der Liebe, '30

Männer und Masken, '30

Erzählung eines Lebens, *autobiog.*, '30

Die göttliche Garbo, '30

Die Lust der Kreatur, '31

Die Gefährtinnen, '31

Talleyrand, '32

BLOCH, ERNST, b. 1885, *philosopher, critic*

Geist der Utopie, '18

Vademekum für heutige Demokraten, '19

Thomas Münzer als Theologe der Revolution, '22

Durch die Wüste, *essays*, '23

Spuren, *sketches*, '30

BÖLSCHE, WILHELM, b. 1861, *naturalist, critic, novelist*

Paulus, *novel*, '85

Die naturwissenschaftlichen Grundlagen der Poesie, '87

Der Zauber des Gönigs Arpus, *novel*, '87

Heinrich Heine, '88

Die Mittagsgöttin, *novel*, '91

Das Liebesleben in der Natur, '00–'03; revised '10 (Love Life in Nature, N. Y. '28, Lon. '31)

Entwicklungsgeschichte der Natur, '92–'95

Charles Darwin, '98

Vom Bazillus zum Affenmenschen, '00; revised '21

Ernst Haeckel, '00 (Haeckel: His Life and Work, Lon. '06)

Die Eroberung des Menschen, '01; revised '23

Goethe im 20. Jahrhundert, '00; revised '09

Die Entwicklungslehre im 19. Jahrhundert, '00; revised '09

Hinter der Weltstadt, '01

Von Sonnen und Sonnenstäubchen, '03; revised '27

Aus der Schneegrube, '03; revised as Naturwende, '25

Die Abstammung des Menschen, '04; revised '21 (The Evolution of Man, Chicago '05; revised as The Descent of Man, N. Y. '23, Lon. '26)

Weltblick, '04; revised '22

Der Sieg des Lebens, '05 (The Triumph of Life, Chicago '05)

Der Stammbaum der Tiere, '05

Naturgeheimnis, '05; revised '22

Was ist die Natur?, '07; revised as Die Vernunft der Natur, '23

Im Steinkohlenwald, '06

Die Schöpfungstage, '06

Tierbuch, '08–'11; Part I, new ed. '23, as Aus der Weltgeschichte des Tieres; Part II, new ed. '23, as Der Liebesroman des Hirsches

Auf dem Menschenstern, '09

Stunden in All, '09

Der Mensch der Vorzeit, vol. I '09, vol. II '11

Komet und Weltuntergang, '10

Festländer und Meere im Wechsel der Zeiten, '13

Stirb und Werde, '13

Tierwanderungen in der Urwelt, '14

Von Wundern und Tieren, '15

Der Mensch der Zukunft, '15

Die deutsche Landschaft in Vergangenheit und Gegenwart, '16

Der Stammbaum der Insekten, '16

Schutz- und Trutzbündnisse in der Natur, '17

Eiszeit und Klimawechsel, '19

Aus Urtagen der Tierwelt, '22

Tierseele und Menschenseele, '24

Erwanderte deutsche Geologie, '25

Von Drachen und Zauberkünsten, '25

Die Abstammung der Kunst, '26

Im Bernsteinwald, '27 (The Amber Forest Primeval, Stuttgart '28)

Lichtglaube, '27

Der singende Baum, '29

Drachen, '29

Termitenstaat, '31

Ausgewählte Werke, '30

Das Leben der Urwelt, '31

BONSELS, WALDEMAR, b. 1881, *poet, novelist, playwright*

Mein Austritt aus der Baseler Missionsindustrie, '04

Madame Potiphar, '04

Ave Vita, *novel*, '06; reissued as Leben ich grüsse Dich!, '18

Mare, *novel*, '07

Das Feuer, *essays*, '07

Frühling, *dramatic poem*, '08

Rote Nacht, Ballade, '08

Aimee (in collab. with Hans Hahn), *novel*, '08

Don Juans Tod, *epic*, '10

Der tiefste Traum, *novelette*, '11

Märztage, *play*, '12

Die Toten des ewigen Krieges, *novel*, '11; reissued as Wartalun, '12

Die Biene Maja und ihre Abenteuer, '12 (Maya, the Adventures of a Little Bee, Lon. '22; Adventures of Maya, the Bee, N. Y. '22)

Das Anjekind, *novel*, '13 (Angel Child, Lon. '27)

Das junge Deutschland und der grosse Krieg, '14

Himmelsvolk, '15 (Heaven Folk, N. Y. '24, Lon. '30)

Indienfahrt, '16 (An Indian Journey, N. Y. '28, Lon. '29)

Kanonier Grimbarts Kriegsbericht, '15

Die Heimat des Todes, '16

Menschenwege, '18 (included in Notes of a Vagabond, N. Y. '31)

Don Juan, '20

Eros und die Evangelien, '21

Norby, '21

Weihnachtsspiel, *dramatic poem*, '22

Kyrie Eleison, '22

Narren und Helden, *novel*, '23

Jugendnovellen, *novelettes*, '23

Menschenwege; aus den Notizen eines Vagabunden, '23 (Notes of a Vagabond, N. Y. '31)

Die Flamme von Arzla, *play*, '25

Die Mundharmonika, *novelettes*, '25

Mario und die Tiere, '27 (The Adventures of Mario, N. Y. '30)

Tiergeschichten, '28

Der Wanderer zwischen Stab und Sternen, '26

Mario und Gisela, '30

Tage der Kindheit, '31

Brasilianische Tage und Nächte (Frhr. v. Dungern), '31

Die Nachtwache, *novel*, '33

BORCHARDT, Rudolf, b. 1877, *poet, playwright, essayist*

Das Gespräch über Formen und Platons Lysis, '05

Walter Savage Landors imaginäre Unterhaltungen, '07

Poetische Erzählungen, '07

Rede über Hofmannsthal, '07

Das Buch Joram, '07

Der Krieg und die deutsche Selbsteinkehr, *speech*, '15

Der Krieg und die deutsche Verantwortung, '16

Der Durant, *poem*, '20

Die Päpstin Jutta, *dramatic poem*, Part I: Verkündigung, '20

Die halbgerettete Seele, *poem*, '20

Krippenspiel, '22

Die Schöpfung aus Liebe, *poem*, '23

Die geliebte Kleinigkeit, Schäferspiel, '23

Schriften, Prosa, vol. I, '24

Der ruhende Herakles, *poem*, '24

Über den Dichter und das Dichterische, '24

Die grossen Trobadors, '24

Vermischte Gedichte, '24

Gartenphantasie, '25

Deutsche Denkreden, '25

Der Deutsche in der Landschaft, '27

Handlungen und Abhandlungen, '28

Die Aufgaben der Zeit gegenüber der Literatur, *speech*, '29

Das hoffnungslose Geschlecht, *four stories*, '29

Die deutsche Literatur in Kampf um ihr Recht, '31

Führung, *speech*, '31

Deutsche Reisende, deutsches Schicksal, '32

BRECHT, Bertolt, b. 1898, *dramatist, poet*

Baal, *drama*, '22

Trommeln in der Nacht, *drama*, '23

Im Dickicht der Städte, *drama*, '23

Leben Eduards II von England (after Marlowe, with Lion Feuchtwanger), *drama*, '24

Mann ist Mann, *comedy*, '27

Die Geburt der Jugend, *play*, '22
Die Exzesse, *comedy*, '23
Die Septembernovelle, '23
Anarchie in Sillian, *play*, '24
Napoleons Fall, *novel*, '24
Katalaunische Schlacht, *play*, '24
Rheinische Rebellen, *play*, '25
Ostpolzug, *play*, '26
Reparationen, *comedy*, '27
Film und Leben Barbara La Marr, *novel*, '28
O.S., *novel*, '29 (S.O.S., Lon. '30)
Kleist's Michael Kohlhaas (*re-written for radio and stage*), '29
Rossbach, *novel*, '30
Erinnerungen an eine Liebe, *novel*, '33
Sonnenberg, *play*, '33

BRUCKNER, FERDINAND (THEO-DOR TAGGER), b. 1891, *drama-tist, poet, novelist*
Von den Verheissungen des Krieges und den Forderungen an den Frieden, '15
Das neue Geschlecht, *essay*, '17
Der Herr in den Nebeln, *lyrics*, '17
Die Vollendung eines Herzens, *novelette*, '17
Über einen Tod, '18
Psalmen Davids, '18
Der zerstörte Tasso, *selected poems*, 2 vols., '19
Auf der Strasse, *novelette*, '20
Harry, *comedy*, '20
  From the dramatic cycle: 1920 oder Die Komödie vom Unter-gang der Welt
Annette, *comedy*, '20
  From the dramatic cycle: 1920 oder Die Komödie vom Unter-gang der Welt
Kapitän Christoph, *drama*, '21
Te Deum, '29
Krankheit der Jugend, *play*, '29
Die Verbrecher, *play*, '29
Die Kreatur, *play*, '30

Elisabeth von England, *play*, '30 (Elizabeth of England, Lon. '31)
Timon, *tragedy*, '32
Die Marquise von O., *play*, '33
Die Rassen, *play*, '33 (Races, N. Y. '34)

CAROSSA, HANS, b. 1878, *novelist, poet*
Stella mystica, '07
Gedichte, '10; enlarged '12
Doktor Bürgers Ende. Letzte Blätter eines Tagebuches, '13
Die Flucht, *poem*, '16
Ostern, *poems*, '20
Eine Kindheit, '22 (Childhood, Lon. '30, N. Y. '32)
Rumänisches Tagebuch, '24 (A Roumanian Diary, Lon. '29, N. Y. '30)
Verwandlungen einer Jugend, '28 (Boyhood and Youth, Lon. '30, N. Y. '32)
Die Schicksale Doktor Bürgers, *short story*, '30
Der Arzt Gion, eine Legende aus dem ärztlichen Leben, '31 (Dr. Gion, Lon. '32, N. Y. '33)
Führung und Geleit, ein Lebens-gedenkbuch, '33

DÖBLIN, ALFRED, b. 1878, *novelist, playwright, essayist*
Die Ermordung einer Butterblume, *novelettes*, '13
Das Stiftsfräulein und der Tod, *novelette*, '13
Die drei Sprünge des Wang-lun, *novel*, '15
Die Lobensteiner reisen nach Böhmen, *short stories*, '17
Wadzeks Kampf um die Dampf-turbine, *novel*, '18
Der schwarze Vorhang, *novel*, '19
Wallenstein, *novel*, 2 vols., '20
Der deutsche Maskenball, *essays*, '21 (pub. under pseud. Linke-Poot)

Dogenglück, *tragedy*, '98

Anna Walewska, *tragedy*, '99

Münchhausen, *play*, '00; new version '25

Leidenschaft, *tragedy*, '01

Künstler und Katilinarier, *play*, '02

Ein halber Held, *tragedy*, '03; revised '28

Kassandra, *drama*, '03

Ritter Blaubart, *play*, '05

Ulrich, Fürst von Waldeck, *play*, '07

Der natürliche Vater, *comedy*, '07

Du darfst ehebrechen, *novelette*, '09

Simson, *tragedy*, '10

Alles um Liebe, *comedy*, '10

Schattenbilder, *essays*, '10; new ed. '33

Das keimende Leben, '10

Deutsche Sonette, '10; enlarged ed. '22

Ein Wanderbuch, '10

Sonderbare Geschichten, '10

Alles um Geld, *play*, '11

Schiller, *speech*, '10

Katinka die Fliege, *novel*, '11

Belinde, *play*, '12

Ikarus und Daedalus, '12

Neue Bilder, *essays*, '12

Ernste Schwänke, '13

Der Frauentausch, *dramatic fantasy*, '14

Zeitwende, *play*, '15

Messalina, *dialogue*, '15

Leidenschaft, *tragedy*, '15

Letzte Bilder, *essays*, '16

Skizzen aus Litauen, '16

Das deutsche Angesicht, '17

Die Insel, *play*, '18

Der Morgen nach Kunersdorf, Krieg dem Krieg, *one-act plays*, '18

Das Ende der Marienburg, *one-act play*, '18

Der Irrgarten, *play*, '18

Die Nachtseite, *play*, '18

Mein Leben für die Bühne, *essays*, '19; revised as Bühnenbilder, '24

Komödien der Ehe, *one-act plays*, '20

Die Nase des Herzogs Restrelli, *anecdotes*, '20

Wie Bismarck seiner Frau beinahe untreu wurde, '20

Kleinselige Zeiten, *farce*, '20

Das grüne Haus, *play*, '20

Mückentanz, '20

Der Bankrott Europas, *short stories*, '20

Der Guckkasten, *essays*, '21

Mächtiger als der Tod, *play*, '21

Wie man's macht ist's richtig, *comedy*, '22

Die Welt ist krank, *play*, '22

Der Übergang, *tragedy*, '22

Erscheinungen, *essays*, '22

Liebesgeschichten, '22

Auf halbem Wege, *novel*, '22

Wir Zugvögel, *novel*, '23

Amerikanismus, '24

Eros, poems, '24

Gestalten und Begebenheiten, '24

Die Familie Feuerbach, *essays*, '24

Ausgewählte Werke, 5 vols., '25

Der rote Mond, *play*, '25

Gegen Shaw, Streitschrift, '25

Freude muss man haben, *play*, '25

Mensch und Meteor, *novel*, '25

Zwischen zwei Frauen, *novel*, '26

Sterblich Unsterbliche, *essays*, '26

Um den Rhein, *novel*, '27

Industrie, *play*, '27

Zwischen zwei Männern, *novel*, '28

Huldigung an Gutenberg, '28

Michel, ein deutsches Heldengedicht, '28

Die Hohenzollern, *essays*, '28 (The Hohenzollerns, Lon. '29, N. Y. '29)

Schubert und die Frauen, '28

Die Aufgabe des Judentums, *essay*,
'33
Marianne in Indien, *short stories*,
'34

FISCHER, SIEGFRIED, b. 1890,
film and literary critic, poet
Die den Fluch Liliths tragen, *short
stories*, '13
Pierrots Kriegsmasken und Ge-
sichte, *poems*, '16
Die Welt des Films (in collab. with
C. Zell), '28
Das belebte Bild; fünf Kapitel
über Film und Kino, *essays*, '31

FLAKE, OTTO, b. 1882, *novelist,
essayist*
Die Leute vom Simplicissimus, '08
Strassburg und das Elsass, '08
Das Mädchen aus dem Osten; Der
unbedachte Wunsch, *novelettes*,
'11
Rund um die elsässische Frage, '11
Schritt für Schritt, *novel*, '12
Der französische Roman und die
Novelle, *essay*, '12
Das Freitagskind, *novel*, '13; later
editions as Eine Kindheit (pro-
jected as Romane um Ruland,
vol. I)
Die Prophezeiung, *short stories*, '15
Horns Ring, *novel*, '16
Das Logbuch, *sketches*, '17
Abenteuerin; Im dritten Jahr, *two
plays*, '18
Die Stadt des Hirns, *novel*, '19
Wandlung, *novelette*, '19
Nein und Ja, *novel*, '20; final ver-
sion, '23
Das Ende der Revolution, *essay*,
'20
Pandämonium, *philosophical es-
says*, '21
Die moralische Idee, *philosophical
essays*, '21
Kaiserin Irene, *drama*, '21

Das kleine Logbuch, '21
Dinge der Zeit, *essays*, '21
Das neu-antike Weltbild, *philo-
sophical essays*, '22
Die Simona, *novel*, '22
Ruland, *novel*, '22 (projected as
Romane um Ruland, vol. II)
Deutsche Reden, *speeches*, '22
Erzählungen, *short stories*, '23
Die Unvollendbarkeit der Welt,
philosophical essays, '23
Zum guten Europäer, *essays*, '24
Der gute Weg, *novel*, '24 (projected
as Romane um Ruland, vol. III)
Die zweite Jugend, *novelette*, '24
Villa U.S.A., *novel*, '26 (projected
as Romane um Ruland, vol. IV)
Der Erkennende, *philosophy*, '27
Sommerroman, *novel*, '27
Unsere Zeit, *essays*, '27
Freund aller Welt, *novel*, '28 (pro-
jected as Romane um Ruland,
vol. V)
Erzählungen, *short stories*, '28
Die erotische Freiheit, *essay*, '28
Es ist Zeit, *novel*, '29
Ulrich von Hutten, *biography*, '29
Marquis de Sade, *essay*, '30
(Marquis de Sade, Lon. '31)
Montijo; oder die Suche nach der
Nation, *novel*, '31
Maria im Dachgarten, *fairy tales*,
'31
Bilanz, *essays*, '31
Christa, ein Kinderroman, '31
Die Geschichte Mariettas, *novel-
ette*, '31
Nationale Erziehung, *essays*, '31
Ausfahrt und Einkehr; Erzäh-
lungen und Reiseskizzen, *short
stories and sketches*, '31
Die französische Revolution, *his-
tory*, '32
Hortense; oder die Rückkehr nach
Baden-Baden, *novel*, '33

Der Strassburger Zuckerbeck, *fairy tales*, '33

Die Töchter Noras, *novel*, '34

Die junge Monthiver, *novel*, '34

FLEISSER, MARIELUISE, b. 1901, *novelist, playwright*

Fegefeuer in Ingolstadt, *play*, '26

Pioniere in Ingolstadt, *play*, '28

Ein Pfund Orangen, *short stories*, '29

Mehlreisende Frieda Geier, *novel*, '31

Andorranische Abenteuer, *sketches*, '32

FRANK, BRUNO, b. 1887, *poet, playwright, novelist*

Aus der goldenen Schale, *poems*, '05

Im dunkeln Zimmer, *novelette*, '06

Gedichte, *poems*, '07

Die Nachtwache, *novel*, '09

Flüchtlinge, *short stories*, '11

Gustav Pfizers Dichtungen, *monograph*, '12

Die Schatten der Dinge, *poems*, '12

Requiem, *poems*, '12

Strophen im Krieg; ein Flugblatt, '15

Die Fürstin, *novel*, '15

Der Himmel der Enttäuschten, *short stories*, '16

Die treue Magd, *comedy*, '17

Die Schwestern und der Fremde, *play*, '18

Die Trösterin, *play*, '19

Ein Abenteuer in Venedig, *novelette*, '19

Von der Menschenliebe, *speech*, '19

Gesichter, *short stories*, '20

Die Kelter, *poems*, '20

Leidenschaften, *short stories*, '21

Das Weib auf dem Tiere, *play*, '21

Bigram, *short stories*, '21

Die Melodie, *short stories*, '24

Tage des Königs, *short stories*, '25 (Days of the King, Lon. '27, N. Y. '27)

Friedrich der Grosse als Mensch, *essay*, '26

Trenck; Roman eines Günstlings, *novel*, '26 (Trenck; the Love Story of a Favorite, N. Y. '28)

Erzählungen, *short stories*, '26

Ein Konzert, *novelettes*, '27

Zwölftausend, *play*, '27 (Twelve Thousand, Lon. '28, N. Y. '28)

Politische Novelle, *novelette*, '28 (The Persians Are Coming, Lon. '29, N. Y. '29)

Perlenkomödie, *comedy*, '28

Der Magier, *novelette*, '29

Sturm im Wasserglas, *comedy*, '30

Alkmene, *novelette*, '30

Nina, *comedy*, '31

Schimmelmanns Brautschau, *play*, '32

Die Fürstin, *novel*, '32

Der General und das Gold, *play*, '32

Cervantes, *novel*, '34 (A Man Called Cervantes, Lon. '34, N. Y. '35)

FRANK, LEONHARD, b. 1882, *novelist, playwright*

Die Räuberbande, *novel*, '14 (The Robber Band, Lon. '28, N. Y. '28)

Der Mensch ist gut, *novel*, '19

Die Mutter, *novelette*, '19

Die Ursache, *novel*, '20 (The Cause of the Crime, Lon. '28, N. Y. '28)

Hermann Büschler, *novel*, '22

Der Bürger, *novel*, '24 (A Middle Class Man, Lon. '30, N. Y. '30)

Auf der Landstrasse, *novelettes*, '25

Die Schicksalsbrücke, *novelettes*, '25

Im letzten Wagen, *novelette*, '25 (included in, In the Last Coach and other stories, Lon. '35)

Karl und Anna, *novelette,* '27 (Carl and Anna, Lon. '29, N. Y. '29)

Das Ochsenfurter Männerquartett, *novel,* '27 (The Singers, Lon. '32, N. Y. '33)

Der Streber, *short stories,* '28

Karl und Anna, *play,* '29 (Karl and Anna, N. Y. '29)

Die Entgleisten, *film novelette,* '29

Die Ursache, *drama,* '29

Bruder und Schwester, *novel,* '29 (Brother and Sister, Lon. '30, N. Y. '30)

Absturz, *novelette,* '29

Hufnägel, *play,* '30

Von drei Millionen Drei, *novel,* '31

FRISCH, EFRAIM, b. 1873, *novelist*

Das Verlöbnis, *novel,* '02

Von der Kunst des Theaters, *essays in dialogue,* '10

Zenobi, *novel,* '27

GLAESER, ERNST, b. 1902, *novelist*

Überwindung der Madonna, *drama,* '24

Jahrgang 1902, *novel,* '28 (Class of 1902, N. Y. '29, Lon. '29)

Fazit, *essays,* '29

Frieden, *novel,* '30

Das dreissigste Jahr, *novel,* '31

Der Staat ohne Arbeitslose (in collab. with F. K. Weiskopf), '31 (Land without Unemployment, N. Y. '31, Lon. '32)

Das Gut im Elsass, *novel,* '32

GOLL, IWAN, b. 1891, *poet, dramatist*

Requiem, *poems,* '17

Der Torso, *Dithyramben,* '18

Der neue Orpheus, *poems,* '18

Die Unterwelt, *poems,* '19

Die drei guten Geister Frankreichs, *essays,* '19

Die Chapliniade, *Kinodichtung,* '20

Die Unsterblichen, *drama,* '20

Gala, '21

Methusalem, *play,* '22

Der Eiffelturm, *selected poems,* '24

Der Stall des Augias, *drama,* '24

Germaine Berton, die rote Jungfrau, *essay,* '25

Die Eurokokke, *novelette,* '27

Der Mitropäer, *novel,* '28

GROSSMAN, STEFAN, b. 1875, *novelist, playwright, critic*

Die Treue, *novelettes,* '01

Die Gasse, *novelette,* '02

Österreichische Strafanstalten,' 05

Der Vogel im Käfig, *play,* '06

Herzliche Grüsse, *novelettes,* '09

Grete Beier, *novelettes,* '13

Der Vorleser der Kaiserin, *novelettes,* '18

Die Partei, *novel,* '19

Der Hochverräter Ernst Toller, '19

Lenchen Demuth, *novelettes,* '25

Chefredakteur Roth führt Krieg, *novel,* '28

Apollo Brunnenstrasse, *play,* '29

Ich war begeistert, *autobiog.,* '30

Die beiden Adler, *drama,* '31

HAAS, WILLY, b. 1891, *critic, journalist*

Die Seele des Orients, *essay,* '16

Eine Ordensübung der Ammaria, '17

Das Spiel mit dem Feuer, *essays,* '23

Gestalten der Zeit, '30

HALBE, MAX, b. 1865, *dramatist*

Friedrich II. und der Päpstliche Stuhl, '88

Ein Emporkömmling, *tragedy,* '89

Freie Liebe, *drama,* '90

Eisgang, *play,* '92

Jugend, *drama,* '93 (Youth, N. Y. '16)

Der Amerikafahrer, *comedy,* '94

Lebenswende, *comedy,* '96

Frau Meseck, Dorfgeschichte, '97

Antigone, *tragedy*, '17

Die Menschen, *play*, '18

Der politische Dichter, *essay*, '19

Die Entscheidung, *comedy*, '19

Die Pest, ein Film, '20

Jenseits, *drama*, '20

Gobseck, *drama*, '22

Gedichte an Frauen, *poems*, '22

Dramen, '24

Mord, *drama*, '26

Ein besserer Herr, *comedy*, '27

Ehen werden im Himmel geschlossen, *play*, '29

Napoleon greift ein, *comedy*, '30

HAUPTMANN, GERHART, b. 1862, *dramatist, novelist*

Promethidenlos, *epic*, '85

Das bunte Buch, '88

Vor Sonnenaufgang, *drama*, '89 (Before Dawn, in "Poet Lore," vol. XX, Boston '09; in Dramatic Works, vol. I, N. Y. '12, Lon. '13)

Das Friedensfest, *play*, '90 (The Coming of Peace, Lon. '00; The Reconciliation, in Dramatic Works, vol. VIII, N. Y. '24, Lon. '25)

Einsame Menschen, *drama*, '91 (Lonely Lives, Lon. '98, N. Y. '98; also in Dramatic Works, vol. III., Lon. '14, N. Y. '14)

Die Weber, *drama*, '92 (The Weavers, Lon. '99, N. Y. '11; also in Dramatic Works, vol. I, N. Y. '12, Lon. '13)

Kollege Crampton, *comedy*, '92 (Colleague Crampton, in Dramatic Works, vol. III, N. Y. '14, Lon. '14)

Der Apostel; Bahnwärter Thiel, *novelettes*, '92

Der Biberpelz, *comedy*, '93 (The Beaver Coat, in D r a m a t i c Works, vol. I, N. Y. '12, Lon. '13)

Hannele, Traumdichtung, '94 (Hannele, Lon. '94; in "Poet Lore," vol. XX, Boston '08)

Florian Geyer, *drama*, '96 (Florian Geyer, in Dramatic Works, vol. IX, N. Y. '29, Lon. '30)

Hanneles Himmelfahrt, *play*, '97 (The Assumption of Hannele, N. Y. '08; also in Dramatic Works, vol. IV, Lon. '14, N. Y. '14)

Die versunkene Glocke, *play*, '97 (The Sunken Bell, Lon. '99, N. Y. '99; also in Dramatic Works, vol. IV, Lon. '14, N. Y. '14)

Fuhrmann Henschel, *drama*, '98 (Fuhrmann Henschel, Chicago '10; Drayman Henschel, in Dramatic Works, vol. II, Lon. '13, N. Y. '13)

Schluck und Jau, *comedy*, '00 (Schluck and Jau, in Dramatic Works, vol. V, N. Y. '15, Lon. '19)

Michael Kramer, *drama*, '00 (Michael Kramer, in Dramatic Works, vol. III, Lon. '14, N. Y. '14)

Der rote Hahn, *tragi-comedy*, '01 (The Conflagration, in Dramatic Works, vol. I, N. Y. '12, Lon. '13)

Der arme Heinrich, *play*, '02 (Henry of Auë, in Dramatic Works, vol. IV, Lon. '14, N. Y. '14)

Rose Bernd, *drama*, '03 (Rose Bernd, in Dramatic Works, vol. II, Lon. '13, N. Y. '13)

Elga, *drama*, '05 (Elga, in "Poet Lore," vol. XVII, Boston '06; also in Dramatic Works, vol. VII, N. Y. '17, Lon. '19)

Buch der Leidenschaft, *novel*, '30 (The Book of Passion, Lon. '30)

Die Spitzhacke, *novelette*, '30

Die Hochzeit auf Buchenhorst, *novelette*, '31

Paralipomena zum Hirtenlied, *eight scenes*, '32

Vor Sonnenuntergang, *drama*, '32

Um Volk und Geist, *speeches*, '32

Goethe, *speech*, N. Y. '32

Die goldene Harfe, *play*, '33

Das Meerwunder, *novelette*, '34

HAUSER, HEINRICH, b. 1901, *novelist, essayist*

Das zwanzigste Jahr, *novel*, '25

Brackwasser, *novel*, '28 (Bitter Waters, N. Y. '29, Lon. '30)

Friede mit Maschinen, *essays*, '28

Donner überm Meer, *novel*, '29 (Thunder Above The Sea, N. Y. '31)

Schwarzes Revier, *essays*, '30

Die letzten Segelschiffe, '30 (Fair Winds and Foul, N. Y. '32, Lon. '34)

Feldwege nach Chicago, '31

Noch nicht, *novel*, '32

Wetter im Osten, *novel*, '32

Ein Mann lernt fliegen, '33

Kampf, *autobiog.*, '34

HAUSMANN, MANFRED, b. 1898, *novelist, playwright*

Die Frühlingsfeier, *novelettes*, '24

Jahreszeiten, *poem*, '24

Orgelkaporgel, *novelettes*, '25

Die Verirrten, *novelettes*, '27

Marienkind, *play*, '27

Lampioon küsst Mädchen und kleine Birken, *novel*, '28

Lilofee, *play*, '29

Salut gen Himmel, *novel*, '29 (Salute to Heaven, Lon. '31, N. Y. '31)

Kleine Liebe zu Amerika, '31

Abel mit der Mundharmonika, *novel*, '32

Die Föhre, *novelette*, '33

Ontje Arps, *novelette*, '34

HERMANN, GEORG, b. 1871, *novelist, playwright, art critic*

Der Simplicissimus und seine Zeichner, '00

Aus dem letzten Hause, *sketches*, '00

Die deutsche Karikatur im 19. Jahrhundert, '01

Skizzen und Silhouetten, *essays*, '02

Jettchen Gebert, *novel*, '06; new ed. '07, as Jettchen Geberts Geschichte, vol. I (Hetty Geybert, N. Y. '24)

Henriette Jacoby, *novel*, '08 (Jettchen Geberts Geschichte, vol. II)

Rudyard Kipling, *essay*, '09

Sehnsucht, ernste Plaudereien, '09

Kubinke, *novel*, '10; new ed. '24

Der Wüstling oder Die Reise nach Breslau, *comedy*, '11

Aus guter alter Zeit—Malerische Winkel aus deutschen Städten, '11

Spielkinder, *novelettes*, '11

Die Nacht des Dr. Herzfeld, *novel*, '12 (reissued as Dr. Herzfeld, vol. I)

Um Berlin, '12

Das Biedermeier im Spiegel seiner Zeit, '13

Jettchen Gebert, *play*, '13

Henriette Jacoby, *play*, '15

Heinrich Schön jr., *novel*, '15

Vom gesicherten und ungesicherten Leben, *essays*, '15

Einen Sommer lang, *novel*, '17 (vol. I of Die steile Treppe)

Mein Nachbar Ameise, *play*, '17

Kleine Erlebnisse, *novelettes*, '19

Randbemerkungen, *epic*, '20

Schnee, *novel*, '21 (vol. II of Dr. Herzfeld)

Die Nacht des Dr. Herzfeld, *tragedy*, '22

Frau Antonie, *play*, '23

Der kleine Gast, *novel*, '25 (vol. II of Die steile Treppe)

Spaziergang in Potsdam, '26

Holland, Rembrandt und Amsterdam, '26

Der doppelte Spiegel, *essay*, '26

Tränen um Modesta Zamboni, *novel*, '28

Die Zeitlupe, '28

Träume der Ellen Stein, '29

Vorschläge eines Schriftstellers, '29

Grenadier Wordelmann, *novel*, '30,

November Achtzehn, *novel*, '30

Das Buch Ruth, *novel*, '31

Ruth's schwere Stunde, *novel*, '34

HERZOG, WILHELM, b. 1894, *essayist, playwright*

Heinrich von Kleist, *biography*, '11

Erzbergers Ermordung und die revolutionären Arbeiter (under pseud. of Junius III), '21

Im Zwischendeck nach Südamerika, '24

Rund um den Staatsanwalt, *revue*, '28

Die Affäre Dreyfus (in collab. with Rehfisch), *play*, '29

Panama, *play*, '31

Der Kampf einer Republik; Die Affäre Dreyfus, '33

HESSE, HERMANN, b. 1877, *novelist, short-story writer, poet*

Romantische Lieder, *poems*, '99

Eine Stunde hinter Mitternacht, *poems*, '99

Gedichte, *poems*, '02

Peter Camenzind, *novel*, '04

Boccaccio, *biography*, '04

Franz von Assisi, '04

Unterm Rad, *novel*, '06

Diesseits, *five stories*, '07

Hermann Lauscher, *novelette*, '08

Nachbarn, *five stories*, '09

Gertrud, *novel*, '10 (Gertrude and I, N. Y. '15)

Unterwegs, *poems*, '11

Umwege, *short stories*, '12

Aus Indien, '13

Rosshalde, *novel*, '14

In der alten Sonne, '14 (In the Old Sun, N. Y. '13)

Anton Schievelbeyn's ohnfreywillige Reise nache Ostindien, '14

Musik des Einsamen, *poems*, '15

Knulp, *novel*, '15

Blick ins Chaos, '15

Am Weg, *short stories*, '16

Brief ins Feld, '16

Schön ist die Jugend, *two stories*, '16; new ed. '34

Die Marmorsäge, '17

Märchen, '19

Umwege, *short stories*, '19

Kleiner Garten, '19

Klingsors letzter Sommer, *novelettes*, '20; reprinted in Weg nach Innen, '31

Zarathustras Wiederkehr, '20

Gedichte des Malers, '20

Wanderung, '20

Blick ins Chaos, *essays*, '20 (In Sight of Chaos, Zurich '23)

Demian, *novel*, '20 (Demian, N. Y. '23)

Elf Aquarelle aus dem Tessin, '21

Siddharta, indische Dichtung, '22; reprinted in Weg nach Innen, '31

Ausgewählte Gedichte, '22

Italien, *poems*, '23

Sinclairs Notizbuch, '23

Die Verlobung, *novelette*, '24

Psychologia balnearia oder Glossen eines Badener Kurgastes, '24

Geschichten aus dem Mittelalter, '25

Kurgast, '25

Bilderbuch Schilderungen, '26

Die Nürnberger Reise, '27

Der Steppenwolf, '27 (Steppenwolf, Lon. '29, N. Y. '29)

Krises, *diary*, '28

Betrachtungen, *sketches*, '28

Trost der Nacht, *poems*, '28

Der Zyklon, *tales*, '29

Narziss und Goldmund, *novel*, '30
(Death and the Lover, Lon. '32,
N. Y. '32)

Zum Gedächtnis unseres Vaters
(in collab. with A. Hesse), '30

Weg nach Innen, *four stories*, '31

Die Morgenlandfahrt, *novelette*, '32

Hermann Lauscher, *short stories*,
'33 (does not include Hermann
Lauscher, *novelette*, '08)

Kleine Welt, *novelettes*, '33

HEUSER, KURT, b. 1903, *novelist*

Elfenbein für Felicitas, *short stories*, '28

Die Reise ins Innere, *novel*, '31
(The Inner Journey, Lon. '32;
The Journey Inward, N. Y. '32)

Abenteuer in Vineta, *novel*, '33

Buschkrieg, *short stories*, '33

Die Landung, *novel*, '34

JACOB, HEINRICH EDUARD, b. 1889,
novelist, essayist

Das Leichenbegängnis der Gemma
Ebria, *novelette*, '12

Reise durch den belgischen Krieg,
diary, '15

Der Zwanzigjährige, *novel*, '18

Das Geschenk der schönen Erde,
Idyllen, '18

Beaumarchais und Sonnenfels,
drama, '19

Die Physiker von Syrakus, *novel*,
'20

Der Tulpenfrevel, *drama*, '20

Das Flötenkonzert der Vernunft,
short stories, '23

Die Leber des General Bonaparte,
novelette, '23

Untergang von dreizehn Musik-
lehrern, *novelette*, '24

Dämonen und Narren, *novelettes*,
'27

Jacqueline und die Japaner, *novel*,
'28 (Jacqueline and the Japan-
ese, Boston '30)

Blut und Zelluloid, *novel*, '29
(Blood and Celluloid, Lon. '30,
N. Y. '30)

Die Magd von Aachen, *novel*, '30

Lieb in Üsküb, *novel*, '32

Ein Staatsmann strauchelt, *novel*,
'32

JOHANNSEN, ERNST, b. 1898,
novelist

Vier von der Infanterie, '29 (Four
Infantrymen on the Western
Front, Lon. '30; Four Infantry-
men, N. Y. '30)

Fronterinnerungen eines Pferdes,
'29

Station Drei, '31

Brigade, *drama for radio*, '32
(Brigade Exchange, N. Y. '32)

JÜNGER, ERNST, b. 1895, *essayist,
pamphleteer*

In Stahlgewittern, '20 (The Storm
of Steel, Lon. '29; Storm of
Steel, N. Y. '29)

Der Kampf als inneres Erlebnis,
'22

Das Wäldchen 125, '25 (Copse 125,
A Chronicle from the Trench
Warfare of 1918, Lon. '30)

Feuer und Blut, '29

Das abenteuerliche Herz, '29

Die totale Mobilmachung, '31

Der Arbeiter, Herrschaft und
Gestalt, '32

Der Krieg als inneres Erleben,
essays, '32

Blätter und Steine, *essays*, '34

KAISER, GEORG, b. 1878, *dramatist*

Die jüdische Witwe, *play*, '11

König Hahnrei, *play*, '13

Der Kongress, *comedy*, '14

Der Fall des Schülers Vehgesack, '14

Die Bürger von Calais, *play*, '14

Europa, '15

Von Morgens bis Mitternacht, *play*, '16 (From Morn to Midnight, Lon. '20, N. Y. '22)

Der Zentaur, *comedy*, '16; new ed. as Konstantin Strobel, '20

Die Sorina, *comedy*, '17

Die Koralle, *play*, '17 (The Coral, N. Y. '29)

Die Versuchung, *tragedy*, '17

Das Frauenopfer, *play*, '18

Rektor Kleist, *tragi-comedy*, '18

Claudius; Friedrich und Anna; Juana, *one-act plays*, '18

Der Brand im Opernhaus, *play*, '19 (The Fire in the Opera House, N. Y. '27)

Hölle, Weg, Erde, *play*, '19

Der gerettete Alkibiades, '20

Er soll dein Herr sein, *comedy* (in collab. with Paul R. Lehnhard), '20

Gas, *play;* part I, '18, part II, '20 (Gas, Lon. '24, Boston '24, N. Y. '31)

David und Goliath, *comedy*, '21

Kanzlist Krehler, *tragi-comedy*, '22

Noli me tangere, *play*, '22

Gilles und Jeanne, *play*, '23

Nebeneinander, *play*, '23

Die Flucht nach Venedig, *play*, '23

Der Geist der Antike, *comedy*, '23

Gats, *play*, '25

Der Protagonist, *one-act opera*, '25

Der mutige Seefahrer, *comedy*, '26

Zweimal Oliver, *play*, '26

Papiermühle, *comedy*, '27

Der Präsident, *comedy*, '27

Oktobertag, *play*, '28 (The Phantom Lover, N. Y. '28)

Die Lederköpfe, *play*, '28

Der Zar lässt sich photographieren, *opera bouffe*, '28

Hellseherei, *play*, '29

Zwei Krawatten, *play*, '30

Mississippi, *play*, '30

Es ist genug, *novel*, '32

KASSNER, RUDOLF, b. 1873, *essayist, novelist*

Die Mystik, die Künstler und das Leben, *essays*, '00

Der Tod und die Maske, '02

Der indische Idealismus, '03

Die Moral der Musik, '05; revised ed. '12

Denis Diderot, '06

Motive, *essays*, '06

Melancholia, eine Trilogie des Geistes, '08

Der Dilettantismus, '10

Von den Elementen der menschlichen Grösse, '11

Der indische Gedanke, '13; new ed. '21

Die Chimäre; Der Aussätzige, '14

Zahl und Gesicht, '19

Englische Dichter, '20

Die Grundlagen der Physiognomik, '22

Essays, '23

Die Verwandlung, *essays*, '25

Die Mythen der Seele, '27

Narciss, '28

Das physiognomische Weltbild, '30

Der Einzelne und der Kollektivmensch, '31

Physiognomik, '32

Buch der Gleichnisse, '34

KÄSTNER, ERICH, b. 1899, *poet, novelist*

Herz auf Taille, *poems*, '28

Lärm im Spiegel, *poems*, '29

Emil und die Detektive, '29 (Emil and the Detectives, a Story for Children, Lon. '30, N. Y. '30)

Leben in dieser Zeit, Kantate, '29

Ein Mann gibt Auskunft, *poems*, '30

Fabian, die Geschichte eines Moralisten, *novel*, '31 (Fabian, Lon. '32, N. Y. '32)

Pünktchen und Anton, Kinderroman, '31 (Annaluise and Anton, Lon. '32, N. Y. '33)

Arthur mit dem langen Arm, '31

Das verhexte Telefon, '31

Gesang zwischen den Stühlen, *poems*, '32

Der 35. Mai oder Konrad reitet in die Südsee, '32 (The 35th of May; or, Conrad's Ride to the South Seas, Lon. '33, N. Y. '34)

Das fliegende Klassenzimmer, Kinderroman, '33 (The Flying Class-Room, Lon. '34)

Drei Männer im Schnee, *novel*, '34

KAYSER, RUDOLF, b. 1889, *biographer, critic, essayist*

Moses Tod, *legend*, '21

Verkündigung, Anthologie, '21

Die Zeit ohne Mythos, '23

Das junge deutsche Drama, '24

Stendhal oder das Leben eines Egotisten, '28 (Stendhal, The Life of an Egoist, N. Y. '30)

Dichterköpfe, *essays*, '30

Spinoza, '32

KELLERMANN, BERNHARD, b. 1879, *novelist, playwright*

Yester und Li, *novel*, '04

Ingeborg, *novel*, '06

Der Tor, *novel*, '09

Das Meer, *novel*, '10 (The Sea, N. Y. '24, Lon. '25)

Ein Spaziergang in Japan, '10

Sassa yo Yassa, '12

Der Tunnel, *novel*, '13 (The Tunnel, Lon. '15, N. Y. '15)

Der Krieg im Westen, '15

Der Krieg im Argonnerwald, '16

Der neunte November, *novel*, '20 (The Ninth of November, Lon. '25, N. Y. '25)

Die Heiligen, *novelette*, '22

Schwedenklees Erlebnis, *novel*, '23

Die Brüder Schellenberg, *novel*, '25

Die Wiedertäufer von Münster, *drama*, '25

Auf Persiens Karawanenstrassen, '28

Der Weg der Götter; Indien, Klein-Tibet, Siam, '29

Die Stadt Anatol, *novel*, '32

Erinnerungen, ein Künstlerleben, *autobiog.*, '32

Jang-tsze-Kiang, *novelette*, '34

KERR, ALFRED, b. 1867, *art critic, essayist*

C. Brentanos Jugenddichtungen, '94

Godwi, '98

Herr Sudermann, der D...Di... Dichter, '03

Das neue Drama, '04

Die Harfe, *poems*, '17

Gesammelte Schriften, 1. Reihe: Die Welt im Drama, 5 vols., '17; 2. Reihe: Die Welt im Licht, 2 vols., '20

Der Krämerspiegel (with music by Richard Strauss), '22

New York und London, '23

O Spanien!, '24

Yankeeland, '25

Caprichos, *poems*, '26

Es sei wie es wolle, es war doch schön, '28

Die Allgier trieb nach Algier, '29

Spanische Rede vom deutschen Drama, '30

Eine Insel heisst Korsika, '33

Was wird aus Deutschlands Theater?, *essay*, '33

KESTEN, HERMANN, b. 1898, *novelist*

Josef sucht die Freiheit, *novel*, '27
(Josef Breaks Free, Lon. '30)

Ein ausschweifender Mensch, *novel*,
'29

Babel oder Der Weg zur Macht,
drama, '29

Die Liebes-Ehe, *novelettes*, '29

Glückliche Menschen, *novel*, '31

Der Scharlatan, *novel*, '32

Der Gerechte, *novel*, '34

KEYSERLING, HERMANN VON, b.
1880, *philosopher*, *critic*

Das Gefüge der Welt, '06

Unsterblichkeit, '07; revised '20

Individuum und Zeitgeist, *speech*,
'08

Entwicklungshemmungen, '09

Prolegomena zur Naturphiloso-
phie, '10

Schopenhauer als Verbilder, '10

Zwei Reden, *speeches*, '11

Über die innere Beziehung zwi-
schen den Kulturproblemen des
Orients und des Okzidents, '13
(The East and West and Their
Search for the Common Truth,
Shanghai '12)

Das Reisetagebuch eines Philoso-
phen, '19 (The Travel Diary
of a Philosopher, Lon. '25, N. Y.
'25)

Europas Zukunft, '19

Deutschlands wahre politische
Mission, '19

Was uns not tut, was ich will, '19

Philosophie als Kunst, '20

Politik, Wirtschaft, Weisheit, '22

Schöpferische Erkenntnis, '22
(Creative Understanding, Lon.
'29, N. Y. '29)

Das Ehe-Buch, '25 (The Book of
Marriage, N. Y. '26, Lon. '27)

Die neuentstehende Welt, '26
(The World in the Making,
Lon. '27, N. Y. '27)

Menschen als Sinnbilder, '26

Wiedergeburt, '27 (The Recovery
of Truth, Lon. '29, N. Y. '29)

Das Spektrum Europas, '28 (Europe, Lon. '28, N. Y. '28)

Darmstadt und Grossherzog Ernst
Ludwig, '29

Amerika, der Aufgang einer neuen
Welt, '30 (America Set Free,
N. Y. '29, Lon. '30)

Südamerikanische Meditationen,
'32 (South American Medita-
tions, Lon. '32, N. Y. '32)

Problems of Personal Life, Lon.
'34, N. Y. '34 (transl. from the
French; no German publ.)

KOKOSCHKA, OSKAR, b. 1886,
dramatist

Dramen und Bilder, '13

Hiob, *drama*, '17

Die träumenden Knaben, *tale*, '17

4 Dramen: Orpheus und Eurydike;
Der brennende Dornbusch;
Mörder, Hoffnung der Frauen;
Hiob, '19

KRAUS, KARL, b. 1874, *satirist, poet,
dramatist, essayist*

Eine Krone für Zion, *essay*, '99

Heinrich von Veldeke, *essay*, '99

Die demolirte Literatur, '99

Sittlichkeit und Kriminalität, *essays*, '02; enlarged ed. '08

Der Fall Hervay, *essay*, '04

Irrenhaus Oesterreich, *essay*, '04

Maximilian Harden, Eine Erledi-
gung, '07

Maximilian Harden, Ein Nachruf,
'08

Sprüche und Widersprüche, *aphorisms*, '09

Heine und die Folgen, *essay*, '10

Die chinesische Mauer, *essays*, '10

Pro domo et mundo, *aphorisms*, '12

Nestroy und die Nachwelt, *speech*,
'12

Worte in Versen, *poems*, vols. I–IV, '16
Die letzte Nacht, *epilogue*, '18
Weltgericht, *essays*, '19
Nachts, *aphorisms*, '19
Die letzten Tage der Menschheit, *tragedy*, '19
Peter Altenberg, *speech*, '19
Ausgewählte Gedichte, '20
Literatur oder Man wird doch da sehen, *operetta*, '21
Untergang der Welt durch schwarze Magie, *essays*, '22
Traumstück, *play*, '23
Wolkenkuckucksheim (after Aristophanes' The Birds), *comedy*, '23
Traumtheater, *play*, '24
Worte in Versen, vols. V–VIII, '22–'25
Epigramme, '27
Die Unüberwindlichen, *drama*, '28
Literatur und Lüge, *essays*, '29
Worte in Versen, vol. IX, '30
Poems (selected translations), Boston '30
Zeitstrophen, *poems*, '31
Adolf Loos, *eulogy*, '33

LAMPEL, PETER MARTIN, 1894, *novelist, essayist, dramatist*
Der Stil in Lyly's Lustspielen, *dissertation*, '12
Bombenflieger, '18
Heereszeppeline im Angriff, '18
Bob, der Pampasflieger, '22
Jungen in Not, '28
Revolte im Erziehungshaus, *play*, '29
Verratene Jungen, *novel*, '29 (Youth Betrayed, Lon. '30)
Patrouillen!, *essays*, '30
Vaterland, *play*, '32
Packt an! Kameraden!, '32
Alarm im Arbeitslager, *play*, '32
Siedeln! Mensch, wie sieht das aus?, *sketches*, '33

LASKER-SCHÜLER, ELSE, b. 1876, *poet, playwright*
Styx, *poems*, '02
Der siebente Tag, *poems*, '05
Das Peter Hille-Buch, '06; new ed. '19
Die Nächte der Tino von Bagdad, '07; new ed. '19
Die Wupper, *play*, '09; new ed. '19
Meine Wunder, *poems*, '11; new ed. '14
Mein Herz, *novel*, '12; new ed. '20
Hebräische Balladen, *poems*, '13; new ed., as Der Gedichte Teil I, '20
Gesichte, *stories*, '13
Der Prinz von Theben, '14; new ed. '20
Die gesammelten Gedichte, '17
Der Malik, '19
Essays, '20
Die Kuppel, *poems*, '20 (Der Gedichte Teil II)
Der Wunderrabiner von Barcelona, '21
Theben, *poems*, '23
Ich räume auf! Meine Anklage gegen meine Verleger, '25
Konzert, '32
Arthur Aronymus, die Geschichte meines Vaters, '32

LEONHARD, RUDOLF, b. 1889, *poet, essayist, playwright*
Angelische Strophen, '13
Der Weg durch den Wald, *poems*, '13
Barbaren, Balladen, '14
Über den Schlachten, *poems*, '14
Äonen des Fegefeuers, *aphorisms*, '17
Polnische Gedichte, '18
Beate und der grosse Pan, *novel*, '18; new ed. '28
Briefe an Margit, *poems*, '19
Das Chaos, *poems*, '19

Katilinarische Pilgerschaft, *poems*, '19

Kampf gegen die Waffe!, '19

Alles und Nichts, *aphorisms*, '20

Spartakussonette, *poems*, '22

Die Prophezeiung, *poems*, '22

Die Insel, *poems*, '23

Die Ewigkeit dieser Zeit, '24

Das nackte Leben, *poems*, '25

Segel am Horizont, *play*, '25

Tragödie von heute, *play*, '27

Das Wort, '32

LERNET-HOLENIA, ALEXANDER, 1897, *poet, dramatist, novelist*

Pastorale, *poems*, '21

Kanzonnair, *poems*, '23

Demetrius, *drama*, '26

Allapotrida, *comedy*, '26

Erotik, *comedy*, '27

Österreichische Komödie, *comedy*, '27

Das Geheimnis Sankt Michaels, *poems*, '27

Parforce, *comedy*, '28

Die nächtliche Hochzeit, *drama*, '29

Die nächtliche Hochzeit, *novel*, '30

Kavaliere, *comedy*, '30

Die Abenteuer eines jungen Herrn in Polen, *novel*, '31 (A Young Gentleman in Poland, Lon. '33)

Ljubas Zobel, *novel*, '32

Ich war Jack Mortimer, *novel*, '33

Jo und der Herr zu Pferde, *novel*, '33

Die goldene Horde, *poems*, '33

Die Standarte, *novel*, '34

LINKE-POOT, *see* DÖBLIN, ALFRED

LOERKE, OSKAR, b. 1884, *novelist, essayist, poet*

Vineta, *novelette*, '07

Franz Pfinz, *novelette*, '09

Der Turmbau, *novel*, '10

Wanderschaft, *poems*, '11

Gedichte, *poems*, '16; new ed. pub. as Pansmusik, '29

Das Goldbergwerk, *novelette*, '19

Chimärenreiter, *novelettes*, '19

Der Prinz und der Tiger, *novelette*, '20

Der Oger, *novel*, '21

Die heimliche Stadt, *poems*, '21

Pompeji, *poems*, '21

Zeitgenossen aus vielen Zeiten, *essays*, '25

Der längste Tag, *poems*, '26

Atem der Erde, *poems*, '30

Der Silberdistelwald, *poems*, '34

LUDWIG, EMIL, b. 1881, *biographer, journalist, novelist, playwright*

Der Spiegel von Shalott, *dramatic poem*, '07

Die Borgia, *play*, '07

Tristan und Isolde, *drama*, '08

Atalanta, *drama*, '09

Ariadne auf Naxos, *drama*, '09

Symphonie, *comedy*, '10

Manfred und Helena, *novel*, '11

Wagner, oder Die Entzauberten, '13

Die Reise nach Afrika, '13

Richard Dehmel, '13

Der verlorene Sohn, *comedy*, '14

Friedrich, Kronprinz von Preussen, *play*, '14

Der Künstler, *essays*, '14

Die Fahrten der Emden und der Ayesha, '15

Die Fahrten der Goeben und der Breslau, '16

Der Kampf auf dem Balkan, '16

Diana, *novel*, '18 (Diana, N. Y. '29, Lon. '30)

Diplomaten, *comedy*, '19

Galatea, *drama*, '20

Meeresstille und glückliche Fahrt, *novel*, '21

Goethe, Geschichte eines Menschen, *biography*, '22 (Goethe, Lon. '28, N. Y. '28)

Bismarck, trilogy: Volk und Krone; 1870; Die Entlassung, *plays,* '22–'24 (Bismarck, trilogy: King and People; Union; Dismissal, Lon. '27, N. Y. '27)

Am Mittelmeer, *travel sketches,* '23 (On Mediterranean Shores, Lon. '29, Boston '29)

Rembrandts Schicksal, '23

Meeresstille, Roman eines deutschen Prinzen, *novel,* '25 (included in Diana, N. Y. '29, Lon. '30)

Genie und Charakter, *essays,* '25 (Genius and Character, Lon. '27, N. Y. '27)

Napoleon, *biography,* '25 (Napoleon, Lon. '27, N. Y. '27)

Wilhelm der Zweite, *biography,* '26 (Kaiser Wilhelm II., N. Y. '26; Wilhelm Hohenzollern, the Last of the Kaisers, Lon. '27)

Bismarck, Geschichte eines Kämpfers, '26 (Bismarck, History of a Fighter, Lon. '27, Boston '27)

Kunst und Schicksal, *biographical essays,* '27 (includes "Rembrandt" and "Beethoven," translated in Three Titans, Lon. '30, N. Y. '30)

Der Menschensohn, '28 (Son of Man, Lon. '28, N. Y. '28)

Tom und Sylvester, *novel in verse,* '28

Juli Vierzehn, *essays,* '29 (July '14, Lon. '29, N. Y. '29)

Lincoln, *biography,* '29 (Lincoln, Lon. '30, Boston '30)

Michelangelo, '30 (included in Three Titans, Lon. '30, N. Y. '30)

Geschenke des Lebens, Rückblick, *autobiog.,* '30 (Gifts of Life, Lon. '31, Boston '31)

Schliemann, *biography,* '31 (Schliemann of Troy, Lon. '31; Schliemann, Boston '31)

Historische Dramen, '31

Dramatische Dichtungen, *collected plays,* '32

Goethe, Kämpfer und Führer, *speech,* '32

Versailles, *play,* Lon. '32 (not publ. in German)

Gespräche mit Mussolini, '33

Gespräche mit Masaryk, '34

Führer Europas, *essays,* '34 (Leaders of Europe, Lon. '34; Nine Etched from Life, N. Y. '34

MANN, HEINRICH, b. 1871, *novelist, essayist, playwright*

Im Schlaraffenland, *novel,* '01 (The Land of Cockaigne, Lon. '29; In the Land of Cockaigne, N. Y. '29)

Die Göttinnen, *trilogy,* 3 vols., '04; reissued in 1 vol., '07
  vol. I: Diana (Diana, N. Y. '29)
  vol. II: Minerva
  vol. III: Venus

Die Jagd nach Liebe, *novel,* '03

Flöten und Dolche, *novelette,* '05 (included in Die Novellen, vol. I, '17)

Professor Unrat, *novel,* '06 (The Blue Angel, Lon. '32)

Zwischen den Rassen, *novel,* '07

Stürmische Morgen, *novelettes,* '07

Die Bösen, '08

Die kleine Stadt, *novel,* '09 (The Little Town, Lon. '30, N.Y. '31)

Variété, *one-act play,* '10 (included in 3 Akte, '18)

Das Herz, *novelettes,* '11 (included in Die Novellen, vol. II, '17)

Die Rückkehr vom Hades, *novelettes,* '11 (included in Die Novellen, vol. II, '17)

Schauspielerin, *drama,* '11

Die grosse Liebe, *drama*, '12

Auferstehung, *novelettes*, '13

Die Armen, *novel*, '17

Bunte Gesellschaft, *novelettes*, '17

Madame Legros, *drama*, '17 (Madame Legros, N.Y. '27)

Brabach, *drama*, '17

Der Untertan, *novel*, '18 (The Patrioteer, N.Y. '21)

3 Akte: Der Tyrann; Der Unschuldige; Variété, *one-act plays*, '18

Der Sohn, *novelette*, '19

Der Weg zur Macht, *drama*, '19

Die Ehrgeizige, *novelette*, '20

Macht und Mensch, *essays*, '20

Die Tote, *novelettes*, '21

Diktatur der Vernunft, *essays*, '23

In einer Familie, *novel*, '24

Der Jüngling, *novelettes*, '24

Abrechnungen, *novelettes*, '24

Der Kopf, *novel*, '25

Kobes, *novelette*, '25

Liliane und Paul, *novelette*, '26

Mutter Marie, *novel*, '27 (Mother Mary, N.Y. '28)

Eugénie, *novel*, '28 (The Royal Woman, N.Y. '30, Lon. '31)

Sieben Jahre, *essays*, '29

Sie sind jung, *short stories*, '29

Der Tyrann, Die Branzilla, *novelettes*, '29

Flöten und Dolche, *novelettes*, '30

Die grosse Sache, *novel*, '30

Geist und Tat, *essays*, '31

Der Freund, *novelette*, '31

Die Welt der Herzen, *novelettes*, '32

Ein ernstes Leben, *novel*, '32

Das öffentliche Leben, *essays*, '32

Das Bekenntnis zum Übernationalen, *essays*, '33

Der Hass, *essays*, '33

Die Jugend des Königs Heinrich IV., *novel*, '34

MANN, Klaus, b. 1906, *novelist, essayist*

Vor dem Leben, *short stories*, '25

Anja und Esther, *romantic play*, '25

Der fromme Tanz, '26 (The Fifth Child, N.Y. '27)

Kindernovelle, '26

Revue zu Vieren, *comedy*, '26

Heute und Morgan, '27

Rundherum, (in collab. with Erika Mann), '29

Abenteuer, *short stories*, '29

Gegenüber von China, *comedy*, '29

Alexander, *novel*, '29 (Alexander, N. Y. '30)

Auf der Suche nach einem Weg, *essays*, '31

Das Buch der Riviera (in collab. with Erika Mann), '31

Kind dieser Zeit, *autobiog.*, '32

Treffpunkt im Unendlichen, *novel*, '32

Flucht in den Norden, *novel*, '34

MANN, Thomas, b. 1875, *novelist, essayist*

Der kleine Herr Friedemann und andere Novellen, *novelettes*, '98 (included in Children and Fools, N. Y. '28)

Buddenbrooks, *novel*, '01 (Buddenbrooks, Lon. '24, N. Y. '24)

Tristan, *novelettes*, '03 (included in Death in Venice, N. Y. '25, Lon. '28)

Fiorenza, *drama*, '05

Bilse und Ich, '06 (Bashan and I, Lon. '23, N. Y. '23)

Königliche Hoheit, *novel*, '09 (Royal Highness, Lon. '16, N. Y. '16)

Der Tod in Venedig, *novelette*, '12 (included in Death in Venice, N. Y. '25, Lon. '28; issued separately, N. Y. '30)

Das Wunderkind, *short stories*, '14 (included in Children and Fools, N. Y. '28)

Tonio Kröger und andere Novellen, *novelettes*, '14 (included in Death in Venice, N. Y. '25)

Friedrich und die grosse Koalition, '15 (included in Three Essays, N. Y. '29, Lon. '32)

Betrachtungen eines Unpolitischen, '18

Herr und Hund; Gesang vom Kindchen, '19 (A Man and His Dog, N. Y. '30)

Rede und Antwort, *essays*, '22 (included in Past Masters, Lon. '33, N. Y. '33)

Novellen, *novelettes*, 2 vols., '22

Goethe und Tolstoi, *speech*, '23 (included in Three Essays, N. Y. '29, Lon. '32)

Von deutscher Republik, '23

Bekenntnisse des Hochstaplers Felix Krull, '22

Okkulte Erlebnisse, '24 (included in Three Essays, N. Y. '29, Lon. '32)

Der Zauberberg, *novel*, '24 (The Magic Mountain, Lon. '27, N. Y. '27)

Bemühungen, *essays*, '25 (included in Past Masters, Lon. '33, N. Y. '33)

Kino, *fragment of a novel*, '26

Lübeck als geistige Lebensform, *speech*, '26

Pariser Rechenschaft, '26

Unordnung und frühes Leid, *novelette*, '26 (Early Sorrow, Lon. '29, N. Y. '30)

Zwei Festreden, *two speeches*, '28

Hundert Jahre Reclam, *speech*, '29

Sieben Aufsätze, *essays*, '29

Die Forderung des Tages, *essays*, '30 (included in Past Masters, N. Y. '33)

A Sketch of My Life, Paris, '30 (not publ. in a German ed.)

Deutsche Ansprache, *speech*, '30

Mario und der Zauberer, *novelette*, '30 (Mario and the Magician, Lon. '30, N. Y. '31)

Goethe als Repräsentant des bürgerlichen Zeitalters, '32

Goethes Laufbahn als Schriftsteller, '33 (included in Past Masters, Lon. '33, N. Y. '33)

Joseph und seine Brüder, *trilogy:*
vol. I: Die Geschichten Jaakobs, *novel*, '33 (The Tales of Jacob, Lon. '34; Joseph and his Brothers, N. Y. '34)
vol. II: Der junge Josef, *novel*, '34

Nocturnes, *stories*, N. Y. '34 [translations of Ein Glück (The Gleam), Schwere Stunde (A Weary Hour), and Das Eisenbahnunglück (The Railway Accident)]

MEHRING, WALTER, b. 1896, *satirist*

Einfach klassisch! Schall und Rauch, *puppet play*, '19

Das politische Cabaret, *poems*, '20

Das Ketzerbrevier, *vaudeville sketches*, '21

Wedding-Montmartre, '22

Europäische Nächte, '24

In Menschenhaut, aus Menschenhaut, um Menschenhaut herum, '24

Abenteuerliches Tierhaus, *fables*, '24

Westnordwest, *novelette*, '25

Algier oder Die 13 Oasenwunder, *novelette*, '27

Paris in Brand, *novel*, '29

Die Gedichte, Lieder und Chansons, '29

Der Kaufmann von Berlin, *poetic drama*, '29

Arche Noah SOS, Neues trostreiches Liederbuch, *poems*, '31

MEIER-GRAEFE, JULIUS, b. 1867,
  art critic, novelist

  Nach Norden, *novel*, '93

  Der Fürst, *novel*, '95

  Prinz Lichtenarm, '95

  Die Weltausstellung in Paris,
    1900, '00

  Manet und sein Kreis, '03

  Der moderne Impressionismus, '03

  Entwicklungsgeschichte der
    modernen Kunst, 3 vols. '04;
    revised ed. '14–'15 (Modern Art,
    Lon. '08, N. Y. '08)

  Der Fall Böcklin und die Lehre
    von den Einheiten, '05

  Corot und Courbet, '05; enlarged
    ed. '12

  Der junge Menzel, '06

  William Hogarth, '07

  Impressionisten: Goya, Manet,
    Van Gogh, Pissarro, Cézanne,
    '07

  Eugène Delacroix, *a catalogue*, '07

  Die grossen Engländer, '08

  Adam und Eva, *drama*, '09

  Hans von Marées, '09

  Spanische Reise, '10 (Spanish
    Journey, Lon. '26, N. Y. '27)

  Vincent van Gogh, '10; revised
    ed. '22

  Paul Cézanne, '10; revised ed. '23

  Nach Norden, eine Episode, '11

  Auguste Renoir, '11

  Orlando und Angelica, *puppet
    play*, '12

  Eduard Manet, '12

  Wohin treiben wir? *two addresses*,
    '13

  Eugène Delacroix, *essay*, '13;
    new ed. '22

  Camille Corot, '13

  Der Tscheinik, '18; new ed. as
    Die weisse Strasse, '29

  Heinrich der Beglücker, *comedy*,
    '18

Degas, '20 (Degas, Lon. '23, N. Y.
  '23)

Cézanne und sein Kreis, '20
  (Cézanne, Lon. '27, N. Y. '27)

Courbet, '21

Vincent, *biography*, '21 (Vincent
  van Gogh, Lon. '22, N. Y. '23;
  new ed., Lon. '26, N. Y. '28;
  revised ed., N. Y. '33)

Geständniss meines Vetters,
  novelette, '23

Stil und Geschmack, *essay*, '24

Die doppelte Kurve, *essays*, '24

Der Zeichner Hans von Marées,
  '25

Dostojewski der Dichter, '26
  (Dostoevsky, Lon. '28, N. Y. '28)

Pyramide und Tempel, '27 (Pyra-
  mid and Temple, N. Y. '30,
  Lon. '31)

Vincent van Gogh, der Zeichner,
  '28

Renoir, '29

Corot, '30

Der Vater, *novel*, '32

Geschichten neben der Kunst, '33

MOLO, WALTER, VON, b. 1880,
  novelist, playwright, essayist

  Als ich die bunte Mütze trug, '04

  Wie sie das Leben zwangen, *novel*,
    '06

  Der Hochzeitsjunker, *novelettes*, '08

  Die unerbittliche Liebe, *novel*, '09;
    revised ed. '19

  Klaus Tiedemann, *novel*, '09; new
    ed. as Die Lebenswende, '12

  Die törichte Welt, *novel*, '10

  Der gezähmte Eros, *novel*, '11

  Das gelebte Leben, *drama*, '11

  Wir Weibgesellen, *novel*, '11; new
    ed. as Wallfahrer zur lieben
    Frau, '19

  Totes Sein, *novel*, '12

  Der Hochzeitsjunker, *novel*, '12

  Ein Schiller-Roman, 4 vols., '12–
    '16; new ed. in 2 vols. '18

Part I: Ums Menschentum, '12
Part II: Im Titanenkampf, '13
Part III: Die Freiheit, '14
Part IV: Den Sternen zu, '16

Die Mutter, *drama*, '14

Deutsches Volk, Flugblatt, '14

Deutsch sein heisst Mensch sein, '15

An unsere Seelen, 3 Flugblätter, '15

Deutschland und Oesterreich, *essays*, '15

An Frederik van Eeden und Romain Rolland, offener Brief, '15

Kriegs-Aufsätze, *essays*, '15; enlarged ed. '20

Der Infant der Menschheit, *drama*, '16

Sprüche der Seele, *poems*, '16

Der Grosse Fritz im Krieg, '17

Die Erlösung, *tragedy*, '17; new ed. as Die Erlösung der Ethel, '18

Im Schritt der Jahrhunderte, geschichtliche Bilder, '17

Die ewige Tragikomödie, *sketches*, '17

Friedericus, *novel*, '18

Der Hauch im All, *tragedy*, '18

Friedrich Staps, *play*, '18

Luise, *novel*, '19

Die helle Nacht, *drama*, '19

Till Lausebums, *romantic comedy*, '21

Die Liebes-Symphonie, *short novels*, '22

Luise im Osten 1806, '22

Im Zwielicht der Zeit, '22

Auf der rollenden Erde, *novel*, '23

Im ewigen Licht, *novel*, '23

Fugen des Seins, *poems*, '24

Lebensballade, *play*, '24

Gesammelte Werke, 3 vols., '24

Vom Alten Fritz, '24

Der Roman meines Volkes, *trilogy*, '18–'24; new ed. in 1 vol., '24

Part I: Friedericus, '18
Part II: Luise, '19
Part III: Das Volk wacht auf, '24

Bobenmatz, *novel*, '25

Die Legende vom Herrn, '27

Hans Amrung und seine Frau, *novelettes*, '27

Das wahre Glück, *novel*, '28

Mensch Luther, *novel*, '28 (Brother Luther, Lon. '29, N. Y. '30)

Ordnung im Chaos, *play*, '28

Die Scheidung, *novel*, '29

Der deutschen Jugend gesagt, '29

Dichterhandschriften, *facsim.*, '29

Im weiten Meer, *novelette*, '29

Zwischen Tag und Traum, *addresses and essays*, '30

Ein Deutscher ohne Deutschland, Friedrich List-Roman, '31

Deutsche Volksgemeinschaft, *speech*, '32

Wie ich Deutschland möchte, *speech*, '32

Holunder in Polen, *novel*, '33

Der Kleine Held, *novel*, '34

MOMBERT, ALFRED, b. 1872, poet, playwright

Tag und Nacht, *poems*, '94; new ed. '22

Der Glühende, *poems*, '96; new ed. '21

Die Schöpfung, *poems*, '97; new ed. '21

Der Denker, *poems*, '01; new ed. '20

Die Blütte des Chaos, *poems*, '05; new ed. '20

Der Sonne-Geist Mythos, '05; new ed. '23

Aeon; dramatischs Trilogie, '07–'11; new ed. '21

vol. I: Aeon, der Weltgesuchte, '07

vol. II: Aeon zwischen den Frauen, '10

PFEMFERT, FRANZ, b. 1879,
essayist
Die deutsche Sozialdemokratie,
bis August 1914, '17
Moskau und wir, '20
Vor zehn Jahren, '24
Wer ist's? eine Gallerie öffentlicher
Menschen, '27
Karl Liebknecht, biography, '31

POLGAR, ALFRED, b. 1875, novelist,
critic
Der Quell des Übels, short stories,
'08
Goethe (in collab. with Egon
Friedell), '08; new ed. '26
Bewegung ist alles, novelettes, '09
Brahm's Ibsen, '10
Soldatenleben im Frieden (in collab.
with Egon Friedell), play, '10
Hiob, novelettes, '12
Kleine Zeit, '19
Max Pallenberg, '21
Gestern und Heute, tales, '22
An den Rand geschrieben, '26
Orchester von oben, '26
Ja und nein, Kritische Schriften,
4 vols., '26
Ich bin Zeuge, '28
Schwarz auf Weiss, '29
Hinterland, '29
Auswahlband, selected prose, '30
Bei dieser Gelegenheit, sketches, '30
Der unsterbliche Kaspar, play, '30
Die Defraudanten, comedy, '31
Ansichten, '33

PONTEN, JOSEF, b. 1883, novelist,
essayist
Jungfräulichkeit, novel, '06
Augenlust, essays, '07
Siebenquellen, novel, '09
Alfred Rethel, biography, '10
Peter Justus, novel, '12
Griechische Landschaften, essays,
'14
Führer durch die Karlsfresken
Alfred Rethels, '15

Der Babylonische Turm, novel, '18
Die Insel, novelette, '18
Die Bockreiter, novelette, '19
Der Meister, novelette, '20
Der Knabe Vielnam, novelette, '21
Der Jüngling in Masken, novelettes,
'22
Studien über Alfred Rethel, essays,
'22
Der Gletscher, novelette, '23
Die Uhr von Gold, novelette, '23
Kleine Prosa, essays, '23
Der Urwald, novelette, '24
Die Fahrt nach Aachen, novelette,
'24
Architektur, die nicht gebaut
wurde, essays, '25
Der Rhein, two essays, '25
Die Luganesische Landschaft,
essays, '26
Die letzte Reise, novelette, '26
Römisches Idyll, poems, '27
Aus deutschen Dörfern, short
stories, '27
Die Studenten von Lyon, novel, '28
Europäisches Reisebuch, essays,
'28
Seine Hochzeitsreise, novel, '29
Wolga, Wolga, novel, '30; repub-
lished with revised version of
Rhein und Wolga as Im Wolga-
land, '33
Rhein und Wolga, novel, '31; re-
published with revised version
of Wolga, Wolga as Im Wolga-
land, '33
Zwischen Rhone und Wolga,
sketches, '31
Die Väter zogen aus, novel, '34

REIMANN, HANS, b. 1889, humor-
ist, playwright
Die schwarze Liste, ein heikles
Bilderbuch, '16
Der Floh, humorous sketches, '18
Tyll, novel, '18
Pax, short stories, '19

Die Kloake, ein heikles Lesebuch, '20

Mit roter Tinte, *sketches*, '20

Die Dame mit den schönen Beinen, *humorous sketches*, '20

Arthur Sünder, Die Dinte wider das Blut, *parody*, '20

Hedwig Courths-Mahler, Schlichte Geschichten für's traute Heim, *parody*, '20

Vampir von Hanns Heinz Ewers, *parody*, '21

Der Engel Elisabeth, *novel*, '21

Sächsische Miniaturen I, '21

Das blinde Huhn, '21

Kaktusse, *grotesque short stories*, '21

Das verbotene Buch, '21

Sächsische Miniaturen II, '22

Mysreium Flip und Ewa, '22

Die sächsische Volkseele in ihren Wallungen, '22

Mein Kabarettbuch, *selections*, '23

Dr Genij, Sächsische Miniaturen III, '23

Das Paukerbuch, *short stories*, '23

Von Karl May bis Max Pallenberg, '23

V. Margueritte, La Garçonne, *parody*, '23

Literarisches Albdrücken, ein lustiges Bilderbuch, '24

Sago, *humorous short stories*, '25

Aquaria, Lohengrin, Neulehmannsland, *parodies*, '26

Komponist wider Willen, *novel*, '28

Die voll und ganz vollkommene Ehe, nach Dr. Th. H. van der Velde, *parody*, '28

Neue Sächsische Miniaturen, '28

Männer, die im Keller husten, *parodies*, '29

Die Gaffeeganne, Sächsische Miniaturen V, '30

Vergnügliches Handbuch der deutschen Sprache, '30

Der Lausbub, '30

Das Ekel (in collab. with Toni Impekoven), *play*, '30

Das Parodienbuch, '30

Das Buch von Leipzig, '30

Das Buch von Frankfurt, Mainz, Wiesbaden, '30

Sächsisch, '31

Quartett zu Dritt, *novel*, '32

Der wirkliche Knigge, '33

REMARQUE, ERICH MARIA, b. 1898, *novelist*

Im Western nichts Neues, *novel*, '29 (All Quiet on the Western Front, Lon. '29, Boston '29)

Der Weg zurück, *novel*, '31 (The Road Back, Lon. '31, Boston '31)

RENN, LUDWIG, b. 1889, *novelist*

Krieg, *novel*, '28 (War, Lon. '29, N. Y. '29)

Nachkrieg, *novel*, '30 (After War, Lon. '31, N. Y. '31)

Russlandfahrten, *sketches*, '32

ROTH, JOSEPH, b. 1894, *novelist, essayist*

Hotel Savoy, *novel*, '24

Rebellion, *novel*, '24

April, *novelette*, '25

Der blinde Spiegel, *novelette*, '25

Juden auf der Wanderschaft, *essays*, '26

Flucht ohne Ende, *novel*, '27 (Flight without End, Lon. '30, N. Y. '30)

Zipper und sein Vater, *novel*, '27

Rechts und Links, *novel*, '29

Hiob, *novel*, '30 (Job, N. Y. '31, Lon. '32)

Panoptikum, *essays*, '30

Radetzkymarsch, *novel*, '31, (Radetzky March, N. Y. '33, Lon. '34)

Tarabas, ein Gast auf dieser Erde, *novel*, '34 (Tarabas, N. Y. '34)

Der Antichrist, *essays*, '34

RUTRA, ARTHUR ERNST, b. 1892, *novelist, poet, playwright*

Aus Oesterreich, *poems*, '15

Russensturm, *poems*, '15

Golgatha, *drama*, '18

Genesis, *poem*, '19

Barrikade, *play*, '20

Die Tat, *play*, '20

Herr Titan trägt Zinsen, *comedy*, '25

Robert Müller, *eulogy*, '25

Der fremde Mann, *novelette*, '26

Zoo, *short stories*, '27

Der Sport siegt! *play*, '27

Der Kronprinz, *tragedy*, '28

Genosse Geld, *play*, '28

Werkspionage, *comedy*, '29

Amokläufer, *play*, '29

Sei schön durch Liebe, *comedy*, '31

Spiel am Abgrund, *essays*, '31

SALOMON, ERNST VON, b. 1902, *novelist*

Die Geächteten, *novel*, '30 (The Outlaws, Lon. '31)

Die Stadt, *novel*, '32

Die Kadetten, *novel*, '33

SCHAFFNER, JAKOB, b. 1875, *novelist*

Die Irrfahrten des Jonathan Bregger, *novel*, '05

Die Erlhöferin, *novel*, '08

Hans Himmelhoch, *letters*, '09

Konrad Pilater, *novel*, '10; revised ed. '22

Der Bote Gottes, *novel*, '11

Die goldene Fratze, *novel*, '12

Der Fuchs, *novelette*, '12

Geschichte der schweizerischen Eidgenossenschaft, *essay*, '15

Das Schweizerkreuz, *novel*, '16

Der Dechant von Gottesbüren, *novel*, '71

Die Weisheit der Liebe, *novel*, '19 (The Wisdom of Love, Lon. '30, N. Y. '30)

Die Erlösung vom Klassenkampf, *essay*, '20

Passionsweg eines Volkes, '20

Grobschmiede, *novelettes*, '20

Kinder des Schicksals, *novel*, '20

Johannes, *novel*, '22

Das Wunderbare, *novel*, '23

Die Brüder, *novelette*, '25

Der Kreiselspieler, *novelette*, '25

Die letzte Synode, *novelette*, '25

Die Glücksfischer, *novel*, '25

Das grosse Erlebnis, *novel*, '26

Festzeiten, *short stories*, '27

Der Kreislauf, *poetry*, '27

Das verkaufte Seelenheil, *novel*, '27

Verhängnisse, *novelettes*, '27

Der Mensch Krone, *novel*, '28

Föhnwind, *short stories*, '28

Die Heimat, *novelette*, '29

Die Jünglingszeit des Johannes Schattenhold, *novel*, '30

Ihr Glück—ihr Elend, *novelettes*, '31

Die Predigt der Marienburg, *novel*, '31

Der lachende Hauptmann, *novelette*, '31

Wie Gottfried geboren wurde, *novelette*, '31

Liebe und Schicksal, *short stories*, '32

Persönlichkeit, *address*, '33

Eine deutsche Wanderschaft, *novel*, '33

Johannes Schattenhold, *novel*, '34

Nebel und Träume, *novelettes*, '34

SCHEFFLER, KARL, b. 1869, *essayist, art critic*

Ludwig von Hofmann, *essay*, '02

Constantin Meunier, *monograph*, '03

Die moderne Malerei und Plastik, *essay*, '04

Konventionen der Kunst, *monograph*, '04

Moderne Baukunst, '06

Max Liebermann, *monograph*, '06

Der Deutsche und seine Kunst, *essay*, '07

Der Architekt, '07

Die Frau und die Kunst, *essay*, '08

Paris, *essay*, '08

Berlin, *essay*, '09

Idealisten, *essay*, '10

Deutsche Maler und Zeichner im XIX. Jahrhundert, *monograph*, '11

Kritischer Führer durch die Berliner Nationalgalerie, '11

Leben, Kunst, Staat, *essays*, '12

Italien, *essays*, '13

Die Architektur der Grosstadt, *essay*, '13

Henry van de Velde, *monograph*, '13

Deutsche Kunst, *essay*, '15

Adolf Menzel, *monograph*, '15

Bildnisse aus drei Jahrhunderten, *essays*, '16

Talente, *essays*, '16

Du sollst den Werktag heiligen, *essay*, '16

Geist der Gotik, *essay*, '17

Was will das werden, *essay*, '17

Die Nationalgalerie zu Berlin, '17

Die Zukunft der deutschen Kunst, *essay*, '18

Bismarck, *essay*, '19

Die Melodie, *essay*, '19

Der deutsche Januskopf, *essay*, '21

Berliner Museumskrieg, *essay*, '21

Zeit und Stunde, *essay*, '26

Die europäische Kunst im XIX. Jahrhundert, '27

Der junge Tobias, '27

L'art pour l'art, *essay*, '28

Holland, *monograph*, '30 (Holland, N. Y. '32)

Berlin, Wandlungen einer Stadt, *essay*, '31

Der neue Mensch, *essays*, '32

Das Land der Deutschen, *essays*, '32

SCHICKELE, RENÉ, b. 1883, *novelist, playwright, poet*

Drei Hefte Lyrik, *poems*, '02

Sommernächte, *poems*, '02

Der Fremde, *novel*, '07

Weiss und Rot, *poems*, '10

Meine Freundin Lo, *novelette*, '11

Schreie auf dem Boulevard, *novelettes*, '13

Die Leibwache, *poems*, '14

Trimpopp und Manasse, *short stories*, '14

Aissé, *novelette*, '14

Benkal der Frauentröster, *novel*, '14

Das Glück, *novelette*, '15

Mein Herz, mein Land, *selected poems*, '15

Hans im Schnakenloch, *drama*, '16

Am Glockenturm, *drama*, '19

Der neunte November, '19

Die Genfer Reise, *essay*, '19

Die Mädchen, *short stories*, '20

Die neuen Kerle, *drama*, '21

Maria Capponi, *novel*, '25; vol. I of Ein Erbe am Rhein (Maria Capponi, Lon. '28, N. Y. '28)

Blick auf die Vogesen, *novel*, '27; vol. II of Ein Erbe am Rhein (The Rhineland Heritage, Lon. '29; Heart of Alsace, N. Y. '29)

Der Wolf in der Hürde, *novel*, '29

Symphonie für Jazz, *novel*, '29

Die Grenze, *novel*, '32

Himmlische Landschaft, *short story*, '32

Die Witwe Bosca, *novel*, '33

Liebe und Ärgernis des D. H. Lawrence, *essay*, '34

SCHIFF, Bert, b. 1890, *playwright, novelist*
Der Bankkrach, *drama,* '25
Das Testament, *comedy,* '26
Elise Ademann, *comedy,* '27
Iwan und Feodora, *novel,* '27
Die Mutter Gottes von Himmelsburg, *novel,* '29

SCHROEDER, Rudolf Alexander, b. 1878, *poet, novelist*
Unmut, *poems,* '99
Sprüche in Reimen, *poems,* '00
Lieder an eine Geliebte, *poems,* '00
Empedokles, *drama,* '01
An Belinde, *poems,* '02
Sonette an eine Verstorbene, *poems,* '04
Elysium, *poems,* '04
Hama, *poems and short stories,* '08
Deutsche Oden, *poems,* '14
Heilig Vaterland, *poems,* '14
Audax omnia perpeti, *poems,* '22
Widmungen und Opfer, *poems,* '25
Jahreszeiten, *poems,* '30
Mitte des Lebens, *poems,* '30
Der Wanderer und die Heimat, *novelette,* '31
Dichterglaube, '31
Racine und die deutsche Humanität, *essay,* '32

SEGHERS, Anna, b. 1900, *novelist*
Aufstand der Fischer von St. Barbara, *novel,* '28 (Revolt of the Fishermen, Lon. '29, N. Y. '30)
Auf dem Wege zur Amerikanischen Botschaft, *essays,* '30
Die Gefährten, *novel,* '32
Der Kopflohn, *novel,* '33

SIDOW, Max, b. 1897, *poet, novelist, playwright*
Der Tageskreis, *poems,* '19
Die Stadt, *drama,* '20
Hermaphrodit, *drama,* '20
Die goldnen Kammern, *poems,* '21

Beiträge zum Werk des Piero della Francesca, *essay,* '23
Spiel mit dem Feuer, *short stories,* '26
Hass, *short stories,* '27
Platen und die venezianische Kunst, *speech,* '28
Das kleine Leben, *poems,* '31
Die Passion der heiligen Elisabeth, *drama,* '32

SPENGLER, Oswald, b. 1880, *philosopher, historian*
Der metaphysische Grundgedanke der Heraklitischen Philosophie, '04
Preussentum und Sozialismus, *essays,* '20
Pessimismus, *essay,* '21
Der Untergang des Abendlandes, vol. I, '19; vol. II, '22 (The Decline of the West, vol. I, Lon. '26, N. Y. '26; vol. II, Lon. '28, N. Y. '28)
Neubau des deutschen Reiches, *essay,* '24
Politische Pflichten der deutschen Jugend, *speech,* '24
Der Mensch und die Technik, *essay,* '31 (Man and Technics, Lon. '32, N. Y. '32)
Denn der Mensch ist ein Raubtier, *essay,* '31
Politische Schriften, *essays,* '32
Jahre der Entscheidung, *essay,* '33 (The Hour of Decision, Lon. '34, N. Y. '34)

STRAUSS, Emil, b. 1866, *novelist, playwright*
Menschenwege, *short stories,* '98
Don Pedro, *drama,* '99
Der Engelwirt, *short stories,* '00
Freund Hein, *novel,* '02
Kreuzungen, *novel,* '04
Hochzeit, *drama,* '08
Hansl und Gretel, *short stories,* '09

Der nackte Mann, *novel*, '12

Der Spiegel, *novelette*, '19

Der Schleier, *novelette*, '20 (included in Der Schleier, *novelettes*, '30)

Vaterland, *drama*, '23

Der Schleier, *novelettes*, '30

Das Grab zu Heidelberg, *novelettes*, '32

Lorenz Lammerdien, *novelette*, '33

Das Riesenspielzeug, *novel*, '34

SÜSKIND, WILHELM EMANUEL, b. 1901, *novelist*

Das Morgenlicht, *short stories*, '25

Tordis, *short stories*, '27

Jugend, *novel*, '29 (Web of Youth, N. Y. '31)

Mary und ihr Knecht, *novel*, '32

THIESS, FRANK, b. 1890, *novelist, essayist*

Die Stellung der Schwaben zu Goethe, *essay*, '15

Der Tanz als Kunstwerk, *monograph*, '20

Lucie Höflich, *monograph*, '20

Der Tod von Falern, *novel*, '21

Gogol und seine Bühnenwerke, *essay*, '22

Die Verdammten, *novel*, '22

Angelike ten Swaart, *novel*, '23

Das Gesicht des Jahrhunderts (Briefe an Zeitgenossen), *essays*, '23

Der Leibhaftige, *novel*, '24 (The Devil's Shadow, Lon. '28, N. Y. '28)

Der Kampf mit dem Engel, *novelettes*, '25

Das Tor zur Welt, *novel*, '26 (The Gateway to Life, Lon. '27, N. Y. '27)

Narren, *short stories*, '26

Abschied vom Paradies, *novel*, '27 (Farewell to Paradise, N. Y. '29, Lon. '30)

Frauenraub, *novel*, '27 (Interlude, Lon. '29, N. Y. '29)

Erziehung zur Freiheit, *essays*, '29

Eine sonderbare Ehe, *novelette*, '29

Der Zentaur, *novel*, '31

Wiedergeburt der Liebe, *novel*, '32

Die Zeit ist reif, *essays*, '32

Die Geschichte eines unruhigen Sommers, *novelettes*, '32

Johanna und Esther, *novel*, '33

Der Weg zu Isabella, *novel*, '34

TIGER, THEOBALD, see TUCHOLSKY, KURT

TOLLER, ERNST, b. 1893, *poet, playwright*

Die Wandlung, *drama*, '19

Requiem den gemordeten Brüdern, *poetry*, '20

Masse Mensch, *drama*, '21 (Masses and Man, Lon. '23; Man and the Masses, N. Y. '24)

Gedichte der Gefangenen, *poetry*, '21

Die Maschinenstürmer, *drama*, '22 (The Machine Wreckers, Lon. '23, N. Y. '23)

Hinkemann, *drama*, '23 (Brokenbrow, Lon. '26, N. Y. '26)

Der entfesselte Wotan, *comedy*, '23

Das Schwalbenbuch, *poems*, '23 (The Swallow Book, Lon. '24, N. Y. '24)

Vormorgen, *poems*, '24

Die Rache des verhöhnten Liebhabers, *cymedy*, '25

Tag des Proletariats, '26

Justiz, Erlebnisse, *sketches*, '27

Hoppla, wir leben!, *drama*, '27 (Hoppla!, Lon. '28)

Feuer aus den Kesseln, *drama*, '30 (included, as "Draw the Fires" in Seven Plays, Lon. '34)

Verbrüderung, *selected poems*, '30

Quer durch, *travel sketches*, '30 (first two sections transl. as

Which World—Which Way?,
Lon. '31)

Nationalsozialismus (in collab.
with Alfred Mühr), *essay*, '30

Wunder in Amerika (in collab.
with Hermann Kesten), *drama*,
'31 (included, as "Mary Baker
Eddy," in Seven Plays, Lon. '34)

Eine Jugend in Deutschland,
autobiog., '33 (I was a German,
Lon. '34, N. Y. '34)

Die blinde Göttin, *play* (The
Blind Goddess, Lon. '34)

TRITSCH, WALTER, b. 1892, *essayist*

Mein Vaterland, 29
Europe im Zwielicht, '31
Erneuerung einer Nation, '31
Weltwirtschaft, '31

TUCHOLSKY, KURT, b. 1890,
satirist, essayist

Rheinsberg, ein Bilderbuch für
Verliebte, '12

Der Zeitsparer (under pseud. of
Ignatz Wrobel), '13

Fromme Gesänge (under pseud. of
Theobald Tiger), '18

Träumereien an Preussischen
Kaminen (under pseud. of Peter
Panter), '30

Pyrenäenbuch, '27

Mit 5 PS, *satirical miscellany*, '28

Das Lächeln der Mona Lisa,
satirical miscellany, '29

Deutschland, Deutschland über
alles!, '29

Lerne lachen ohne zu weinen, '31

Schloss Gripsholm, *novelette*, '32

ULITZ, ARNOLD, b. 1888, *novelist*

Die vergessene Wohnung, *short
stories*, '15

Die Narrenkarosse, *novelettes*, '16

Der Arme und das Abenteuer,
poetry, '19

Ararat, *novel*, '20

Die ernsthaften Toren, *novelettes*,
'21

Die Bärin, *novel*, '22

Das Testament, *novel*, '24

Der Lotse, *poetry*, '24

Der verwegene Beamte, oder Was
ist die Freiheit?, *short stories*,
'25

Barbaren, *novel*, '26

Christine Munk, *novel*, '26

Der Bastard, *novel*, '27

Der Schatzwächter, *novelettes*, '28

Aufruhr der Kinder, *novel*, '29

Worbs, *comical novel*, '30

Boycott, Scharlach, *two novelettes*,
'30

Die Unmündigen, *novelettes*, '31

Eroberer, *novel*, '34

UNRUH, FRITZ VON, b. 1885, *playwright, novelist, essayist*

Offiziere, *drama*, '11

Louis Ferdinand, Prinz von Preussen, *drama*, '12

Stürme, *drama*, '14

Vor der Entscheidung, *poem*, '14

Opfergang, *novelette*, '16 (Way of
Sacrifice, Lon. '28, N. Y. '28)

Ein Geschlecht, *tragedy*, '16

Platz, *play*, '20

Stirb und werde!, *speech*, '22

Reden an die Jugend, *lecture*, '23

Flügel der Nike, *travel book*, '25

Heinrich aus Andernach, *play*, '25

Bonaparte, *play*, '27 (Bonaparte,
N. Y. '28, Lon. '29)

Phäa, *comedy*, '30

Berlin in Monte Carlo, *comedy*, '31

Zero, *comedy*, '32

Politeia, *speeches*, '32

VALLENTIN, BERTHOLD, b. 1877,
essayist

Napoleon, *biography*, '22

Napoleon und die Deutschen,
essays, '26

Heroische Masken, *essays*, '27

Winckelmann, *biography*, '31

VRING, GEORG VON DER, b. 1889, *novelist, poet*

Südergast, *poems*, '25

Der Zeuge, *novelette*, '27

Soldat Suhren, *novel*, '27 (Private Suhren, Lon. '28, N. Y. '28)

Adrian Dehls, *novel*, '28

Camp Lafayette, *novel*, '29

Verse, '30

Station Marotta, *novel*, '31

Der Wettlauf mit der Rose, *novel*, '32

Argonnerwald, *play*, '32

Blumenbuch, *poems*, '33

Einfache Menschen, *short stories*, '33

Der Schritt über die Schwelle, *novelette*, '33

Schwarzer Jäger Johanna, *novel*, '34

WALDEN, HERWARTH, b. 1878, *poet, critic, dramatist*

Opernwegweiser der Schlesinger-'schen Musikbibliothek, *essay*, '07

Richard Strauss, *essay*, '08

Das Buch der Menschenliebe, *novel*, '16

Kunstkritiker und Kunstmaler, *essays*, '16

Weib, *drama*, '17

Die Härte der Weltenliebe, *novel*, '17

Kind, *drama*, '18

Trieb, *drama*, '18

Menschen, *drama*, '18

Unter den Sinnen, *novel*, '19

Die neue Malerei, *essays*, '20

Glaube, *drama*, '20

Einblick in Kunst, *essays*, '20

Sünde, *drama*, '20

Die Beiden, *drama*, '20

Erste Liebe, *drama*, '20

Letzte Liebe, *drama*, '20

Im Geschweig der Liebe, *poems*, '25

Expressionistische Dichtungen vom Weltkrieg bis zur Gegenwart (in collab. with Silbermann), *critical essays*, '32

WEISS, ERNST, b. 1884, *novelist*

Die Galeere, *novel*, '13

Franziska, *novel*, '15

Tiere in Ketten, *novel*, '18; revised ed. '22

Mensch gegen Mensch, *novel*, '19

Tanja, *drama*, '20

Versöhnungsfest, *poetry*, '20

Stern der Dämonen, *novel*, '21

Nahar, *novel*, '21

Olympia, *tragic comedy*, '22

Atua, *short stories*, '23

Feuerprobe, *novel*, '23

Hodin, *short story*, '23

Daniel, *novelette*, '24

Der Fall Vukobrankovics, *essay*, '25

Männer in der Nacht, *novel*, '25

Boëtius von Orlamünde, *novel*, '28

Das Unverlierbare, *essays*, '28

Dämonenzug, *novelette*, '28

Georg Letham, Arzt und Mörder, *novel*, '31

WERFEL, FRANZ, b. 1890, *novelist, poet, playwright, essayist*

Der Besuch aus dem Elysium, *drama*, '11

Der Weltfreund, *poems*, '12

Versuchung, *poems*, '12

Wir sind, *poems*, '13

Einander, *poems*, '14

Troerinnen, *drama*, '14

Gesänge aus den drei Reichen, *selected poems*, '14

Nicht der Mörder, der Ermordete ist schuldig, *novel*, '15

Der Gerichtstag, *poems*, '16

Die Mittagsgöttin, *drama*, '17

Spielhof, *drama*, '19

Spiegelmensch, *drama*, '20

Bocksgesang, *drama*, '21 (Goat Song, Lon. '26 N. Y. '26)

Beschwörungen, *poems*, '22

Schweiger, *drama*, '22

Verdi, Roman der Oper, *novel*, '24 (Verdi, N. Y. '25, Lon. '26)

Juarez und Maximilian, *drama*, '24 (Juarez and Maximilian, N. Y. '26)

Paulus unter den Juden, *drama*, '25 (Paul Among the Jews, Lon. '28)

Der Tod des Kleinbürgers, *novelette*, '26 (The Death of a Poor Man, Lon. '27; The Man Who Conquered Death, N. Y. '27)

Geheimnis eines Menschen, *novelettes*, '27

Gesammelte Gedichte, '27

Der Abituriententag, *novel*, '28 (The Class Reunion, Lon. '29; Class Reunion, N. Y. '29)

Gesammelte Dramen, '28

Barbara, oder die Frömmigkeit, *novel*, '29 (The Hidden Child, Lon. '31; The Pure in Heart, N. Y. '31)

Das Reich Gottes in Böhmen, *drama*, '30

Realismus und Innerlichkeit, *essay*, '31

Kleine Verhältnisse, *short stories*, '31

Die Geschwister von Neapel, *novel*, '31 (The Pascarella Family, Lon. '32, N. Y. '32)

Das Geheimnis des Laverio, *novelette*, '32

Können wir ohne Gottesglauben leben?, *address*, '32

Die vierzig Tage des Musa Dagh, *novel*, '34 (The Forty Days, Lon. '34; The Forty Days of Musa Dagh, N. Y. '35)

WILLE, HANSJÜRGEN, b. 1902, *short-story writer, novelist*

Rosenkavalier, *novelette*, '27

Juan Sorolla, *novel*, '28

Mitmenschen, *short stories*, '28

Karusselfahrt, *ballet*, '29

Harald Kreuzberg, Yvonne Georgi, *essays*, '30

WOLFENSTEIN, ALFRED, b. 1888, *poet, essayist, dramatist*

Die gottlosen Jahre, *poems*, '13

Die Freundschaft, *poems*, '17

Die Nackten, *poems*, '17

Der Lebendige, *novel*, '18

Menschlicher Kämpfer, *poems*, '19

Sturm auf den Tod, *drama*, '21

Der Mann, *drama*, '22

Jüdisches Wesen und neue Dichtung, *essays*, '22

Mörder und Träumer, '23

Der Flügelmann, *poems*, '24

Unter den Sternen, *novelette*, '24

Der Narr der Insel, *drama*, '25

Bäume in den Himmel, *drama*, '26

Die Celestina, *drama*, '26

Bewegungen, *selected poems*, '28

Die Nacht vor dem Beil, *drama*, '29

WROBEL, IGNATZ, *see* TUCHOLSKY, KURT

ZECH, PAUL, b. 1881, *novelist, poet, playwright*

Der Wald, *poem*, '10

Waldpastelle, *poems*, '10

Die eiserne Brücke, *poems*, '12

Das schwarze Revier, *poem*, '13; new ed. '22

Der schwarze Baal, *novelette*, '16

Das Grab der Welt, '18

Golgatha, *poem*, '19

Der feurige Busch, *poems*, '19

Das Terzett der Sterne, *poems*, '19

Das Ereignis, *novelette*, '20

Die Jacobsleiter, *poem*, '21

Die ewige Dreieinigkeit, *poems*, '24

Die Reise um den Kummerberg, *short stories*, '24

Das törichte Herz, *short stories,* '24
Das trunkene Schiff, *drama,* '24
Sebastian, *drama,* '24
Die Geschichte einer armen Johanna, *novel,* '25
Die Mutterstadt, *two stories,* '25
Stiefkinder Gottes, *poems,* '25
Erde, *drama,* '25
Peregrins Heimkehr, *novel,* '25
Der Kuckucksknecht, *drama,* '25
Omnia mea mecum porto, *ballad,* '26
Ich bin Du, *novel,* '26
Gesammelte Gedichte, '27
Jean-Arthur Rimbaud, *monograph,* '27
Zuletzt bleibt Hiob, *drama,* '28
Das Baalsopfer, *short stories,* '29
Rotes Herz der Erde, *ballads,* '29
Rainer Maria Rilke, *biography,* '30
Neue Balladen von den wilden Tieren, '30
Terzinen für Thino, *poems,* '32
Das Schloss der Brüder Zanowsky, *novelette,* '33

ZOLLIKOFER, FRED VON, b. 1898, *poet, novelist*
Die frühen Tage, *poems,* '21
Die Nacht von Mariensee, *novel,* '27
Über Maschinen das Licht, *poems,* '28
Schwarzfahrt, *short stories,* '31

ZUCKMAYER, CARL, b. 1896, *dramatist, novelist, poet*
Kreuzweg, *drama,* '21
Der fröhliche Weinberg, *comedy,* '25
Der Baum, *poem,* '26
Ein Bauer aus dem Taunus, *novel,* '27
Schinderhannes, *drama,* '27
Katerina Knie, *drama,* '29
Kakadu-Kakada, *play,* '30
Der Hauptmann von Köpenick, *drama,* '30

Die Affenhochzeit, *novelette,* '32
Der Schelm von Bergen, *play,* '34
Eine Liebesgeschichte, *novelette,* '34

ZUR LINDE, OTTO, b. 1873, *poet, critic*
Heinrich Heine und die deutsche Romantik, '99
Gedichte, Märchen, Skizzen, '01
Fantoccini, '02
Die Kugel, eine Philosophie in Versen, '09; enlarged ed. '23
Gesammelte Werke, vols. I–V, '10–'13
vol. I: Thule, Traumland
vol. II: Liebe und Ehe
vol. III: Stadt und Landschaft
vol. IV: Charontisches Mythos
vol. V: Wege, Menschen und Ziele
Arno Holz und der Charon, '11
Gesammelte Werke, vol. VI: Das Buch Abendrot, '20
Gesammelte Werke, vols. VII–VIII: Lieder des Leids, '24
Gesammelte Werke, vols. IX–X: Denken, Zeit und Zukunft, '25

ZWEIG, ARNOLD, b. 1887, *novelist, essayist, poet, dramatist*
Aufzeichnungen über eine Familie Klopfer, *novelette,* '09
Novellen um Claudia, *novel,* '12 (Claudia, Lon. '30, N. Y. '30)
Abigail und Nabal, *drama,* '12
Ritualmord in Ungarn, *drama,* '15; republished as Die Sendung Semaels, '20
Geschichtenbuch, *short stories,* '16
Das ostjüdische Antlitz, *essays,* '20
Drei Erzählungen, *novelettes,* '20
Gerufene Schatten, *novelette,* '23
Söhne, *short stories,* '23
Lessing, Kleist, Büchner, *biogr. essays,* '25
Frühe Fährten, *short stories,* '25

Die Umkehr des Abtrünnigen, *play*, '25

Das neue Kanaan, *essay*, '25 (included in Herkunft und Zukunft, '29)

Der Regenbogen, *short stories*, '26

Der Spiegel des grossen Kaisers, *novel*, '26

Die Umkehr, *play*, '27

Caliban; oder, Politik und Leidenschaft, *essay*, '27

Der Streit um den Sergeanten Grischa, *novel*, '27 (The Case of Sergeant Grischa, Lon. '28, N. Y. '28)

Juden auf der deutschen Bühne, *essay*, '28

Pont und Anna, *novel*, '28

Herkunft und Zukunft, *essays*, '29

Knaben und Männer, *short stories*, '31

Junge Frau von 1914, *novel*, '31 (Young Woman of 1914, Lon. '32, N. Y. '32)

Mädchen und Frauen, *short stories*, '31

De Vriendt kehrt heim, *novel*, '32 (De Vriendt Goes Home, N. Y. '33, Lon. '34)

Spielzeug der Zeit, *short stories*, '33

Bilanz der deutschen Judenheit, *essay*, '33

Erziehung vor Verdun, *novel*, '34

ZWEIG, STEFAN, b. 1881, *essayist, novelist, dramatist, poet*

Silberne Saiten, *poems*, '01

Die Liebe der Erika Ewald, *short stories*, '04

Verlaine, *monograph*, '05 (Paul Verlaine, Lon. '13, Boston '13)

Die frühen Kränze, *poems*, '07

Tersites, *drama*, '07

Emil Verhaeren, *monograph*, '10 (Emile Verhaeren, Lon. '14, Boston '14)

Erstes Erlebnis, *short stories*, '11 (the following transl. in Kaleidoscope, Lon. '33, N. Y. '33: Die Gouvernante as The Governess; Brennendes Geheimnis as The Burning Secret; Sommernovelette as The Fowler Snared)

Das Haus am Meer, *play*, '11

Der verwandelte Komödiant, *comedy*, '13

Jeremias, *tragedy*, '18 (Jeremiah, N. Y. '22, Lon. '29)

Das Herz Europas, *essay*, '18

Drei Meister, *essays*, '19 (Three Masters, N. Y. '30)

Legende eines Lebens, *play*, '19

Romain Rolland, *monograph*, '20 (Romain Rolland, Lon. '21, N. Y. '21)

Fahrten, *essays*, '20

Marceline Desbordes-Valmore, *biography*, '21

Brief einer Unbekannten, *story*, '22 (A Letter from an Unknown Woman, N. Y. '32, Lon. '33; originally pub. in Passion and Pain, Lon. '24)

Amok, *novelette*, '22 (Amok, N. Y. '31, Lon. '32)

Sainte-Beuve, Literarische Charakterbilde, '23

Die gesammelten Gedichte, '24

Frans Masereel, *monograph*, '24

Ernest Renan, Kinderheitserrinerungen, '25

Angst, *novelette*, '25 (transl. as Fear, in Kaleidoscope)

Der Kampf mit dem Dämon, *essays*, '25

Die Augen des ewigen Bruders, *legend*, '25 (transl. as Virata, in Kaleidoscope)

Verwirrung der Gefühle, *novelettes*, '26 (Conflicts, Lon. '28, N. Y. '28)

Volpone, *comedy* (after Ben Jonson), '27 (Volpone, Lon. '28, N. Y. '28)

Erinnerungen an Emile Verhaeren, '27

Abschied von Rilke, *speech*, '27

Die unsichtbare Sammlung, *essay*, '27 (The Invisible Collection, N. Y. '26)

Sternstunden der Menschheit, *essays*, '28

Josef Fouché, *biography*, '29 (Joseph Fouché, Lon. '30, N. Y. '30)

Das Lamm des Armen, *tragedy*, '30

Die Heilung durch den Geist, *essays*, '31 (Mental Healers, N. Y. '32, Lon. '33)

Drei Dichter ihres Lebens, *biogr. essays*, '28 (Adepts in Self-Portraiture, N. Y. '28, Lon. '29)

Marie Antoinette, *biography*, '32 (Marie Antoinette, Lon. '33, N. Y. '33)

Erasmus von Rotterdam, *biography*, '34 (Erasmus, Lon. '34, N. Y. '34)

INDEX